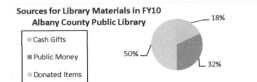

Sources for Library Materials in FY10
Albany County Public Library

- Cash Gifts
- Public Money
- Donated Items

18%
50%
32%

The

Million-Dollar
Financial Services Practice

A Proven System for Becoming
a Top Producer

David J. Mullen, Jr.

AMACOM
American Management Association
New York • Atlanta • Brussels • Chicago • Mexico City • San Francisco
Shanghai • Tokyo • Toronto • Washington, D.C.

Special discounts on bulk quantities of AMACOM books are
available to corporations, professional associations, and other
organizations. For details, contact Special Sales Department,
AMACOM, a division of American Management Association,
1601 Broadway, New York, NY 10019.
Tel.: 212-903-8316 Fax: 212-903-8083
E-mail: specialsls@amanet.org
Website: www.amacombooks.org/go/specialsales
To view all AMACOM titles go to: www.amacombooks.org

This publication is designed to provide accurate and authoritative
information in regard to the subject matter covered. It is sold with the
understanding that the publisher is not engaged in rendering legal,
accounting, or other professional service. If legal advice or other expert
assistance is required, the services of a competent professional person
should be sought.

Library of Congress Cataloging-in-Publication Data

Mullen, David J., Jr.
    The million-dollar financial services practice : a proven system for becoming a top
producer / David J. Mullen, Jr.
        p.   cm.
    Includes index.
    ISBN-13: 978–0-8144–8052–6
    ISBN-10: 0–8144–8052–7
    1. Financial planners.   2. Financial services industry.   3. Investment advisors.
I. Title.

HG179.5.M85   2008
—dc22   2007031495

Printing number

10   9   8   7   6   5   4   3   2   1

To my loving family, which has always provided unconditional love and support. Thank you Cynthia, Nathan, David, John, and Katie. Also to my parents, the late Dave Sr. and Rosemary Mullen. Not only were they wonderful parents but both were teachers who inspired in me the sharing of knowledge to others.

Contents

Acknowledgments   vii

Part 1 The Foundation   1
    1. Overview   3
    2. Motivation   11
    3. The Numbers You Need to Succeed   19
    4. Niche Marketing   27
    5. Getting the Appointment   34
    6. The Appointment   48
    7. Turning Prospects Into Clients   59
    8. The Wealth-Management Process for New Advisors 75
    9. Time Management for New Financial Advisors   85

Part 2 Taking It to the Next Level:
    Building a Million-Dollar Practice   95
    10. Balancing Clients and Prospects   97
    11. Getting More Assets from Existing Clients   104
    12. Leveraging Clients to Get New Ones   110
    13. Expanding the Client Relationship   124
    14. Your Natural Market   135
    15. Client Retention   143
    16. Time Management and the Client Associate   155
    17. Teams   164
    18. What Millionaires Need   176
    19. Beyond a Million-Dollar Practice   186

Part 3 Market Action Plans   199
    20. Seminars   201
    21. Event Marketing   212

22. Networking   223
23. Past Experience and Personal Contacts   233
24. Adopt a Town   241
25. Business Owners   245
26. Professionals: Medical, Legal, and Sales   251
27. Executives   258
28. Influencers   263
29. Diverse Markets: Women, Hispanics, and Asians   270
30. Retirement Plans   282
31. Retirees   290
32. Money in Motion   293
33. Mortgages   299
34. Nonprofits   305

Appendix   Resources   315

Index   337

Acknowledgments

To the financial advisors I have worked with over the past twenty-six years: You have been my teachers and students. Without you, this book would not have been possible.

To my many mentors: Al Thornton, Morris Copeland, Bill Crawford, Jim Billington, Larry Biederman, Rob Knapp, Bob Sherman, Dave Middleton, Mike Thompson, Bob Mulholland, and John Dozier. You have been the role models I have learned from and who shaped my career as a manager.

To Jan Jones, who helped me in countless ways.

To Joe Yanofsky, for being my partner in developing many of the concepts presented in this book.

To Race Cowgill at Zenith Management Consulting, for being my business consultant and editing partner. His organizational skills and fine editing made a significant difference in this book.

To Wendy Keller, my agent, for her support and confidence in me.

To AMACOM, for believing in me for my first book.

PART 1

The Foundation

Overview

Y ou are about to read a book that can change your career.

Building a million-dollar financial services practice is not complicated, but I'm not going to pretend that it is easy. If it were, there would be a lot more financial advisors making millions. In the twenty-six years that I have been in the business, I have seen hundreds of people fail to make it past the first two years and few who reached the million-dollar level. Yet those who reach or exceed $1 million in business have one of the best jobs imaginable. The autonomy and income of, and the excitement experienced by, million-dollar and multimillion-dollar producers are unparalleled.

- This book will give you every tool you need to build your financial services practice to a million dollars and beyond, no matter where you are in your career—and show you when to use each tool, how to use it, and how often to use it.

- There are many books and training programs that claim to help you build your financial services practice. However, this book is different because it gives you step-by-step instructions for carrying out a *comprehensive, tactical process that has been proven* to make your practice more successful.

- The process I present here has for twenty-one years been able to double, in many cases, the income of financial advisors at any stage of their career. It has been refined hundreds of times to be sure it is as effective as it can possibly be.

- This book is tactical; it contains specific templates, scripts, contact plans, lists, tasks, marketing plans, letters, and resources, and all these tools are integrated into the overall process.

- This book covers every aspect of a financial advisor's job, from prospecting to client service.

- This book addresses every stage of an advisor's career, from the first day on the job to becoming a multimillion-dollar producer.

There are three distinct stages of an advisor's career:

Stage one is building the foundation. This is done during the first two years of the advisor's career. During this stage, the advisor should spend the majority of his time on marketing, with the objective of building a "book" of fifty client relationships and a prospect pipeline of one hundred. About 70 percent of the new advisor's time should be spent on marketing, with the objective of getting eight new appointments a week.

Stage two runs from the third year through the fifth year of service. Now the advisor must balance client service with marketing. The number of client relationships should be increased to one hundred, and the client relationships and the one hundred prospects should be upgraded. The advisor needs to spend at least 50 percent of her time on marketing—on client-leveraging activities, on natural marketing techniques, and on attempting to identify and get all her existing clients' assets. The advisor should have four appointments per week with new prospects.

Stage three is beyond five years. The advisor should continue to upgrade the one hundred client relationships throughout his career. A minimum of fifty prospects should be in the active pipeline, and they should continue to be upgraded. The advisor should spend a minimum of 25 percent of his time marketing, and he needs to see at least one new prospect per week.

The road to a million-dollar practice is a series of steps that build on one another, and you must take the first ones first. The new advisor needs to understand that building the right foundation greatly increases the chances of building a million-dollar practice and greatly reduces the time required to get there. An advisor can commit to the million-dollar road at any stage of her career, but the fastest and easiest way is to take the proper steps at the beginning. As your practice grows, the fundamentals remain the same, but how you allocate your time to each one changes.

In this chapter, I will give you a brief overview of the journey to building a million-dollar practice; in subsequent chapters, I will go into greater detail about every aspect of building a million-dollar practice and beyond.

Book Outline

This book is divided into three parts.

Part 1: The Foundation

Chapters 1 through 9 make up this part. It will be of particular interest to new advisors. It outlines the first things you need to do on the pathway to building a million-dollar practice; it shows you how to build the foundation you need for a million-dollar business. However, I encourage any advisor no matter how much experience she has, to review the information in this section. The importance of motivation (Chapter 2) and the marketing process (Chapters 3–7) outlined in this part of the book applies to experienced advisors as well as new ones.

Part 2: Taking It to the Next Level: Building a Million-Dollar Practice

This part includes Chapters 10 through 19. More experienced advisors will find it particularly useful—you will find everything you need to do once you have built the proper foundation. It will also be useful for new advisors to read these chapters because they provide a vision for how to reach a million-dollar practice once the new advisor has built the foundation.

Part 3: Market Action Plans

This part, Chapters 20 through 34, includes over fifty approaches to fifteen different markets. Each market action plan gives you all the tools you need to succeed in that market, including when the action plan is appropriate, case studies, how to implement the plan, and sample phone scripts and letters.

Appendix

At the end of the book, the appendix gives you resources for finding names and directories for each market.

The Concept Behind the Process

As you can see from these descriptions, each chapter will guide you through a comprehensive, tactical process for improving your practice.

Before you begin, however, it is important that you understand the five characteristics of million-dollar producers and the five fundamentals of growth, which together are the foundation on which the million-dollar practice is built.

The Five Characteristics of Million-Dollar Producers

1. They set business and activity goals and track their progress.
2. They are motivated.
3. They market relentlessly.
4. They manage their time effectively.
5. They make establishing relationships with affluent individuals their first priority.

My observations of successes and failures in this business have led me to the conclusion that million-dollar producers do not possess any extraordinary skills; however, they have different characteristics from advisors who do not reach the million-dollar level. These are the five characteristics, and they show you what multimillion-dollar producers are like, their basic approach, and how they work day to day. These characteristics apply to any advisor who wants to build a million-dollar practice, no matter where he is in his career.

Characteristic 1: They Set Business and Activity Goals and Track Their Progress

Studies done on the differences between more successful and less successful people indicate that the most successful people set goals. To reach a million dollars in business, you must set goals and measure your progress.

The first step is to understand that your business corresponds to the number of affluent households (households with more than $250,000 in investable assets) you have and the total amount of assets you manage. The average million-dollar producer I have worked with manages at least $120 million in assets for about one hundred affluent households.

Take the number of affluent households (100) and the amount of assets ($120 million). Subtract from that the amount of assets and the number of households you have now, if any. The result is the amount of assets and number of households that you need to add in order to reach

$1 million. If you divide that number by the number of years within which you want to reach $1 million, you will see the number of households and the amount of assets that you need to add to your practice each year in order to reach your goal by that time.

I tell new advisors that building a million-dollar practice in ten years is a challenging but realistic time frame. Certainly, advisors can do this in less time, but I have seen very few do so—most advisors who reach $1 million take at least twenty years. However, if a new advisor is trained to develop the five characteristics described here from the beginning and to understand and execute the five fundamentals introduced later in this chapter, she can realistically expect to reach $1 million in ten years.

Those advisors who want to reach $1 million and who have been in the business for a while can expect that the training in this book, if they follow it, can add at least $100,000 in business each year. As an example, if you are currently producing $500,000 per year, following and executing the five fundamentals should result in your reaching $1 million within five years.

Once you have set your overall production goal, you should set goals in the following two areas:

1. You have set your goals for the number of affluent households and the amount of managed assets required to reach a million-dollar practice; now you should break down these goals into daily, weekly, monthly, and annual goals, and you should monitor your progress at least every week—track the difference between your goals and where you currently are.

2. You should set activity goals every week for the number of client contacts to make, the number of prospect contacts to make, and the number of new appointments to have.

Characteristic 2: They Are Motivated

Once you have established your goals and your time frame for reaching them, you must make sure that you have a truly high level of motivation to fuel the process. Merely understanding the five fundamentals of building a million-dollar practice is not enough. In order to execute the five fundamentals every day, you must have a very high level of sustainable motivation.

Executing the fundamentals is no easier for the million-dollar producer than for those who never reach that level; instead, the successful advisor can *make* himself execute the fundamentals, and the less successful advisor cannot. Million-dollar producers make themselves do the more difficult tasks that this business sometimes requires, in spite of the rejection they receive. Less successful advisors do not. Remember what I said at the beginning: Building a million-dollar practice is not complicated, but it is difficult. Having a high and sustained level of motivation is essential if the advisor is to do the difficult things required to succeed in this business.

Characteristic 3: They Market Relentlessly

After you have made your commitments (motivation) and set your goals (and the time frame for reaching them), you must understand that the most important characteristic is sustained and relentless marketing. The most successful million-, multimillion- and decamillion-dollar advisors I have worked with never quit marketing. Their individual marketing processes may be different, but they always do them. The only way to reach a million-dollar practice is to understand that you must always be carrying out effective marketing.

This book provides a proven marketing process, as well as fifteen different marketing plans, that any advisor at any point in her career can implement. This is certainly not the only marketing process that works, but it has been used by hundreds of advisors, and it has been proven to work very well.

Characteristic 4: They Manage Their Time Effectively

It is essential that you have sound time-management techniques, especially in order to perform—every day—the "five fundamentals," which are discussed in the next section.

- You should divide your day between client service and marketing.
- You should use your client associate to protect your time throughout the day and to help increase your service to your existing clients.
- You should have an automated, well-thought-out wealth management process.
- You should keep track of how you spend your time and be accountable for spending time doing the right things.

- You should become a master at executing the three basics of time management: prioritization, delegation, and time blocking.

Characteristic 5: They Make Establishing Relationships with Affluent Individuals Their First Priority

This is primarily a relationship business, and million-dollar producers focus more on their relationships with affluent individuals than do less-successful advisors. Without strong relationships and all the elements that strong relationships are based on, it is very difficult to reach the million-dollar level.

The Five Fundamentals of Growth: LEARN

Leverage: Leverage current clients to get new ones.

Expand: Expand the products and services each client uses.

Assets: Get all of your clients' assets.

Retain: Retain your clients by providing extraordinary service.

Niche: Develop your niche and natural markets and build a marketing process around them.

Niche: Develop Your Niche Markets and Build a Marketing Process Around Them

The most important fundamental is to develop your niche market and to build a marketing process that you can automate—that you incorporate every day. This process:

- Should include one to five marketing plans for different niches.
- Should make getting a face-to-face appointment right away a first priority.
- Should have a follow-up process that is tailored to each prospect's needs.

In order to open the number of new accounts that will lead to a million-dollar practice, you should be servicing between fifty and one hundred prospects. Most prospects are underserviced by their existing advisor, and if you service these prospects better, you will convert them to clients. This means providing them with consistent follow-up tailored to their personal and financial needs.

Once you have at least fifty affluent client relationships of at least $100,000 each, you can now tackle the other four fundamentals of growth:

Leverage: Leverage current clients to get new ones.

Expand: Expand the products and services each client uses.

Assets: Get all of your clients' assets.

Retain: Retain your clients by providing extraordinary service.

Knowing what the five fundamentals are and developing a plan to incorporate these fundamentals every day is how a million-dollar practice is built in the shortest time possible.

What It All Adds Up To

The formula for building a million- and multimillion-dollar practice is not a complicated one. It involves building the right foundation first, then taking it to the next level by ongoing marketing, developing strong relationships with clients, and providing outstanding service. This formula is much easier to understand than to execute. It takes a high level of commitment and motivation to do the activities necessary to build a million-dollar practice every day. It takes strong organization and time-management skills to fit these activities in every day, to build an effective team, and to build processes that support the practice. It takes making the highest priority that of building relationships. This can all be condensed into the following equation:

The Formula for a Million-Dollar Practice

The right foundation + marketing + strong client relationships + outstanding service = $1 million practice

---

There are so few million-dollar advisors and even fewer multimillion-dollar advisors not because the formula for success is complicated, but because it is so hard to carry out the right activities every day. If you are committed, develop the characteristics of million-dollar producers, and follow the fundamentals I have outlined in this book, then a million-dollar and multimillion-dollar practice can be yours.

Motivation

The five fundamentals that I mentioned at the end of the last chapter form the foundation of a million-dollar-plus practice. These five fundamentals are the foundation, and motivation is their cornerstone.

Everyone who enters the financial services business wants to succeed. However, to truly succeed, an advisor must have more than simply the *desire to succeed*. There must be a far deeper level of motivation. An advisor's motivation will be tested over and over throughout her career, and her motivation reservoir must always be deep enough to replenish her. It is possible to write down all the correct processes and techniques for succeeding in this business, but without deep motivation, none of it works.

There are two components to motivation:

1. Building and keeping motivation
2. Time allocation

Building and Keeping Motivation

In order to achieve a million-dollar practice in financial services, you *must* market, and if you market, you *must* be ready to face rejection. This is especially true at the early stages of your career. Marketing is difficult, and over the course of your career, you may not feel that your motivation level is high enough to do it. You are not lost, though, because you can renew or increase your motivation any time. In order to build and keep your motivation, you need to do two things:

1. You must understand the low-percentage/high-payoff dynamic of the business.
2. You must clearly understand your own personal reasons for wanting to have a million-dollar-plus practice.

The Low-Percentage/High-Payoff Dynamic

A fundamental aspect of the financial services business is that it is a low-percentage/high-payoff business: A high number of rejections (low percentage) is required to reach the reward (high payoff). Notice that I used the word *required*: It is *required* that you have a high number of rejections in order to reach the high payoff. The payoff is so high because the number of rejections is so high. They go hand in hand.

Every affluent investor has a current provider; it is difficult to disrupt an existing relationship, and it takes time. You face an uphill battle to capture affluent investors, which means that you must market as effectively as you possibly can in order to succeed. The most effective marketing practice I have seen is the "Rolodex technique" (calling the list of personal contacts you have built over the years), which generates a 50 percent call-to-appointment ratio (50 percent of calls lead to appointments); the worst is a mailing, which generates about 1 percent. Cold calling generates about 5 percent. These numbers reflect a low-percentage success rate, which means that doing these tasks every day requires a very high level of motivation. However, the payoff is very high. For example, in the Denver Metropolitan Statistical Area, there are approximately 30,000 households that have investable assets of $1 million or more. To have a million-dollar practice, an advisor needs to have only twenty-five $1 million-plus households. While it is very hard to get a new million-dollar household (low percentage), it takes only two or three per year to put you on track to build a million-dollar practice (high payoff).

If you understand this dynamic, it is easier to accept rejection. You are prepared for it because you know that only a few successes have a significant impact on the growth of your business, and that in order to get those few successes, you *must* go through a lot of rejection. Please take note: *It is easier to be rejected than to fail.* In other words, you pay a greater psychological price if you fail than if you are rejected.

Your Reasons for Wanting a Million-Dollar Practice

Think through and even write down why reaching a million-dollar-plus practice is important to you. Your reasons might be:

•   Professional accomplishment and status

•   The extra things the income could provide, such as a new dream car, a European vacation, a second home, a bigger home, remodeling your home, a country club membership, or a boat or plane

- Financial independence at a younger age
- Charitable giving
- A top college education for your children

Your reasons should be very definite and very clear. You need to fill a very deep motivation reservoir with a clear idea of what reaching this goal will mean. In too many cases, advisors set a goal and have not spent much time thinking through why they want to reach it. Setting general goals without thinking through the details and without generating real desire leads to superficial motivation and is not enough to make a behavioral difference.

Once your goals are set and your desire is high, you have the ammunition you need to make the right time-management choices. As you work through the day, when the time comes for you to choose to risk rejection or not, you must be able to draw on your reservoir of motivation to make the right choice: You must vividly recall why it is important to you to grow your business, you must call up strong images that fuel your desire to grow, and you must remember that doing the difficult tasks is worth more than failing or not growing.

Each day, you will face the decision whether or not to do those tasks that expose you to rejection, and each time, your deep motivation will push you toward the choices that fuel growth. The tasks that expose you to rejection and that build your business are marketing tasks, because when you are marketing, you are putting yourself in the position of asking for new money from a client or a prospect. Marketing activities are the ones that require deep motivation.

You should decide in advance at what times during the day you will market. Interestingly, once you start on marketing tasks, they actually get easier and require less motivation. Once you make marketing a daily practice and do it for at least a month, starting the marketing activities requires less motivation. One of the reasons for this is that you get better and more relaxed by doing them. As with anything else, "practice makes perfect."

You must have high motivation to engage in activities that have a high risk of rejection. You must have high motivation to engage in marketing activities. At the same time, if you don't perform these marketing activities, you will not reach a million-dollar practice.

Time Allocation

Most people in financial services have a superficial level of motivation. Superficial motivation is the simple desire to do well and to work hard. This alone will not lead you to a million-dollar-plus practice. You need a deeper level of motivation: motivation not only to work hard, but to spend a high percentage of your time every day risking being rejected.

Deeply motivated advisors spend their time doing the tasks that build their business most effectively, and they spend little time doing tasks that do not. How you spend your time, then, will be a good indicator of how motivated you are. Another way of looking at this is that when you choose how you will spend your time, you are really choosing how successful you are going to allow yourself to be—how you spend your time is the most important choice in building a million-dollar practice.

There are no shortcuts to building a million-dollar practice. In the end, it is simple math. To have a million-dollar practice, you should have:

- Between $100 million and $150 million in investable assets
- At least one hundred relationships that have over $250,000 in investable assets
- At least twenty-five of those one hundred relationships with assets over $1 million.

To *build* a million-dollar practice, you should bring in:

- At least $12 million net new assets per year (net means assets in minus assets lost)
- Nine $250,000-plus relationships per year
- Three $1 million-plus relationships per year

This seems like a simple formula, and it is, but it is also very hard to reach these numbers every year.

The only way to bring in $1 million in new assets and one new $250,000-plus household every month is to spend time marketing. It is a cause-and-effect relationship: Do those tasks that are effective in bringing in this new money, and the effect will be that you will reach a million-dollar practice.

The only way to market effectively is to get in front of affluent prospects, follow up with affluent prospects, or get more money from existing clients. For most advisors, the time they spend marketing is "hard time" because they are putting themselves in the position of being rejected.

If your level of motivation is high, you will do these tasks. If it is not, you will not, and you will not achieve a million-dollar practice. The choice you make will be obvious each day when you choose how you will spend your time.

You have to spend a much greater percentage of your time marketing when you are building a new practice. However, no matter where you are in your career, if you want your practice to grow at an above-average rate, you must market. As a guideline, in the first two years, you should spend 70 percent of a ten-hour day, or seven hours, directly on marketing activities. In years three through five, you should spend 50 percent of a ten-hour day (five hours daily); and in years six and after, you should spend 25 percent of an eight-hour day (two hours per day). As your experience and expertise increase, you will be able to leverage your clients more, which means that it will take less time to get each new affluent household. Upgrading a household to a $250,000 household counts as one of the twelve households you need; this is much easier for an experienced advisor to do than for a new advisor.

Motivation becomes the cornerstone of success when, each day, you make choices about how to spend your time. Some tasks put you at risk of being rejected. These are hard tasks and require high motivation. These are also the marketing tasks that will advance your practice most effectively. The hard tasks put you at risk of being rejected, but they also lead to a high payoff—building a million-dollar practice. As I stated earlier, high rejection and high payoff go hand in hand.

Some tasks do not put you at risk; these are easier tasks and require little motivation. These are nonmarketing tasks. They do not put you at risk of being rejected, but they also do not advance you to building a million-dollar practice. Worse, they take time away from doing the things that *will* lead you to building a million-dollar practice.

If your level of motivation is high enough, you will spend time doing the things that put you at risk of being rejected. Here are some examples of common tasks and the motivation they require:

Activity	Motivation Level Required
Reading, doing paperwork, problem solving	Low
Returning calls	Low
Solving an operational problem	Low
Research, portfolio work	Low
Portfolio or client performance reviews	Low
Database, computer time	Low
Marketing preparation or thinking about marketing	Low
Client events that are not marketing-based	Low
Mailings*	Low
Training	Low
Professional designation training/studying	Low
Preparing lists to call	Low
Seminar preparation	Low
Prospect proposals	Low
Team meetings on marketing, pipeline, or idea sharing	Low
Study time	Low
Proactive client calls†	Medium
New prospect appointments	High
Prospect drop-bys	High
Calls to new prospects	High
Following up with existing prospects	High
Calls or client meetings asking for more money	High
Calls or client meetings asking for help in getting new clients	High
Putting on seminars	High
Networking meetings and asking for names	High
Client/prospect events	High
Centers-of-influence contacts or events	High
Reestablishing a business relationship with a past contact	High
Following up on new prospects from a seminar	High
Cold-calling a business owner	High
Prospect follow-up appointments	High

---

* Mailings require a low level of motivation, but they are marketing. Mailings are, however, some of the least effective marketing you can do.

† Making proactive client calls and meeting with clients require a higher level of motivation than reactive tasks, but not as much as marketing tasks.

Notice that the tasks in this list that require high motivation are all marketing tasks. If you are highly motivated, you are willing to spend time, and in some cases the majority of your time, every day doing the hard, low-percentage/high-rejection activities instead of the easier activities. This is a difficult choice that you must make every single day. It is not easier for successful professionals. It's just that they are capable of *making themselves do these things.* This is the heart of motivation in financial services.

If you have the right mindset, it is not difficult to make the right time-management choices. You will make the right time-management choices if you are willing to risk rejection, if you understand the low-percentage/high-payoff dynamic, and if you realize that your willingness to accept that dynamic will lead to a million-dollar practice.

In the end, the high level of turnover in financial services has more to do with a lack of deep motivation than with a lack of talent. Most people are not willing to face, over the long term, the low-percentage/high-payoff dynamics of this business—they cannot stand the pain of rejection long enough to reap the big rewards. The advisor must want, at the deepest level, this kind of success and be very clear about why that success is so important; that desire is the essence of the motivation you must have to face rejection and to ensure success.

There is such an information overload in financial services that it is easy to get distracted and not focus on the right activities and the right numbers. No matter where you are in building a million-dollar practice, it is critical that you understand the numeric measures that lead to it; this understanding will allow you to focus on the right activities and to set the right goals. In Chapter 3, I will explain these numeric measures and goals.

Summary

- To succeed in financial services, you must market, and to market, you must have deep motivation.

- How you spend your time shows how motivated you are.

- The activities required to build a million-dollar practice put you in the position of being rejected, which is hard.

- Financial services is a low-percentage/high-payoff business.

- You must spend time on direct marketing activities every day in order to build a million-dollar practice and beyond.

- The price you pay to risk being rejected must be less than your fear of failure.

- The key to deep motivation is being clear on how important success is to you and what tangible results you will receive.

- You make a hard choice every day of how to spend your time. Your motivation must be high for you to make the right choice.

- The more time you spend on marketing, the easier it gets.

- It is not easier for successful advisors to face rejection, but they can make themselves do it.

The Numbers You Need to Succeed

Any advisor in financial services can build a million-dollar practice. Reaching the million-dollar level generates a level of income that few other occupations provide. However, only about 10 percent of financial advisors who survive two years or more reach $1 million or greater, and only about 1 percent of those hired as financial advisors ever achieve a million-dollar practice. If every advisor aspires to the million-dollar goal, why do so few reach it? There are two reasons:

1. A lack of deep motivation—not being willing to pay the price of facing rejection to achieve a million-dollar practice
2. Not knowing how to build a million-dollar practice, or building a practice that limits growth

What I am about to outline is how to build a million-dollar practice within ten years of starting in the business, or, for advisors who are not just starting out, how to add $12 million in assets and $100,000 in business each year.

Building a million-dollar business starts with understanding the six numeric elements you should have in order to reach that level.

The Six Numeric Elements of a Million-Dollar Practice

Element 1. You should have at least $120 million in assets under management.

Element 2. You should have one hundred relationships with affluent investors ($250,000+).

Element 3. You should set relationship minimums.

Element 4. You should have at least one $1 million-plus client for every three clients in the $250,000 asset class.

Element 5. You should constantly raise the minimums.

Element 6. You should have broad relationships.

If you have all six elements, then you will have built the right business practice to reach $1 million in business; you should be generating about 80 basis points on all assets under management under most circumstances and market conditions. An advisor can manage a conservative practice and still generate 80 basis points in most financial cycles. Generating less business is a sign of a practice that is missing one of these elements. Here is how these six elements work.

Element 1: You Should Have at Least $120 Million in Assets Under Management

It takes approximately $120 million in assets to generate $1 million in business (with a velocity of 80 basis points; velocity equals fees divided by assets).

Element 2: You Should Have One Hundred Relationships with Affluent Investors

It is nearly impossible to manage more than a total of 100 relationships effectively:

- If you contact each client once a month, and if three of these contacts include a quarterly review and one includes an annual review with a planning session, then you will be spending approximately nine hours per year on each client relationship. Given one hundred relationships, this is 900 hours per year.

- If you have between fifty and one hundred prospects and you spend thirty minutes on each prospect per month, you need to spend twenty-five to fifty hours a month on your existing prospects. This is 300 to 600 hours per year.

- This adds up to 1,200 to 1,500 hours that you need to spend on your current clients and prospects.

- The average advisor works approximately 2,000 hours per year, which leaves only 500 to 800 hours (between 10 and 16 hours per week, or 2 to 3 hours a day) for all administrative work, client service, and marketing.

There are physically not enough hours in the day to service more than one hundred relationships properly. The same principle applies to the advisor's client associates. To keep these one hundred clients, you should provide "raving fans" service, which limits the number of total relationships you and your client associates can have.

Element 3: You Should Set Relationship Minimums

- Every relationship should have at least $250,000 in investable assets, or that potential. If you are an advisor with a length of service of five years or less, it's fine to have accounts with less than $250,000 as you build up to a total of one hundred total relationships, as long as those relationships are over $100,000.
- Every relationship should generate at least $1,000 in fees per year. Million-dollars-plus relationships should average at least $10,000 per year.

These numbers should be relatively easy to achieve if you contact each relationship twelve times per year and you expose each one to a broad mix of products and services. If a client does not generate the minimum level of business during the course of a year, consider replacing him with a client who will.

Element 4: You Should Have at Least One $1 Million-Plus Client Ratio for Every Three in the $250,000 Asset Class

- You need to have approximately seventy-five relationships with *at least* $250,000 but less than $1 million in investable assets, with an *average* of $600,000 to $700,000 in assets.
- You need to have *at least* twenty-five relationships that have *at least* $1 million in investable assets, with an *average* of $2.5 million in assets.

Element 5: You Should Constantly Raise the Minimums.

Constantly raise the minimums for assets and business. Your number of client relationships should always be constant—one hundred—but you should keep raising the minimum level of assets and business.

To continue to increase these minimums, and grow at the rate of $100,000 per year, you should keep a pipeline of one hundred active prospects at all times (fifty for advisors with a length of service of six years or more). You should spend time daily contacting the prospects in this pipeline and setting appointments with new ones. These prospects will ultimately replace the lower end of your existing one hundred client relationships as you increase the minimums each year.

Your goal should be to have one hundred client relationships that are above your minimums, and fifty to one hundred prospects that are all more qualified than your smallest and least productive client relationships. To grow your business at the rate that will lead to a million-dollar practice, you need to upgrade both your client list and your prospect list every year.

Fundamental Truth:

You grow your business by raising the level of minimum assets, not by increasing the number of relationships.

Element 6: You Should Have Broad Relationships

Maximize the number of different products and services that each relationship has. In many cases, if you double the products and services that a client uses, you can *triple* the business that that client generates. It is also the case that if a relationship has over $250,000 and uses six or more services and products, retention is close to 95 percent.

Note: These six elements are interrelated. Having relationships of this size automatically limits the total of relationships you can have; clients at this level of affluence want and need a greater variety of products and services and require more contact and a higher level of service.

How New Advisors Need to Start Out

If you are a new advisor and you want to reach a million-dollar practice in the shortest time possible, you need to understand from the outset how the numbers work. This increases the probability of building a million-dollar practice and decreases the time it will take.

As a new advisor, you have two goals above all others:

Goal 1. Build a pipeline of one hundred qualified prospects quickly.

Goal 2. Bring in $1 million in net new assets per month.

Goal 1: Build a Pipeline of One Hundred Qualified Prospects Quickly

First and most importantly, you need to build a pipeline of one hundred qualified prospects as soon as possible. The definition of a qualified (or "legitimate") prospect is a person who:

- Has met you.
- Meets your minimum level of investable assets.
- Agrees to a second appointment and/or will return your phone call.

It should take six to twelve months to build this pipeline. Remember that once you build this pipeline of a hundred prospects, you will continue to upgrade it throughout your entire career. The number of a hundred prospects should never change. If your length of service is six years or more, your goal should be at least 50 qualified prospects.

After six months, you, as a new advisor, should set a goal of acquiring one new $250,000 client a month, and within a year, one of those should be at least a $1 million client. This means that by the end of your first twelve months of production, you should have:

- One hundred qualified prospects
- Five $250,000-plus relationships
- One $1 million-plus relationship
- At least ten $100,000-plus relationships

Goal 2: Bring In $1 Million in Net New Assets per Month*

The other important goal is assets under management. Your goal should be to bring in $1 million net in new assets per month (with net meaning assets in minus any assets lost) after the first six months. Any affluent clients or large assets you capture in less than six months is mostly the result of luck, because in most cases, it takes six months to cultivate a prospect's trust to the point that she will let you manage his money. Therefore, you should have at least $6 million in assets after your first

---

*Market appreciation or depreciation is not factored into any asset goal referenced in this book.

twelve months in order to be on track to reach a million-dollar practice within ten years.

After the first twelve months, a new advisor's numbers stay essentially the same. You need to add an average of one new affluent relationship ($250,000-plus) per month, of which three, after twelve months, should be $1 million-plus. Additionally, you need to bring in $12 million net in new assets per year. Note that existing clients who turn over new money to you count toward new assets and new affluent households if they cross the $250,000 or $1 million mark; this gives the more senior advisor an advantage because at least 50 percent of these goals can be achieved by upgrading current clients, which is much easier that bringing in new ones.

The following tables show how your length of service (LOS) and production goals affect your numbers.

NUMBER OF PROSPECTS AND THEIR MINIMUMS FOR DIFFERENT LENGTH OF SERVICE

Advisor Experience (LOS in Years)	Minimum Prospect Qualification	Number of Prospects
0–2	$100,000	100*
3–5	$150,000	75 **
6+	$250,000	50 **

MINIMUMS FOR DIFFERENT PRODUCTION GOALS

Production Goal (in millions)	Prospect Qualification	Number of Clients with $250,000–$1 Million	Minimum Number of Clients with $1 Million+
1	$250,000	75	25
2	500,000	50	50
3	1,000,000	25	75
4	1,000,000	0	100

What It All Means

Any advisor who is motivated to reach $1 million needs to set a goal of adding approximately one new $250,000-plus household per month net (of which three per year need to be $1 million +) and $1 million in new assets per month. This will lead to a million-dollar practice.

Reminder: Upgrades of clients and additional client assets count toward these goals.

Now that you understand the numbers, move on to the next step, which is to have a good overall marketing process for reaching those numbers. Without a good process, all you have are goals and motivation. Chapter 4 covers that marketing process, called *niche marketing*.

Summary

- It takes a deep level of motivation to build a million- or multimillion-dollar business.

- With the right focus and motivation, a new advisor can expect to reach a million-dollar practice within ten years from starting.

- With the right focus and motivation, an experienced advisor can expect to increase her business $100,000 per year.

- To support a million-dollar practice, you need to bring in $12 million net new assets per year and add at least ten net new $250,000 households per year, of which two or three are $1 million-plus.

- You should limit your total number of relationships to one hundred; teams of three or more should consider limiting each member's total number of relationships to fifty.

- For a million-dollar practice, no relationship should be below $250,000.

- Deep penetration of each relationship is important; make it a goal to have five to six different products and services per relationship.

- To grow beyond $1 million, you should limit the number of affluent client relationships to 100, but always increase the minimums.

- In most market conditions a well-managed financial practice that follows all six elements should generate 80 basis points on assets managed.

- Set a minimum amount of business for a relationship to qualify as one of your one hundred. As a guideline, set a $1,000 revenue minimum for relationships with $250,000 to $1 million in assets, and $10,000 for relationships with over $1 million.

- Depending on your experience level, keep fifty to one hundred active prospects in your pipeline at all times.

- Set a minimum for a prospect of at least $100,000 in assets for length of service of zero to five years, and $250,000 in assets for length of service of six years or more until you reach $1 million. Never have more than one hundred prospects at once, but increase the qualifying minimums constantly.

- Upgrading an existing relationship to above $250,000 is just as valuable as bringing in a new one. It all counts the same in building a million-dollar practice.

Niche Marketing

f you want to build your business to $1 million-plus, you must develop
an effective marketing process. The first step in doing this is to identify
the markets you want to focus on. Once you have identified your markets, the second step is to develop a well-thought-out market action plan.
These two steps create what is called a *niche marketing plan* because the
plan is focused on a small number of specific markets.

Part 3 of this book gives market action plans that advisors can choose
from, complete with sample scripts and sources of names.

Why Niche Marketing Works Best

Niche marketing works because each market requires a high level of expertise and experience to capture it effectively. The more you understand
the dynamics of a particular market, the easier it is to get appointments
with prospects in that market. You will capture your market most effectively if you select only a few markets (narrow) and understand and work
them deeply—niche marketing is narrow and deep. As your familiarity
and expertise with a market increase, so will your confidence and ability
to build trust with potential investors.

The goal is to build depth within the markets you choose. How?

- Join their professional associations
- Subscribe to their trade journals
- Attend their professional meetings

These activities will enable you to "talk the talk" and "walk the walk"
of your target markets. They will give you credibility and visibility so you
can build trust with potential investors in those markets.

Typically, each market has individuals who are leaders and centers of
influence within that market. The only way you can identify and connect

with these centers of influence is to have a level of expertise in their market and to know who the "movers and shakers" are. It is hard to do this for more than three to five markets.

Elements of an Effective Market Action Plan

An effective niche market action plan should have three parts.

Part 1: Approach

The approach is a description or set of ideas regarding how best to approach the target market. Develop this description by:

- Interviewing the most successful advisors for that market about what they do to succeed
- Reading books on the target market
- Collecting information from local management, wholesalers, home-office training, and other sources

Your objective is to get appointments with affluent investors within your niche markets. Whenever possible, these should be "warm calls," not cold calls. To make the initial contact warmer, try:

1. A referral from someone whom that person knows
2. A connection—something you have in common
3. Knowing something about your contact's area of expertise

One way of developing this information is to enter the name of the person you will contact in an Internet search engine before contacting her. This can provide some interesting background that can make the contact "warmer." Warm calls go much farther than cold ones; making warm contacts is what niche marketing is all about.

Part 2: Scripts

The second part of the market action plan is the scripts. These scripts link the theory of the market action plan to reality by getting appointments. You develop these scripts from the market intelligence you gathered in Part 1.

Part 3: List of Names

The third part of the market action plan is a list of names of potential prospects that are in the target market. The source for these names can be the library, the Internet, or leads lists you purchase (see appendix/resources). Try to screen each person on this list to be sure he fits your qualifications before the first contact is made. (See how in Chapter 5.) The more time spent developing and prescreening these names, the more productive each contact will be. There are few things more valuable than a prescreened list of qualified names within a target market.

The market action plan is complete and ready to execute once it has all three parts. All that's left is to execute by contacting the qualified names. In order to do that, you must have a deep level of motivation that pushes you through the inevitable rejection you will get.

An Example of Developing a Market Action Plan

Let us say you choose to target attorneys. In Part 1 of your market action plan, you might discover that attorneys are generally too busy to spend much time on investing because they are paid for billable hours. You might also find out that most attorneys are responsible for their own retirement plans and that by becoming an expert in retirement plans, you become more valuable to this market. In Part 3 of the action plan, you could start a list of all attorneys in your market with the Yellow Pages (which is only one example of the many sources for finding names of attorneys), and you could use an Internet search to narrow that list to the most experienced and successful attorneys in town. You might also identify and read local publications or trade magazines that your local attorneys read and attend the meetings of the bar associations they belong to; as you do, you will quickly find out who the centers of influence within that market are. Let's say that you then make a connection with one of these centers of influence—she can then refer you to other qualified attorneys, which is invaluable. Armed with the information you have gathered, write out several scripts that you will use when contacting the attorneys on your list to set up initial appointments.

The Marketing Process for New Advisors

I recommend that new advisors initially target five markets and have five market action plans. I believe that new advisors need to focus on more markets than experienced advisors because at the early stages of your career, you may not be certain which markets you will be most effective with. You need to experiment to see what works best; then, over the course of your first two years, you can narrow your five initial market action plans to two or three, based on your success.

I further recommend that every new advisor have the following two market action plans among their first five:

1. *Past-experience market action plan* (see Chapter 23). As a new advisor, one of your first market action plans should be based on your past experience. For example, if you were previously in the software business, then one of your market action plans should focus on people in the software industry. You know who the most qualified prospects are in that industry; use your insider knowledge and contacts to make a connection with those prospects.

2. *Personal contacts market action plan* (see Chapter 23). Your second market action plan should be based on personal contacts, which is essentially a list of all potentially qualified personal contacts. This approach is also called "Rolodex marketing," and it has the highest ratio of contacts to appointments: 50 percent of contacts lead to appointments.

Choose your other three market action plans based on the types of markets you are interested in or you think you would do well with. Part 3 of this book contains fifteen market action plans and over fifty approaches. Find ones that appeal to you and develop them fully, complete with sources of names, before you receive a production number. You should have at least 3,000 names among all five market action plans. If possible, do all this work in advance so that when you receive your production number, all you have to do is execute your plans.

The Marketing Process for Experienced Advisors

Experienced advisors can choose from among the six market action plans I outline here. (You don't need all six to be successful, and you can choose others that may suit you better—see the fifteen market action plans in Part 3 of this book.) These six are based on leveraging your current client relationships and on your outside interests. Parts 2 and 3 of this book have more detail on each of the six market action plans, but I will outline each of them here.

1. *Referrals* (see Chapter 12). Every senior advisor must have an active referral program in place. A proactive referral plan is essential, because the
   majority of new relationships are opened as a result of referrals. Furthermore, the majority of clients would refer if they were asked to do so by
   their advisor. Most clients indicate, however, that they are never asked.

2. *Influencers* (see Chapter 28). All experienced advisors should have a network of CPAs and attorneys who refer prospects to the advisor. The
   number-one way millionaires get their financial advisor is by referral
   from their CPA or attorney. The best way to build this network is
   through the CPAs your current clients use—take advantage of this natural leverage point of the mutual acquaintance. Many advisors who are
   successful in building this kind of network find that between three and
   ten CPAs and attorneys generate a good number of referrals. Support
   and strengthen this network by offering these people continuing education sessions and fun events, by being an information resource, by educating them about the business, and by showcasing the strengths of your
   practice.

3. *Seminars* (see Chapters 12 and 20). Most of your clients belong to outside organizations, such as chambers of commerce, garden clubs, and
   business service clubs, such as Rotary and Kiwanis clubs. Offer to speak
   to these ready-made audiences about investing, and follow up with a
   response card after the seminar. This way, you can reach 240 new potential prospects per year (twelve organizations with twenty participants
   in each organization).

4. *Prospect events* (see Chapter 21). The experienced advisor should host
   client events focused on their clients' interests, and invite his clients to
   bring a friend to these events. These events can be educational or
   activity-based. People like to be with other people who share common
   interests—this is a nonthreatening way for clients to introduce you to
   potential referrals.

5. *Natural-market board of directors* (see Chapter 14). If you look at your
   clients' demographics, you will see that many of your clients are clus-
   tered in the same occupation or the same stage of life; these groupings
   are your "natural market." Form a marketing board of directors, with
   the directors coming from this natural market, then ask these clients how
   to market to people like them. They will give you good ideas, and it's an
   ideal time to ask them for a referral to someone they know or work with.
        You can take your natural market further by using the same narrow
   and deep approach within this niche market: Read publications, join
   local organizations, network within your natural market, become the fi-

nancial services expert that everyone in that market knows about and contact qualified prospects in it.

6. *Nonprofits* (see Chapter 34). In this market action plan, you take a leadership role in an organization that you have a passion for. This can be a philanthropic, civic, or social organization. The key to making this work is to be in a *leadership* role and to be *committed* to the organization. Qualified investors who have a similar passion will be in this organization, and they will be drawn to you.

Marketing Effectiveness

The following table gives approximate ratios of how many contacts each technique requires in order to produce one appointment:

Marketing Method	Contact-to-Appointment
Mailing	100:1
Cold call	20:1
Influencer networking*	10:1
Seminar follow-up	5:1
Referrals	2:1
Personal contacts (Rolodex)	2:1
Networking**	2:1

* Number of influencer meetings need to get one referral.
** Referral from a network member.

The key to reaching a million-dollar practice is to increase your business by twelve new affluent investors ($250,000 in investable assets or more) per year and $12 million in new assets. The first step to achieving that goal is to identify specific market niches and to develop market action plans for these niches. Each action plan should contain a well-thought-out approach, scripts, and qualified names. Niche marketing is effective at all stages of your career.

Once you have your action plans, your next step is to contact the names in each plan. As you do this, be very clear about why you are making the contact and that your objective is a face-to-face meeting; otherwise, you will squander all your hard work, and you will not be effective. In Chapter 5, I outline how you go from your list of names to actually getting an appointment with each person you contact.

Summary

- The first step in growing your practice is to identify three to five niche markets and develop a market action plan for each one.

- Each market action plan should include a detailed plan for how to approach the niche market, scripts to get appointments with people in that market, and sources of names.

- Economies of scale work in favor of going deep and narrow in each niche market. Knowing local centers of influence in each one provides great leverage for penetrating that market effectively.

- You must be deeply motivated to execute the market action plan each day.

- The key focus of each market action plan is getting appointments with new prospects in that market.

- All experienced advisors should choose among six market action plans and consider using one or several of the other market action plans in Part 3. These six plans are: referrals, a CPA/attorney network, seminars for clients' organizations, client/prospect events, developing prospects within your natural market, and taking a leadership role in nonprofit organizations.

CHAPTER 5

Getting the Appointment

I n building the foundation for a million-dollar business, a new advisor's highest priority should be to get as many appointments with affluent prospects as possible. In fact, getting new appointments with affluent prospects should be one of your highest priorities throughout your entire career.

You Must Meet Your Prospects Face to Face

The ability to build a million-dollar practice has more to do with psychology than with financials. This is a people business, and your success is determined by building relationships with people, affluent investors in this case, and opening accounts with them in a reasonable time frame (six to twelve months).

Next to physical health, their fiscal health is people's highest priority. An affluent investor has so many choices of advisors that he would never enter into a relationship without trusting and liking the advisor he will be working with. This is especially true if he is currently working with another advisor, which most affluent investors are.

> **Fundamental Truth:**
> You cannot build a relationship without meeting a prospect face to face.

Understanding that nothing good will happen without your first meeting a qualified investor face to face is essential. The first important skill for achieving marketing success and building a million-dollar practice is to be able to get an initial face-to-face appointment with a qualified prospect.

Any activity that postpones the face-to-face appointment delays building the relationship that leads to doing business with the prospect. Appointments with affluent prospects should be priority 1.

Most advisors will do anything to get a "feel-good" response from a prospect and will delay rejection for as long as they can. This tendency to get a feel-good response is like a one-yard play in football—the ball is moving down the field, but after four one-yard plays, you lose the ball. Examples of one-yard plays include mailing a prospect something or calling her back before you have met her. Getting a first appointment is harder to do, but in the end, it is much more productive. It is like getting a first down—it is harder to do, but you are moving the ball and you *keep* the ball.

If you focus on getting the appointment, then you are absolutely clear about what you want when you first contact the prospect. The mistake most advisors make when they are prospecting is that they do not really know what they want to get out of the initial contact. They want to get a positive response, but they are unclear about where they want the contact to go. If you know with absolute clarity where you want the first contact to go, your probability of success is much higher. When you contact the prospect, he has no idea where the contact is going; if you make a strong case initially about the value of an appointment, the prospect is much less likely to object.

You might assume that giving the highest priority to getting an appointment applies only to cold calling. That is absolutely not the case. Whatever your market action plans are, your first priority must be to get a face-to-face appointment. Remember the Fundamental Truth just given; it applies to networking, seminars, prospect events, CPA referrals, or any other market action plan. Consider cold calling as a last resort when you can't get an appointment any other way.

Prequalifying Your Prospects

It is important that you prequalify the prospect before contacting her to get an appointment. It is a complete waste of time to set appointments with unqualified prospects. When developing your market action plan and building the lists to support the plan, spend as much time as you can qualifying the prospects on the list. You can do this in a variety of ways:

- Determine what job title the prospect holds. An executive who holds the title of vice president or higher is most likely qualified.

- If the prospect owns a business, find out if it is generating $2 million or more in revenue, or if it is consistently profitable and has been in existence for five years or longer.

- Find out where the prospect lives; for example, many qualified investors live in older neighborhoods that have larger homes.

- If the prospect is a professional (attorney or physician), find out if he owns the practice or is a partner. Determine how long he has been in practice.

- If the prospect is an executive of a public company, check public records for information on his holdings and compensation.

- It is also possible to purchase or lease lists of people who have been prescreened for different selectors (income, job title, value of home, and so on).

Qualifying Referrals

Try to prequalify prospects who have been referred to you by others as tactfully as possible. To do this, you can ask questions of the person making the referral, such as:

- "Do you believe the net worth of the prospect you are referring is similar to yours?"

- "Do you believe the referred prospect has at least [minimum qualification] in investable assets?"

- "I find I am most valuable to prospects who have investable assets of [minimum qualification]. Do you believe the referred prospect has at least that amount?"

Qualifying on the First Contact

If you have not prequalified your list or if you want to confirm that the prospect is qualified before making the appointment, you can do it during the initial contact. Here are some examples of how to do that:

- "I am looking forward to meeting you, and I have found that I provide the most value to investors who have [minimum qualification] or more. Would that apply to you?"

- "Before our meeting, it would be helpful for me to have some preliminary information; would you estimate that you have over or under [minimum qualification] in investable assets?"

- "In preparing for our appointment, it would be helpful for me to have an estimate of your investable assets. Would you be comfortable providing me with an estimate?"

- "In preparing for our appointment, it would be helpful to know some preliminary information about your situation. Currently, do you invest in mutual funds or use separate account managers? Do you invest in municipal bonds? Do you have any concentrated stock positions?"

I recommend that you do as much prequalification as you can in advance because having to qualify the prospect during the first contact can be awkward and might offend the prospect. However, you should prequalify the prospect before the appointment, and if the only way to do it is during the initial contact, do it then to avoid wasting time with an unqualified prospect.

The bottom line is that the more time you spend prequalifying your list before you contact a prospect, the more hours you will save by avoiding meeting with unqualified prospects. Your ability to prequalify is limited only by the time you are willing to spend researching the qualification level.

How to Determine the Minimum Qualification

Determine the minimum qualification level based on the size of your current clients. A rule of thumb is that a prospect should have at least as many investable assets as your one-hundredth/least-affluent, client. A new advisor has very few, if any, client relationships, so the minimum qualification should be at least $100,000 in investable assets. Another guideline is based on your length of service (LOS):

LOS (in years)	Minimum Investable Assets Guidelines
0–2	$100,000
3–5	$150,000
6+*	$250,000

* If over $1 million in production, prospect minimum should increase. See table in Chapter 3

If the Prospect Is Not Qualified, "Unsell" the Appointment

If you have to "unsell" an appointment because the prospect does not meet the minimum qualification, it is okay to do so. The following script gives some idea of how to do this:

> Mr./Ms. Prospect, based on what you told me about your investments, I am not sure an appointment makes sense right now. I would like to send you some information on what we have available, and you can call me if you are interested.

Making the Contact and Getting the Appointment

The objective of your contact is to get the prospect to commit to a short meeting so that you can make a connection with her face to face to discuss her investments—only a face-to-face investment discussion counts here. You should understand this and remember it at all times.

Most affluent investors are bombarded with offers to invest their money—they are bombarded by solicitations in the mail, in newspapers and magazines, on television, from telemarketers, and so on. Other obstacles are that the affluent investor most likely already has an advisor, and affluent investors tend to be very busy people.

On the other hand, take confidence from the fact that the majority of investors are underserviced and will change advisors at some point. Also, despite the obstacles, getting an appointment is not complicated, although it is difficult. You will greatly increase the probability of getting an appointment when you contact a prospect to ask for one if you:

- Remember that your first priority is to get a face-to-face meeting.
- Quickly describe why it is in the prospect's best interest to take some time to meet you ("value-added").
- Provide a sincere compliment.

Remember that the objective of the appointment will be to make a personal connection, which will set the stage for building a strong relationship with the prospect; that, in turn, will become the catalyst for the prospect to transfer at least a portion of his assets to you. In order to make this connection during the appointment, add value by focusing on the prospect's needs. This is why niche marketing, and the research behind it, is so important. The value you will give to the prospect when he meets with you is based on your understanding of that prospect's needs.

The more you know about the prospect in advance, the stronger the case you can make for why the prospect should meet with you. If you have any common connection with the prospect, that will further increase the value of the appointment. The following are some examples of how you can add a sense of value when you contact a prospect to set up your appointment:

Examples of Scripts for Getting an Appointment

Mr./Ms. Business Owner, this is Joe Advisor from XYZ Financial. The reason for my call is that I know that as a successful business owner, you are always trying to improve your bottom line, and I specialize in helping business owners get more profits. I know you are successful, and if you give me the opportunity to meet with you, I am convinced that I can show you how I could add to your bottom line. Would you be available next Thursday to meet with me?

• • • • • • • • • • •

Mr./Ms. Business Owner, my name is Jane Advisor from XYZ Financial, and the reason I am calling you is that I specialize in working with successful owners of dry cleaners like you. I understand your business, and I am convinced that if you give me the opportunity to meet you and find out more about your circumstances, I could show you some ways to improve your bottom line. I will be in your area next Thursday. Could we schedule a brief appointment?

• • • • • • • • • • •

Mr./Ms. Prospect, my name is Joe Advisor, and I work with XYZ Financial, and the reason for my call is that I used to do what you do now. If I had known then what I know now, I would have done better with my business and personal investments. I know you are successful and could benefit from someone like myself who understands the dynamics of your profession/business/industry. If you would give me some time, I know I could provide value. Would you be available next Thursday for a brief introductory meeting?

*This script assumes you were a former business owner in that particular industry.

• • • • • • • • • • •

Mr./Ms. Executive, my name is Jane Advisor, and I work with XYZ Financial, and the reason for my call is that I specialize in working with successful and highly compensated executives like you. I understand that there is a lot of complexity in your deferred compensation, stock options, and retirement plans. If you would be willing to give me the opportunity, I know I could provide you with valuable information on how to maximize your benefits and minimize your taxes. Would you be available for a brief introductory meeting on Thursday?

. . . .

Mr./Ms. Past Contact, this is Joe Advisor, and I wanted to have the opportunity to reconnect with you. I have always respected you professionally and personally. I am currently working with XYZ Financial and have been very impressed with the training I have received and the unique wealth-management process that we offer our clients. I would like to have the opportunity to visit with you to find out more about your circumstances and see if I could provide some value. Would you be receptive to meeting with me and taking the opportunity to reconnect?

. . . .

Mr./Ms. Prospect, my name is Jane Advisor, and I work with XYZ Financial. My firm has asked me to cover your town/suburb. You have the reputation of being a successful business owner/professional/individual, and I would like to meet you and get your opinion on how I should best approach your town/suburb. I also could provide you with a contact with our firm and all the resources we have. Would you have time for a brief introductory meeting when I am in your area next Thursday?

. . . .

Mr./Ms. Investor, my name is Joe Advisor, and I am with XYZ Financial. The reason for my call is that I know you are a successful investor and I wanted to offer to be a contact for you with our firm. We have excellent research, a good inventory of bonds, and a very broad product line. I know that in the long term I would be an excellent resource for you; and at the very least, I could offer a second opinion. I am going to be in your area next Thursday and was hoping to schedule a brief introductory meeting. Would you be available?

The Four Elements Scripts Need to Have

These scripts all have four things in common:

1. *Connection.* The advisor draws a connection between the prospect's needs or situation and the advisor's specialization or capabilities.

2. *Recognition.* The advisor compliments the prospect on her success or reputation.

3. *Value.* The advisor quickly states how he can provide some value to the prospect given the prospect's current situation.

4. *Commitment.* The advisor asks for a commitment to having a brief introductory appointment.

These are the four elements most initial contacts should have in order to get the appointment. Please note that some market action plans require a softer, longer-term approach; examples of these are action plans that involve social networking and networking through organizations.

If you include these elements in your contacts, with experience and practice, you should average one appointment per ten contacts. This will be an average of the blend of techniques you use. For example, the Rolodex technique delivers about five appointments per ten contacts, while cold calling delivers one per twenty. Using a mix of techniques, as you will in real life, you will average around one per ten.

> **Fundamental Truth:**
> The more contacts you make seeking appointments, the better your contact-to-appointment ratio will be.

The more experience you have getting initial appointments, the higher your success ratio will be. In our business, as in everything else, practice makes perfect. With experience comes skill and flow. The advisor who makes many contacts seeking appointments will naturally become more relaxed and more comfortable asking for, and getting, appointments. It is important to remember the low-percentage/high-payoff dynamic of this business (see Chapter 4). It is okay if you get only a 10-to-1 contact-to-appointment ratio—it takes only eight appointments with new prospects per week to build a million-dollar practice, and at a 10-to-1 ratio, you need to make only eighty contacts per week, or sixteen per day, to build a million-dollar practice.

A Confident Style Gets Better Results

One of the reasons that practice and experience improve results is that your confidence will increase over time and create a more fluid style.

These phone contacts should be friendly, relaxed, and filled with "give and take" and, when possible, humor. A confident style projects experience, and experience is what the prospect wants. A tight, scripted-sounding, nervous style projects inexperience and insecurity, which is not what the prospect wants in a future advisor. The only way to be relaxed and confident is to practice and gain experience.

For most advisors, if you practice diligently and make several hundred contacts, you will have the right level of confidence within three months. If it takes eighty effective contacts a week to build the foundation for a million-dollar practice, in three months you will have made about 1,000 contacts, in six weeks, almost 500.

Handling Objections

You need to know how to overcome objections. You should be like a black-belt martial arts master who anticipates objections in advance and has a practiced move to deflect them. Prospects object in predictable ways, and you can prepare to handle them in advance.

"No" is an overall objection that you will encounter in many different forms. The response that most people give to a stranger asking for their time is no. It is like walking into a store and the clerk asks, "Can I help you?" Our first reaction is, "I am just looking," even if we want help. Initially contacting a prospect in this business is the same. In many cases, the prospect will reflexively respond with, "No, I am not interested," whether she has a need or not. The key is to catch the prospect off guard and build a case for why it is to her advantage to spend time face to face with you in as short a time as possible.

In some cases, prospects have trouble saying no and will delay saying it by sidetracking you: They will ask you to send something or to call them back. All the prospect is doing is delaying the "no" response. The trap the advisor falls into is that he wastes precious time following up with an uninterested prospect who will never commit to an appointment. You should either get an appointment or move on to a prospect you can get an appointment with. Here are the most common forms "no" takes, and how to respond:

Prospect: "I don't have the time to see you right now."
Advisor: "I understand you are busy. Most successful people are. But

this brief appointment will be time well spent for you. My intention is just to meet you and find out more about your circumstances. In return for your time, you will have free access to all of our research and other resources, and free access to me. I only expect us to do business together if I earn that privilege over time by providing you better service than you have now."

Prospect: "I don't have any money to invest right now. It would be a waste of your time."

Advisor: "I did not expect you would have anything to invest immediately. My only intention is to have a brief introductory meeting so that we can meet each other and so that I can find out more about your circumstances. Over time I hope I can earn a portion of your business if you feel that I offer you value and if you feel that there is a good fit."

Prospect: "I am taken care of. I have an advisor."

Advisor: "I would be surprised if a successful investor like you did not already have an advisor. My intention is just to have a brief introductory meeting so that we can make a connection face to face, and so that I can find out more about your situation. I am confident that over time I could earn a portion of your business by providing superior service and by creating value for you."

Prospect: "I am not interested in seeing you now."

Advisor: "My only intention is to make a quick connection and find out more about your circumstances so that I can provide you, at no cost, my time, our resources, and our research. I am confident that over time I could give you more value than you are currently getting. Would you consider giving me that opportunity?"

These responses will cover 90 percent of the objections you will receive. Prospects do not think about objections in advance; this is simply a reflex response. By being prepared and practicing the objection responses, you can often overcome the objection and improve your appointment ratio by 25 percent. If the prospect responds negatively to your objection response, close the call by asking the prospect if she knows anyone else who might be interested in getting to know an honest, hardworking advisor.

Recontacting a Prospect Who Won't Meet with You

If, after you try to overcome her objections, the prospect is not interested, you should ask for a referral and then move on. After you make a well-rehearsed contact in which you offer value with a minimum time commitment, if you cannot convince the prospect, she is no longer a prospect and you should recycle her name to be contacted several months later. You can *profitably* contact her again later because her circumstances may have changed and the law of receptivity may apply (which is that as circumstances change, the same prospect may become much more receptive); thus, there is good reason to recontact the prospect in several months and to ask for an appointment again. Qualified names are too scarce to discard a good potential prospect.

However, what will *not* work is to follow through with a prospect who will not commit to an appointment. Sending an uncommitted prospect a follow-up mailing or doing any other follow-up activity before you have an appointment is a waste of time. The only exception to that is if the prospect indicates an interest in the appointment but physically cannot make an appointment in the next several weeks. Under those circumstances, it is a good idea for you to recontact the prospect in order to schedule an appointment at a more convenient time (within thirty days). There are so many prospects who will meet with you that you cannot waste time on those who will not. Move on.

Keeping the Appointment

Between the time you make the appointment and the time the appointment occurs, many prospects will have second thoughts, but because an appointment has been made, most prospects will keep it—they committed to doing so. Once a prospect commits to seeing you face to face, in most cases he will keep that commitment.

Do not reconfirm the appointment because that gives the prospect an easy out, and he may cancel.

How Many Prospects to Meet With

You should expect that 50 percent of the prospects you meet with will convert to qualified prospects, i.e., meet, commit to second appointment, and/or return calls. Qualified prospects are your future clients, and if you follow up with them at the right frequency, 25 percent of them should become clients within twelve months.

The total number of qualified prospects in your pipeline should never exceed one hundred. You cannot properly contact and service more than one hundred prospects. Once you have one hundred prospects in your pipeline, you should replace the smallest and least likely to do business with more qualified prospects. If you are a senior advisor with a length of service of six years or more, your prospect pipeline can include a total of only fifty prospects, because they will typically be more qualified—as they will have a higher minimum qualification.

In your first two years, you should meet a minimum of eight *new* prospects a week. This is a challenging but completely achievable goal, and there is no excuse for not meeting it. As I stated earlier, at a 10-to-1 contact-to-appointment ratio, it takes only sixteen effective contacts per day to reach this goal.

Advisors in their third to fifth year should set a goal of four new prospect appointments per week, and senior advisors with length of service of six years or more should set a goal of one to two new prospect appointments per week. At a 10-to-1 ratio, you can achieve these goals with eight contacts per day and four per day, respectively.

It is important for you to understand that most affluent investors are underserviced and many are not completely satisfied with their current advisor. Your goal is to get an appointment in order to start building a case for why the investor is better off with you. You want to position yourself as "a strong number two": Even if you do not open the account in the short term, you are positioning yourself to be the next in line for the account, right after the prospect's current provider. Be aware that there is little competition for the number two spot.

Now that you have the appointment, what do you do in the appointment? This is your golden opportunity, where you can create a connection with a prospect that will lead to his becoming a client. How do you do this? See the next chapter for the answer.

Summary

- From the first day of your career, make as many new appointments with new affluent prospects as you possibly can.
- You cannot build the right relationship with affluent investors without meeting them face to face.

- Your first priority in prospecting is to get an appointment.
- Any marketing activity that delays an initial face-to-face appointment is a waste of time.
- You will get a much higher contact-to-appointment ratio if you focus right away on getting an appointment.
- Most prospects are underserviced. The key first step is to get a foot in the door through an appointment, and position yourself as number two in line for their business.
- Before you make the contact, spend time prequalifying your prospects. If that is not possible, or if you want to verify her qualification, you can do so during the initial contact.
- Do not get sidelined by anything other than getting an appointment. If you cannot convince a prospect to meet you, recycle the name and move on.
- The minimum qualification for a prospect should be assets greater than your 100th client or $100,000, whichever is greater.
- Cold calling for appointments can be effective, but it has one of the lowest contact-to-appointment ratios of any direct-marketing approach.
- Every initial contact with a prospect should have four elements: connection (with the prospect's situation), recognition (of the prospect's success), value (what benefit the prospect will derive from meeting with you), and commitment (to meet).
- You should anticipate and have ready responses to objections that prospects may raise about meeting with you. If the response does not work, ask for a referral and move on. There are plenty of prospects who will see you.
- A relaxed, confident style is essential to success in getting an initial appointment. This comes with practice and experience.
- Weekly appointment goals:

Length of service 0 to 2 years	Eight appointments per week, minimum
Length of service 3 to 5 years	Four appointments per week
Length of service 6 years or more	One–two appointments per week

- About half of your meetings will be with contacts who meet your qualification minimums and agree to a second appointment. These are true prospects. A quarter of those (or 13 percent of all meetings you have) are likely to become clients within twelve months, with proper follow-up.

- You should never have more than one hundred qualified prospects in your prospect pipeline. (That's for advisors with zero to two years of service; those with three to five years LOS need seventy-five, and those with LOS of six years and over need only fifty prospects in their pipeline.) After your pipeline is full, you can add a prospect to it only if you also drop one from the bottom of the pile.

CHAPTER 6

The Appointment

The initial face-to-face appointment is like gold: It is hard to get, but it is extremely valuable. Because of the potential value of every face-to-face appointment, you must maximize this golden opportunity; in order to do so, you should know exactly what you need to cover in the initial appointment:

- You should make a positive connection by building rapport.
- You should gather all the information possible about the prospect. You will use this information in the important follow-up.
- You should get a commitment for a second appointment.

You can achieve all these objectives through the same technique: by asking a lot of questions.

Start Off Right

You are a guest of your prospect, and you are asking for the privilege of asking her questions, so you should begin with a brief introduction that will let your prospect know your agenda. Here are some examples of how to set the stage:

> Mr./Ms. Prospect, thank you for taking the time to see me. The purpose of the appointment from my standpoint is to get the chance to know you better and to find out as much as I can about your current investment situation. Hopefully, by understanding your situation better, I can follow up and provide some real value to you. As I mentioned on the phone, I hope to earn a portion of your business by offering my services and the resources of our firm at no cost to you. The best way for me to accomplish that is to ask you some questions. It is clear to me that you are successful—could you share your story with me?

. . . .

Mr./Ms. Prospect, it is clear to me that you are successful, and I know your time is at a premium. By finding out more about your circumstances, I am confident that I can add value to your current financial situation. The best way I can accomplish that is to ask you some questions about your current situation. Could you share your story with me?

. . . .

Mr./Ms. Prospect, I know that you are a successful individual and that you are busy. I hope that over time I can earn a portion of your business by offering you my time and the resources of our firm at no cost to you, in order to fill in the service gaps you may be experiencing. The best way for me to get started is to ask you as many questions about your current financial circumstances as you are comfortable with. May I ask you about your story and how you have been so successful?

. . . .

Mr./Ms. Prospect, I appreciate your time today. I know that since you are a successful individual, your time is at a premium. My intention is to position myself over time as a strong number two in line behind your current advisor, and to earn the right to a portion of your business by providing you with access to me and to the resources of our firm at no cost. I can best accomplish that by asking you some questions about your current financial circumstances and long-term objectives.

. . . .

It is important that you use an approach that does not appear to be an interrogation. Start with softer, more general questions and gradually become direct. Be sure to be aware of the dynamics during this process and "give and take" as needed. Let the prospect set the pace. If the prospect wants to expand or elaborate, give him plenty of leeway to do so. Stay engaged throughout the appointment, and keep a relaxed, confident style. This comes only with practice and experience.

When appropriate, ask for a tour of your prospect's business or operation. The prospect will usually accept the offer and will show you her operation with pride. This is a great rapport-building, fact-finding technique that you should use whenever possible. At the end of the appointment, ask the prospect if she knows anyone else you should be talking to, and ask if she could possibly introduce you personally if that person works at the same location.

Ask Questions

The appointment should be a fact-finding mission. The facts you gather will become the basis of the all-important follow-up process. You will build rapport and gather the facts you need if you focus on asking the prospect questions. If the prospect talks, he will like you; if you talk, the opposite occurs. Most successful people like to tell their story, but too often no one is really interested in their story, and they do not get the opportunity to tell it enough.

This is your chance to make a good first impression, and you can best do that if the prospect believes that you are experienced and confident, and at the same time empathetic and sincere. You can accomplish all this by becoming a master of asking questions.

Note that the first two objectives of the first appointment are to build rapport and to gather information on which to set up the follow-through. There is a fine line between building rapport (asking more general questions) and asking too much (and turning the prospect off. During the first appointment, be careful how specific your questions regarding the exact amount of money the prospect has are. Many people are uncomfortable disclosing this kind of information without first building a relationship with you. If you ask the fifty questions I recommend (at the end of this chapter), you should be able to develop a sense of whether you have a qualified prospect or not without asking about the specific amounts of money she has invested. Use your own judgment about how specific you should be on the first appointment—if the rapport you have created seems particularly strong, you may be in a good position to be more specific.

If this is not the case, however, your opportunity comes a bit later. Note once again that the third objective of every first appointment is to get a commitment to a second, follow-up appointment; if the prospect agrees to the second appointment, it is at that appointment that you will present your wealth-management process and explain how different it is from the way the prospect is probably investing. If you do this properly, in most cases you will have created doubt in the prospect's mind about his current situation and have caused him to consider whether it might make more sense to work with you. In this case, I recommend that as part of the second appointment, you outline the next steps and ask for permission to get much more specific about the dollar amounts, the specific investments that the prospect has, and his net worth. If the second appointment does not turn out to be the place for such specific questions either, that is fine; put the prospect into your follow-up process (see Chapter 7)—the opportunity will come as you build his trust in you.

To some degree, this is more of an art than a science; your own judgment will dictate when you should become more specific about dollar amounts.

Ask About the Prospect's Personal Situation and Interests

Remember the three objectives I stated at the beginning of this chapter— rapport, information, and commitment. One way to achieve all three is to gather as much information as possible about the prospect's personal interests. This provides essential information to use for the later follow-up process. Gather information about the prospect's family, her marital status and her spouse, how many children and grandchildren she has, and the interests and activities of those offspring. Gather information about her hobbies, such as hunting, golfing, fly-fishing, or tennis. All of this information will be useful during the follow-up stage.

As the questions progress, I strongly recommended that you pay attention to the prospect's surroundings. Pictures, trophies, and awards are important clues to the prospect's interests. You can build rapport by referring to these areas of interest throughout your questions; this will also help the prospect relax and feel more open. Everyone likes to talk about his personal interests and passions.

You cannot give too many sincere compliments throughout the appointment. Some of the best rapport building happens when you and your prospect share interests.

Pitfalls

If the prospect asks you for your opinion about the markets, make your answers general and brief—this is not the time to impress the prospect. Be sure to get back to your goal of gathering information about the prospect. If the prospect persists and asks a question that you do not know the answer to, offer to get back to her after you have had time to research or think about the answer.

One of the fears all new advisors have is that the prospect will ask about their level of experience. The best response is to be truthful, but to emphasize the resources and training of your firm and its unique wealth-management process, and to emphasize your commitment to, and the time you can provide for, servicing the prospect. Remember, most senior advisors are short on time and long on accounts; the junior advisor has plenty of time to provide the much-needed service that the prospect is often not receiving.

If you discover during the appointment that the prospect does not meet the minimum qualification, you should politely make the appointment as short as possible. There is no value to either you or the prospect in having a long appointment if he is not a qualified prospect.

How Long to Meet

A good appointment can last from thirty minutes to an hour or more. Never cut short an appointment with a qualified prospect; the opportunity is too valuable, and there is too much information that it is impossible to get otherwise.

If you have multiple appointments during the day, schedule your appointments loosely (preferably in the mornings or afternoons) so that you do not run into problems. You should never be late, but if you schedule appointments every hour, you may have to choose between being late and having to cut short a good appointment (or even end up doing both).

Close the Appointment

The best way to close the appointment is to thank the prospect for her time and her willingness to share information. Restate the purpose of the appointment, which was to find out as much information as possible so that you can tailor your advice and the resources of the firm to add value to the prospect's situation. Restate your confidence that over time, you will add value and hopefully earn a portion of the prospect's business—again, your objective is to be a strong number two in line, at no cost to the prospect.

Before you part, try to set up a face-to-face appointment at which you will present your preliminary thoughts and recommendations. Remember that one of your primary objectives on the first appointment is to get a commitment from the prospect to a second appointment, in which you can present your wealth-management process tailored to that particular prospect. If you cannot schedule a second appointment, try to set up a follow-up call.

When you get back to the office, be sure to enter the prospect into the contact management system for the follow-up process.

The Bad Appointment

You should expect that about half of your appointments will not be good ones. In a bad appointment, the prospect will be abrupt and will not give you the time to ask the questions you need to ask or to build rapport. However, only 50 percent of the appointments need to be good ones to make the process work; if you have a bad appointment, you should be willing to cut your losses and move on to a potentially good appointment as soon as possible. The best tactic to use on a bad appointment is to thank the prospect for his time, ask him for a referral, and then leave.

If the appointment is a no-show, leave your card, go to another appointment, then drop by again to catch the prospect. No-shows give you the right to drop in anytime that day. If you miss the prospect throughout the day, call the next day and try once more to reschedule.

Follow Up Right Away

Send a follow-up letter the next day. Thank the prospect, restate the purpose of the appointment, and reconfirm the follow-up appointment.

Follow-Up Letter

Dear Mr./Ms. Prospect:

I wanted to sincerely thank you for taking the time to see me last Thursday. I was impressed by you and your success. I know your time is valuable, but by your giving it to me, I was able to gain some insights into how I might help you in the future.

I appreciate your willingness to meet again, to give me the opportunity to share with you some of my recommendations and thoughts on how you might improve your current investment situation. My objective over time is to *earn* a portion of your investment business by providing you valuable ideas and outstanding service.

> Thank you again for giving me the opportunity to visit with you. I look forward to our next meeting.
>
> Sincerely
Joe Advisor

Follow-Up Call

Use this script in the event that you could not get a commitment to a second appointment during your first meeting.

> Mr./Ms. Prospect, this is Joe Advisor with XYZ Financial. I wanted to thank you again for seeing me last week.
>
> Based on the information you gave me, there are a couple of suggestions I want to give you that I believe make sense.

Immediately after you say that last sentence:

- Offer to do a free plan for her.
- Share the top one or two action steps that are most timely.
- Suggest another appointment to review her situation in more detail.

Most prospects will not become clients during your first meeting with them. You have set the best possible conditions for them to become clients, but then you must do the proper things after that to finally convert them. I will cover what those things are, and how and when to do them, in the next chapter.

Fifty Sample Questions

The following questions should serve only as guidelines for questions that you might ask during the appointment. You can and should modify them to suit your own style, and to the circumstances of the first appointment. I recommend that you memorize the questions you are going to ask, although it is not necessary—if you ask your questions spontaneously, it can seem less formal and more relaxed. Feel comfortable writing down notes on the information you gather.

I recommend that when you ask questions, you use the different categories in the order given—personal questions are easier to answer and can help build rapport, making it easier for the prospect to answer financial questions later on. I also recommend that within any particular category, you ask less personal and more general questions first, then move on to more personal and more specific questions.

Feel free to add more specific questions based on the circumstances and your prospect. It is okay to ask fewer questions if the prospect is getting impatient or seems pressed for time. You need to rely on your expertise in your target market to develop additional, more specific questions. Markets that could require additional questions could include business owners, executives, retirees, and professionals.

Personal Information

1. Where did you grow up? How did you get here (this town/city)?
2. Where do you live? How long have you lived there?
3. Where did you go to school?
4. How did you end up in this line of work?
5. Are you involved in any community, service, or charitable groups?
6. Do you belong to any social organizations (e.g., a country club)?
7. What do you do in your spare time (outside interests)?
8. Do you have a CPA and an estate planning attorney that you are comfortable with?

Investment Information

9. What keeps you up at night regarding your investments?
10. What are your personal long-term investment goals?
11. What are your short-term goals?
12. What do you like about your current investment situation?
13. What would you change if you could about your investments?
14. How would you describe your risk tolerance?
15. What is your highest priority for your investments?
16. What do you consider an acceptable long-term rate of return (annual percentage rate)?
17. How have you determined asset allocation?
18. Have you had a financial plan done? Have you followed it? How do you feel about your most recent financial plan?
19. How have you invested for your short-term cash-flow needs?
20. How satisfied are you with your investments?

21. What could your current advisor do better?

Family Information

22. Tell me about your family.

23. Are you married?

24. Do you have children? Grandchildren?

25. How old are they?

26. Do you anticipate that your children/grandchildren will go to college? Where would you like to see them go?

27. Have you set up funding for their education? Do you have an idea of the cost?

28. Are your parents still alive? Do you anticipate having to support your parents?

29. Do you have any gifting strategies for your children?

30. What is your spouse's involvement in your investments?

31. Does your spouse have the same goals and risk tolerance as you?

Retirement Information

32. When do you anticipate retiring?

33. What plans do you have in place to prepare for your retirement?

34. Does your company have retirement plans? Do you participate?

35. Do you contribute to an IRA or a Roth IRA? Does your spouse?

36. Are you on track with your retirement goals?

37. What rate of return do you expect to have in your retirement that will keep your principal intact?

38. How much money do you expect to need every year to support your retirement lifestyle?

Insurance and Estate Planning Information

39. What type of protection do you have in case of death or disability?

40. What type of life insurance do you have?

41. When was the last time you had your life insurance reviewed?

42. Have you made plans for the transfer of assets if something were to happen to you or your spouse?

43. Have you established a trust or will? When was the last time you had it reviewed?

44. How long has it been since you reviewed your beneficiary designations on your life insurance policy and retirement plans?

45. Do you or your parents (if living) have long-term-care insurance?

46. Do you have a charity you are committed to, and if so, have you developed any charitable gifting strategies?

Liability Information

47. Do you have a mortgage? What are the terms? How long has it been since you refinanced?

48. Have you established a home equity line of credit? What is the interest rate?

49. Do you have any other lines of credit? What rates are you paying?

50. Do you have a second home? If not, do you have any goals to purchase one?

Optional: Net Worth

51. Would you be comfortable sharing your net worth with me?

52. How much of that is investable assets (equities, fixed income, cash)?

53. What is your real estate equity value?

54. What is the value of your other types of investments?

55. What are your liabilities and their amounts?

Finally, ask the prospect if there is anything else you haven't talked about that he would like to discuss.

Summary

- The objectives of the appointment are to build rapport, make a connection and gather personal and investment information, and get a commitment for a second appointment.

- The best way to accomplish the objectives of the appointment is to begin with a simple framing statement followed by questions.

- A relaxed, spontaneous, confident style is important for the appointment. You will achieve this with practice and experience.

- Be prepared for specific questions; answer generally and offer to get back to him on unanswered questions; then get back on track.

- Expect 50 percent of the appointments to be good ones and accept that bad appointments do occur. Be prepared to leave politely but promptly if the appointment is a bad one.

- Under no circumstances make a presentation on the first appointment. The second appointment is when you can present your wealth-management process and indicate what an investment experience with you would be like.

- Ask for a tour of the operation if appropriate.

- Always ask for a referral.

- Pay attention to the surroundings—they are clues to the prospect's main interests. Try to make a connection to these interests and refer to them during your questions.

- Personal information can be as valuable as investment information and uncovers important areas to follow up on.

- A good appointment will last from a half hour to an hour. If it goes longer with a qualified prospect, do not rush through the appointment.

- Do not commit to an exact time for the appointment when you have multiple appointments in one day. Simply setting morning or afternoon is best to give you maximum flexibility. Do not be late for an appointment if a time is set.

- If a prospect is not qualified, minimize appointment time.

- Get a commitment to follow up within a week to share your thoughts and provide preliminary recommendations based on the information you gathered.

- Send a letter the next day. Thank the prospect for her time, review the purpose of the appointment, commit to follow through, and remind the prospect of the follow-up appointment.

- Enter the prospect in the follow-up contact management process.

- Have your fifty questions prepared and memorized whenever possible. This permits a more relaxed approach.

Turning Prospects Into Clients

n Chapter 6, I explained that one of your objectives during the appointment is to get a commitment for a second, follow-up appointment. If you have built good rapport and have asked questions, you have set the stage for the second appointment.

The Second Appointment

The second appointment is where you share how you can improve the prospect's investment experience. In the second appointment, you use all the information you gathered in the first appointment and give the prospect a customized presentation on why he is better off working with you. Keep these points in mind:

- The presentation should not be long; thirty minutes total is ideal. Make it concise and full of impact.
- The presentation can be as informal or formal as you think appropriate for the particular prospect.
- In the presentation, give a brief overview:
  - Of yourself and what you bring to the investment experience
  - Of your wealth-management process
  - Of the tools and resources you have that will improve the prospect's investment experience
  - Of the potential next steps

You have now set the stage for either opening an account with the prospect or positioning the follow-up process. Clearly, not all prospects will commit to the next steps and open a new account. In fact, the majority will not, and that is when you will use the process I outline in this chapter for turning prospects into clients. The cornerstones of this process are the monthly contact and the drop-by. I should warn you, however, that you need to be patient: When this process is done properly, it can take from six to twelve months to convert 25 percent of your prospects into clients.

What Is a Qualified Prospect?

Being sure that a prospect meets the minimum assets level will increase your chances of converting the prospect to a client. I tell my new advisors that prospects should have at least $100,000 to invest. The more business you currently have, the higher this minimum should be; a rule of thumb for experienced advisors is that every new prospect should have more assets to invest than the advisor's one-hundredth largest client has, but always at least $100,000.

Fundamental Truth:
A qualified prospect will become a client if she trusts you and likes you, and if she believes that you will do a better job than her current advisor.

A prospect will become a client when you provide better service and build a stronger relationship with him than his current advisor has, and do so in the shortest time possible. You will achieve this if you make a minimum of two contacts with each prospect per month.

Contacting each prospect twice a month is frequent enough to build a relationship, but not so frequent as to be overly aggressive. Clearly there will be times when the prospect requests that you follow up or talk with her more than twice monthly; if a prospect is ready to take action immediately, then more frequent contact is appropriate.

One of the two contacts each month with each prospect is a *monthly prospect contact,* and the other is a *drop-by.*

The Monthly Prospect Contact

The monthly prospect contact is probably the most important part of the prospecting process. Before going into the mechanics of these contacts, it is important to spend time understanding the proper mindset and what the objective is.

The objective of these contacts is to build a relationship with the prospect, and to create the perception that you will provide a higher level of service and be more attuned to his needs than his current advisor. The contact is either a phone call or an e-mail or mail piece followed by a phone call. (Personal visits are the drop-bys.)

As you have met with the prospect, you have determined what his investment and personal objectives are. As an example, let's say that on the initial appointment with a prospect, you discovered the following:

Your prospect is a male executive employed by a publicly traded company; he has an interest in retiring within five years; he has three teenagers for whom he has not set up a college education fund; he is an avid skier and golfer, and he loves baseball.

With this basic information, you can set up an effective twelve-month contact system tailored to him. After the second appointment, you could call him and say:

- "I'm calling you with the latest earnings forecast our firm has on your company."

- "I'm calling to invite you to a seminar titled 'Retirement Checklist— What Does It Take?'; do you know anyone else who might be interested in attending?"

- "I'm calling to tell you about a college funding idea: the 529 plan."

- "I'm calling to invite you to a major league/minor league baseball game next week."

- "I'm calling you about an article in *Golf* magazine that I am sending you that I thought you might be interested in."

- "I'm calling to congratulate you on your son's making the honor roll, and on his being recognized in the community paper for that."

- "I'm calling you with an idea that I am sharing with my best clients, and I thought you might be interested."

Each of these calls provides valuable information and acknowledges the prospect's interests. Relationships are built by listening to and understanding the prospect, and responding to his needs and interests. Unless the prospect's existing advisor is one of the very best, she is no longer taking the time to do these things, if she ever did—she takes most of her clients for granted. You, on the other hand, have made the commitment to the prospect, and your mind is "tuned into" your prospect's needs all the time.

Any time you see something or think about something that will be of interest to your prospects, send it to them, call them, or drop by. Over time, usually within six to twelve months, many of your prospects will come to the obvious conclusion that they would be better off with you than with their current advisor. You have earned this trust through the attention and service you provided.

As an advisor who is committed to growth by taking the time to follow up with your prospects, you are capitalizing on another fundamental truth.

Fundamental Truth:

Most affluent investors know that there is little difference between competitors when it comes to the products and services they offer.

Portfolio performance matters, but it is not all that matters. Service and relationships matter too: Good performance without a strong relationship and good service isn't enough, and good service and a strong relationship without good performance are also not enough. It takes all three.

Most firms manage investments in similar ways, and affluent investors tend to know this. The biggest difference, then, is in the strength of the relationship (trust) and in personal service. The combination of a strong relationship, excellent service, and good performance can give the prospecting advisor an edge.

The most successful advisors I have worked with were the ones who recognized that it was trust and service that set them apart and who made these their highest priority. Make no mistake, these advisors had established a wealth-management process and followed it in a disciplined way, but they understood that the fundamental difference was not in their wealth-management process, but in the depth of the relationship and the level of service that they provided. Most advisors do not give the relationship and service a high enough priority; this weakness works to the advantage of the prospecting advisor who focuses on these aspects through the monthly prospect contacts and drop-bys.

> **Fundamental Truth:**
> **Most advisors do not spend enough time servicing their accounts.**

What these two fundamental truths are saying is that you will have a higher success rate if you provide better service and develop better relationships than the prospect's current advisor does. This concept is particularly true for the new advisor who is long on time and short on clients. By spending time with a *manageable number of prospects,* the new advisor is capitalizing on his strength (time) and the current provider's weakness (lack of time). This dynamic is the engine that drives the prospecting process, and it will greatly increase the rate of converting prospects to clients. The more experienced advisor may not have as much time, but focusing on a manageable number of prospects still allows this process to work.

The Drop-By

The drop-by is dropping by the prospect's home or office with some research or printed material that would be of specific interest to the prospect, and hand-delivering the information to her. Do this once a month for each prospect. This takes perceived service to the highest level. I recommend to my advisors that they look for reports, articles, and other interesting information to use for drop-bys. Do the drop-bys when going to or from an appointment or to or from work.

Organize your prospects geographically so that when you are in a particular area, it is convenient to drop by. If the prospect is in, deliver the information to him by hand with a brief acknowledgment: "I was thinking of you and wanted to deliver this timely information personally." If the prospect is not in, then attach a note stating essentially the same thing and give this to his assistant to give to the prospect. The impact is the same: The prospect sees that you took the time to think about him, you found useful information connected to his interests, and then you personally delivered that information to him.

This is a powerful message regarding the level of service you provide your clients. The prospect will compare the level of interest and service you are providing with the interest and service he is currently getting;

over time, this will convince him that you are the better provider and that it is time to change.

My experience has shown that service and the relationship are the most frequent catalysts for change. The prospect cannot compare investment performance because she does not have an account with you yet, but the service you provide and the relationship you build are tangibles that she can measure her current advisor against.

I recommend doing drop-bys once a month for each prospect in your pipeline. This will be more of a challenge for the experienced advisor, in which case I recommend that you do a drop-by whenever it is practical.

How Many Prospects to Have at Any One Time

A key here is exactly that: to focus on a manageable number of prospects. To build your practice as quickly and strongly as possible, you must have enough prospects at one time so that *ten prospects could be converted to clients each month*, but not so many that you cannot follow through enough to build a strong relationship.

To have ten potential opportunities and actually convert at least one prospect to a client each month, you need one hundred prospects in your pipeline all the time (this applies mainly to new advisors—experienced advisors should have at least fifty). Remember that you need to contact each prospect twice a month—one drop-by and one a monthly prospect contact. Reaching all one hundred prospects with both a drop-by and a contact each month requires five phone calls and five drop-bys per day.

One hundred prospects is the number I recommend because that is the most that an advisor can handle. There simply is not enough time to do everything for more than one hundred prospects: contacts for new appointments, calls to existing clients, follow-up calls to prospects, and drop-bys to prospects.

It should take approximately six to eight months for the new advisor to build his prospect pipeline to one hundred. The more experienced the advisor, the fewer the number of prospects he can handle because the client service demands are higher; also, the experienced advisor can afford to be more selective. However, I recommend that under no circumstances should the total number of prospects be less than fifty at any one time.

Once you have one hundred prospects, you can drop the weakest prospects as you add new ones. Over time, you will upgrade your prospects by raising the minimum qualification; this will further accelerate the growth of your practice to a million-dollar business.

In my experience, an advisor has room for 150 to 200 relationships. One hundred of these relationships should be your clients, and fifty to one hundred should be your prospects.

When and Why Your Prospects Will Switch to You

Fundamental Truth:

Money is easy to transfer, and there are many opportunities for the current advisor to make mistakes; if you are a strong number two in line, over time you will have a chance to become number one.

The prospect's current advisor is number one, and you, as the one wanting her business, are number two. If you are a strong number two and you have no competition for the spot, you will have the opportunity to replace number one for all or a portion of the prospect's assets when the inevitable problems occur. By following the prospecting process I recommend, you will have been doing all the things that will allow you to take over the relationship. This requires patience and an organized process, two things the majority of your competitors don't have. This should also serve as a strong motivation for the established advisor to always continue to prospect—client attrition is inevitable.

Unlike in other industries, in financial services it is very easy to transfer an account from one firm to another—in most cases, it is as simple as signing transfer forms. This works to the advantage of the prospecting advisor: If you are able to establish that the prospect is better off working with you, it is very easy for that prospect to give you a chance because of the ease of transferring.

The very nature of financial services leads to perceived mistakes, which means that it is impossible for the current advisor not to lose some of his affluent clients over time. The most common reasons are:

• Operational problems exist in every organization, and sooner or later a client will experience them.

- Client associate turnover is high in our business, and the quality of the associate will affect the client's experience, good and bad.
- The firm itself can experience bad publicity that can affect the relationship.
- Fee increases can weaken the relationship.
- The current advisor can change firms, retire, or leave the business.
- The attention the client receives can be less than satisfactory.
- Investment performance can be less than desirable.

All these factors can *and will* lead the prospect to have some level of dissatisfaction with her current advisor. *This is inevitable.*

Most advisors, if they spend time prospecting at all, either do not make the time commitment necessary or are not organized enough to do it right. If you make yourself a strong number two with fifty to one hundred prospects at any given time, you will at some point have a chance to replace number one. With most prospects, there are no competitors for the number two spot because the other prospecting advisors have long ago given up. You, on the other hand, through your monthly prospect contacts, drop-bys, and constant attention to your prospect's needs, will be in a very strong position when number one makes a mistake, which will surely happen.

Service Your Prospects Like Clients

Fundamental Truth:
Treat your prospects as if they were already your clients.

You should think about prospects the same way that you think about your clients, and you should treat them the same way too. Your prospects are your future clients; the only difference is that they have not yet done business with you. Ask your prospects for referrals, such as who their CPAs are, just as you do your clients. Ask them all the same questions you ask your clients. Seeing prospects as clients is the basis of your monthly prospect contacts and drop-bys.

One of the most effective calls you can make to a prospect is calling him to offer the same idea that you are offering your clients:

Mr./Ms. Prospect, I had an investment idea that I am sharing with my best clients, and I thought of you. The idea is _____, and I was wondering if you would be interested.

The Right Attitude

This leads to the important question of "style" or attitude when dealing with prospective clients. From the beginning of the relationship, it is important that you come across as confident, professional, empathetic, and responsive. Your prospects will respond best if they sense that you are confident. No prospect wants to work with an advisor who seems desperate for business, or who shows little confidence.

Remember that your objective is to have fifty to one hundred prospects. Once you have reached this objective, no single prospect will make or break your career. This will give you the confidence to come across as the kind of professional a prospect wants to work with.

This same confidence will carry you when a prospect does not call you back after the second try. If you are able to reach this prospect, it is important to confirm in a friendly, professional way whether or not she is still interested in your calling her. If a prospect does not return your calls, or if she tells you that she is no longer interested in hearing from you, drop her from your list of one hundred and replace her with a new prospect. With one hundred qualified prospects, you are never dependent on any one prospect—if a prospect is not qualified or doesn't return your calls, it is okay to drop her.

The psychology of converting prospects to clients is very important. After the initial appointment, there is an excitement about adding another prospect and about what a good client this prospect will eventually become. Most advisors in this business are optimistic by nature and believe that good things will happen. However, it is easy to get discouraged after a few follow-up calls when the prospect has still not become a client. At the initial point of discouragement, most advisors give up; that is why it is so easy for those who follow the process I am recommending to be in the number two position.

It is nearly impossible to build a good relationship quickly. Most prospects will unconsciously, and in some cases consciously, test you in order to answer these critical questions:

- Can I really trust this person?
- Will he follow up reliably?

- Would I be better off with him?
- Is he willing to be patient?
- Is he willing to earn my business?

Rather than getting discouraged, your thoughts should be that you are laying the foundation that will convert your prospect to a client. If you lay this foundation properly, *then you should convert 25 percent of your prospects to clients in six to twelve months.*

Replacing Prospects

If it is taking longer than twelve months and you have been following the process of monthly prospect contacts and drop-bys, you need to decide whether or not to replace this prospect with a new one. Remember, the limit is one hundred prospects; once you have reached one hundred, one of two things must happen before you can add more:

1. You convert the prospect to a client.
2. You drop the prospect.

I recommend that you drop a prospect:

- If she no longer returns your calls
- If you determine that you do not want to work with her
- If you discover that she is not qualified
- If it has been over twelve months since your first appointment

In some cases, you may decide that the prospect is worth keeping beyond twelve months. If you feel that he is very qualified and you like working with him, then he is probably worth keeping. However, if you have more qualified prospects that you believe are more likely to do business with you, then it makes sense to drop the prospect after twelve months.

If you are considering keeping a prospect longer than twelve months, you can find out if it's a good idea with one of three questions:

• • • • • • • • • • •

Mr./Ms. Prospect, we have been working together for over a year, and I hope I have shown you how committed I am to earning your business as a client. If you were me, how should I approach you going forward?

• • • • • • • • • • •

Mr./Ms. Prospect, I have been working toward earning your business for over a year, and I know I would do a great job for you as your financial advisor. What will it take for us to do business together?

• • • • • • • • • • •

Mr./Ms. Prospect, I have enjoyed working with you for the past twelve months, and I am sure you can tell that I would very much like to have you as my client. I would like you to be candid with me—do you see us working together, and if so, in what time frame do you see that happening?

• • • • • • • • • • •

These questions are all appropriate after you have been building the relationship for twelve months. If you have been following the process for twelve months, you have built the kind of relationship that has earned you the right to be candid and ask these questions. How the prospect answers will determine whether or not you will keep him beyond twelve months. It is also appropriate to use these scripts between six and twelve months as a trial close with your prospects.

Customizing This Process for New Advisors and Experienced Ones

This process can be applied by any advisor at any stage of her career as long as she is willing to prospect. The numbers, however, change based on the advisor's experience level.

1. An advisor who is just starting in the business (and through his their second year) should be having eight appointments per week with new prospects who have at least $100,000 to invest; this should result in acquiring four new prospects each week. After the first six months, the advisor should be adding at least twenty-five new client relationships per year.

2. The advisor with between three and five years length of service should be having four appointments per week with new prospects who have either at least $100,000 to invest or more than the advisor's hundredth largest client, whichever is greater; this will result in acquiring two new prospects and one new client relationship per month (twelve new client relationships per year).

3. The advisor who has six or more years length of service has less time to devote to prospecting because of the time needed to service existing clients. Nonetheless, she should be having at least one, and ideally two, appointments per week with new prospects who have at least $250,000 to invest. This will typically lead to twelve new affluent relationships per year, eight with investable assets of $250,000 or more and four with $1 million or more; this will result in $10 million in new assets and $80,000 in new business. Note: a number of these new affluent relationships will come as the result of upgrading nonaffluent existing client relationships.

An experienced advisor can spend less than half the time prospecting that a new advisor spends and have less than half the number of appointments, and still open twelve new affluent relationships. This is for three reasons:

1. In general, the more experience an advisor has, the greater his skill in closing.
2. Experienced advisors' new prospects tend to come from referrals from clients and influencers, and these kinds of prospects have a much higher closing rate.
3. An experienced advisor can upgrade a lower-asset relationship into a higher-asset one by bringing in assets held somewhere else (see Chapter 11), which is essentially the same as bringing in a new high-asset relationship.

Prospecting in financial services is a low-percentage/high-payoff business. The prospecting process I describe will raise the percentage of success in converting prospects to clients. There is no magic in the process; it is just based on building good relationships, working with a manageable number of qualified prospects, and positioning yourself as a strong number two. The process will work and should result in a minimum of 25 percent of your prospects being converted to clients within twelve months. Over time, these results should lead to a million-dollar-plus practice.

What you are actually selling in financial services is a wealth-management process. For new advisors, wealth management can be an area of uncertainty. This is unnecessary. In Chapter 8, I will show you how to turn wealth management into an organized process that you can have confidence in.

Examples of Monthly Prospect Contacts

Letter (first follow-up contact)

Dear Mr./Ms. Prospect, I wanted to sincerely thank you for taking the time to see me last Thursday. I was impressed with you and your success. I know your time is valuable, but by giving it to me, I gained some insights into how I might help you in the future.

I look forward to our second appointment where I can share some of my initial thoughts and recommendations with you.

Thank you again for giving me the opportunity to visit with you. I look forward to talking to you shortly.

Planning Contact

Mr./Ms. Prospect, this is Jane Advisor at XYZ Financial. I am calling to encourage you to let me do a free planning session with you. I am convinced that the most successful investors know where they are and where they want to go, and have a clear plan for getting there. This preliminary planning session is a great way to start that process (even if you have done one before, it makes sense to update it). If I could spend fifteen minutes asking you some questions, I can share the results with you next week. Would you be interested? I also want to share a business idea that I am talking to my best clients about that I thought you would be interested in.

Research Contact 1

Mr./Ms. Prospect, this is Joe Advisor with XYZ Financial. I hope things are well with you. I recently sent you some research that I knew you would be interested in. What do you think? [Let the prospect answer.] Is there any other information I could provide you with? Has anything changed in your investment circumstances? Is there any service I can provide that you are not getting? [Let the prospect answer.] By the way, I have been contacting my best clients with an idea that you might be interested in. [*Example: It is a muni-bond fund paying* _____ *percent tax free and has an average duration of* _____ *years.*] Would you like the details?

[Change the idea each time you contact that prospect.]

Mr./Ms. Prospect, you know that my objective is to one day earn a portion of your business. I would appreciate your letting me know of anything I can do to help you. Thanks for taking the time. I will talk to you next month.

Research Contact 2

Mr./Ms. Prospect, this is Joe Advisor with XYZ Financial. I want to offer you the opportunity to get a weekly research report from one of our top investment strategists. He offers a great perspective on the markets. It comes through e-mail and would be with my compliments. Are you interested? [Let the prospect answer.] By the way, I have a great idea I want to share with you. [Provide details.]

Event Contact

Mr./Ms. Prospect, this is Joe Advisor from XYZ Financial. I want to invite you to [fun event, date, time]. I thought it would be a great way to get to know each other better. I am also inviting some of my good clients and friends. Would you like to join us?

Seminar Contact

Mr./Ms. Prospect, this is Jane Advisor with XYZ Financial. I am hosting a seminar for my good prospects and clients, to provide an update on XYZ Financial's view of the current investment environment. I know that we will touch on some areas that you are interested in. [Give time, date, and place.] Would you like to attend?

Portfolio Analysis Contact

Mr./Ms. Prospect, this is Jane Advisor with XYZ Financial. The purpose of my call is to offer you a free analysis of all the equities/mutual funds we cover in your portfolio. XYZ Financial provides broad research coverage, and I thought you might be interested in what our best people think of your current holdings. Would you be interested? [Let prospect answer.] By the way, I want to share an investment idea I thought you might be interested in. [Give details.]

Retirement Analysis Contact

Mr./Ms. Prospect, this is Joe Advisor with XYZ Financial. We have a preretirement/retirement analysis available that serves as a progress check to make sure you are doing everything you can to take advantage of the current tax laws and benefits. This analysis will also include reviewing your beneficiary designations to make sure they are set up to your best advantage. Do you have a few minutes where I could ask you some questions? I will be glad to provide you with the analysis after I complete it. Would you be interested? [Let the prospect answer.] By the way, I want to share an investment idea that I thought you might be interested in. [Provide details.] Is there any other information or service I can provide you? My objective is to give you the best service possible.

Send a Book Contact

Mr./Ms. Prospect, this is Joe Advisor with XYZ Financial. I have sent you a book that I thought you might enjoy, as it puts a great perspective on successful investing. Let me know what you think after you read it. By the way, I want to share an investment idea that I thought you might appreciate. [Provide details.]

Suggested books (available at www.barnesandnoble.com and www.amazon.com):

1. *The Only Investment Guide You'll Ever Need*, by Andrew Tobias
2. *The Intelligent Investor*, by Benjamin Graham
3. *Grow Rich Slowly: Merrill Lynch Guide to Retirement*, by Don Underwood
4. The "Finish Rich" Series of Books, by David Bach
5. *Consider Your Options*, by Kaye Thomas

Summary

- Prospects should have at least $100,000 to invest or more than your one-hundredth-largest client, whichever amount is greater.
- The key to conversion is focusing on building the relationship and providing better service than the current provider.
- The ideal number of prospects is between fifty and 100, depending on your experience and the number of clients you service.
- Most clients are underserviced by their existing advisor; you should take advantage of this.
- As a new advisor, turn a weakness into a strength: Your lack of clients translates into more time to service prospects.

- The second appointment is your opportunity to make a presentation that shows the prospect he would be better off working with you. It also sets the stage for follow-up prospecting.

- Drop-bys are invaluable in demonstrating to the prospect your commitment to a high level of service.

- Listen closely to your prospect's objectives and interests. Follow up constantly by connecting to her objectives and interests.

- You will convert prospects to clients through relationships and service, not by competing on investment performance.

- Your actions speak louder than words. Show the prospect your commitment to service by serving his needs before he is a client.

- Contact the prospect at least once a month by phone and, when possible, once a month via drop-by.

- Position yourself as a strong number two in line. You will have no competition for the spot. The number one in line will inevitably make a mistake.

- Treat your prospects like your clients. Be confident, and provide leadership in an uncertain investment environment.

- This process should provide 25 new $100,000-plus clients annually to advisors with zero to two years length of service, twelve new $150,000-plus clients annually to advisors with two to five years length of service, and twelve new $250,000 clients annually to advisors with six or more years length of service (some of whom will be upgrades of existing clients).

The Wealth-Management Process for New Advisors

Financial services is about managing clients' money. This is the core element of the business. But most new advisors face important hurdles regarding this core element:

- *Expertise.* Most new advisors are not expert in investing or in investment strategy. The new advisor can be overwhelmed by all the investment options and products that are available. When new advisors are presented with a new idea or learn about a new product, they often abandon whatever investments they have used before and end up with a jumble of investments and a different investment strategy for each client. Some new advisors try to be portfolio managers, investing the money in individual equities themselves, but it's hard for a new advisor to have time to be a good money manager. In most cases, your time is best spent marketing. Your clients' investment results will be better if you delegate money management to professional money managers. This is not always true for more experienced advisors.

- *Priorities.* Every new advisor needs to spend most of her time marketing. For the first two years, you should be focused on getting as many new appointments as you can and on converting prospects to clients. During this period, you are building the foundation for a million-dollar practice; this takes an enormous amount of time and energy, and you have little time available for nonmarketing activities.

- *Uncertainty.* Most new advisors feel uncertain about being able to capture an affluent prospect if they are not confident of their ability to successfully invest money for their clients.

Investing is actually more about emotions than about financials. An advisor who understands this and who can take the emotion out of investing is invaluable, because the investor will get a reasonable return without taking more risk than he can tolerate.

Everyone wants high returns with no risk. This is not realistic, but it is a mindset that many investors have. They *think* they have a high risk tolerance because they want high returns, but in reality, they often have a very low risk tolerance. When the market drops, these investors panic and sell at a loss.

I want to describe a wealth-management process that takes the emotion out of investing and brings investing into reality. Further, it is an easy-to-use and easy-to-automate process that will keep you marketing and provide good performance to your clients.

The Wealth-Management Process

Throughout this book, I have used the term *wealth-management process*. The following section describes this process. By being disciplined in following each of these steps, you will differentiate yourself from most other advisors. A particularly strong differentiating point is spending a lot of time up front on the long-term plan. Explaining your wealth-management process to prospects will lead them to compare it to their current advisor's strategy, and will plant the first seed suggesting that they will do better with you.

Step 1. (A) Determine your client's objectives and risk tolerance, and (B) set her expectations.

Step 2. Create an investment strategy for each client based on Step 1, including selecting funds and money managers. (A note on terms: This entire four-step program is the *wealth-management process*. One of those steps is to create an *investment strategy*.)
A. Allocate funds among equities, fixed income, and cash.
B. Diversify by investment size and style in equities.
C. Diversify internationally in equities.
D. Select bonds by maturity or select professionally managed bond funds.
E. Select money managers by expertise in size and style.
F. Determine the probability of reaching goals based on proposed allocation. Adjust either allocation or goals accordingly.

Step 3. Monitor performance and review with the client how it is all working.

Step 4. Reallocate if necessary.

In this process, your job, as an advisor, is to be a manager of managers—you manage the professional money managers, who, in turn, actually manage your clients' money day to day.

Step 1A: Determine Your Client's Objectives and Risk Tolerance

The client relationship needs to start with the wealth-management process. The most important part of the wealth-management process is to have a clear understanding of your client's objectives and risk tolerance. The investment strategy that you create during the wealth-management process will be a good one only if it is tailored to the client's risk tolerance and objectives; undertaking an assessment of your client—creating an investment plan—gives you all the information you need to allocate the portfolio properly.

A good investment plan does three things:

1. It gives a high priority to allocation, which most investors do not realize accounts for up to 90 percent of a portfolio's success.
2. It helps the client focus on the long term, which is fundamental to successful portfolio management.
3. It provides a document that you and your client can review every quarter and use in the context of the long-term plan.

This plan can be as formal as you like. The key ingredients are:

• Understand the client's complete investment circumstances.

• Determine the client's risk tolerance.

• Define the client's long-term and short-term objectives.

Mention your ability to create an investment plan and your wealth-management process frequently as you prospect because it will differentiate you and will show your prospects some of the value they will receive once they become a client.

Step 1B: Set Your Client's Expectations

It is important for you to set realistic expectations from the beginning and manage your clients' expectations properly. You do this at the beginning of the relationship by explaining to the client historical returns, asset allocation, risk tolerance, and the benefits of a long-term approach. If you explain portfolio management and corresponding realistic returns from the beginning, you can explain short-term declines and subpar performance much more easily when they occur. If a client has unrealistic return expectations, this is certain to cause problems later on. You are better off declining to work with a client like this—there are plenty of other potential clients you can work with.

Step 2A: Allocate Funds Among Equities, Fixed Income, and Cash

It is essential to good portfolio performance that you allocate assets in a way that is consistent with your client's risk tolerance. And remember that up to 90 percent of a portfolio's success can be tied to proper asset allocation. Be confident that if you allocate the assets properly and rebalance when necessary, the portfolio will do very well over time.

Step 2B: Diversify by Investment Size and Style in Equities

It is not complicated or time-consuming to diversify by investment size and style. Diversification is a cornerstone of good portfolio performance, and every equity portfolio should have, at a minimum, value and growth components, and in most cases, these should be of equal weight. For higher-net-worth individuals, consider alternative investments in the portfolio—as a non-equity-correlated asset class, alternative investments can, over time, reduce risk and add to the return of the portfolio. Examples of alternative investments include hedge funds, private equity, and managed futures.

There is a place in most portfolios for different products. For example, annuities are an ideal investment for many conservative investors. Structured products that provide protection are also attractive for some investors.

Some advisors will set aside 10 percent for special opportunities. If the investor wants to take additional risk by holding equities with a potentially high return, concentrated positions, or junk bonds, it is okay to do so with a small portion of the equity portfolio (10 percent as a guideline). These investments can often be the client's idea and as a result do not take much time to manage.

All the principles I have described should also govern these investments—they must fit the client's risk tolerance and fit within the investment strategy's diversification plan by asset class. As an example, variable annuities with equities should be part of the equity asset allocation that fits with the investor's risk tolerance.

Step 2C: Diversify Internationally in Equities

Most portfolios should also have both international and small-cap exposure. These components should have a smaller weighting, but will add to the portfolio's performance over time.

Step 2D: Select Bonds by Maturity or Select Professionally Managed Bond Funds

Fixed-income management is relatively simple. Most affluent investors should have high-quality municipal bonds of varying maturities in nonretirement accounts. As a rule of thumb, you can provide a hedge against interest-rate risk and generate a good income flow by allocating one-third of the bonds to five-year or under maturity, one-third to five-year to ten-year maturity, and one-third to ten-year maturity or more. Nontax-exempt bonds are appropriate in retirement accounts or for investors who are in a low tax bracket. In all cases, bonds should be of investment-grade quality or higher; bonds are not an asset class that should expose your client to default risk.

Professionally managed bond funds or diversified bond unit trusts are an excellent choice for fixed-income management. Bond management does not require much time once the portfolio is set up, so bond funds are not as essential as professional equity money management. However, you should seriously consider any way to save time when it comes to money management.

Step 2E: Select the Individual Money Managers by Expertise in Size and Style

Most firms perform extensive due diligence on the professional money managers they choose, and carefully monitor these managers and their personnel to ensure that their performance and management are as advertised. Most firms have an open architecture and offer hundreds, if not thousands, of mutual funds. You should have absolute confidence that with this many choices and the due diligence done by your firm, there is a high probability that those money managers will perform well relative to the markets.

Selecting a professional money manager is not complicated. Select two separate account managers and mutual funds for each equity size and style class. Be sure that in doing so, you also provide your client with some international exposure. Each manager and fund will have its past performance numbers available, as well as Sharpe ratios, volatility numbers, and other such information. Spend some time researching managers and funds to select the final one or two that you will use for each size and style class. This is a task that you should undertake periodically (because manager changes are inevitable), but it should not be a time-consuming one.

You should become an expert on the managers you select and stay abreast of important developments that warrant your changing managers. Resist the temptation to change managers frequently—money managers and fund performance are based on the long term, and they should be given time to perform. If you change, do so because of long-term underperformance, key personnel changes, or style changes. Select at least one alternative manager and fund for each size and style class in the event that a change needs to be made.

The decision whether to use mutual funds or separate account managers depends on what the client has to invest. For most clients with under $400,000 to invest, mutual funds make the most sense.

It is difficult to properly diversify a portfolio that has less than $400,000 using separate account managers who have a $100,000 minimum. If a value manager and a growth manager are part of the portfolio, then $200,000 is required, and if the client has a 50 percent equity allocation, the other 50 percent needs to be allocated to fixed income and cash. Mutual funds have very low minimums, and a portfolio with $100,000 can be properly diversified regardless of allocation.

There is an alternative, however, as separate money managers can be diversified for less than $100,000 each when they are part of a separate account manager product that provides size and style diversification. There is typically a manager of managers involved, and this can provide diversification for less money. The benefits of separate account managers include better tax management and the ability to customize the portfolio better than with mutual funds.

An important note about small-cap and international exposure: Because these portions of the equity portfolio are smaller, you can use separate account managers for the value and growth portions and mutual funds for the international and small-cap portions of a portfolio.

You are a manager of money managers and fund managers. That is the value that you provide your clients, and that is what you are paid to do. A good manager of managers is worth paying a premium for.

Step 2F

Once the asset allocation has been determined, run a Monte Carlo simulation on the probability of the proposed portfolio delivering on the client's goals. Based on this probability report, you and the client may decide to adjust the allocation or the goals. If your firm does not have access to a Monte Carlo simulation program, there are companies that provide, for a cost, access to programs that will run it.

Step 3: Monitor Performance and Review with the Client How It Is All Working

Update the client on the performance of the portfolio compared to the client's objectives. This is an important way to reassure the client, and to relate the performance to a reasonable rate of return that is consistent with her long-term plan.

Step 4: Reallocate If Necessary

If one class or style of assets outperforms or underperforms, it is easy for the allocation to get out of balance. To keep the allocation intact, rebalance the portfolio when these changes occur.

Easy to Set Up and Maintain

An important part of this wealth-management process is that it does not take a great deal of time to set up and maintain. The new advisor must spend the majority of his time marketing, and although the wealth-management process is very important, it does not take much time to set up and maintain. Set up the wealth-management process while you are still in training—all the time you need is available then. If you set up the process while you are in training, you will not need to spend much time on it once you have your production number. If you're out of training, you should take the time to set up this process during nonmarketing hours.

I recommend that, if possible, you do all your research on the managers during training, and select all the money managers and funds you will use. Then set up an investment matrix that categorizes all the money managers and funds you have selected by asset type and class. The matrix should include mutual funds for clients with fewer assets and separate account managers for clients with more assets.

Develop a risk-tolerance questionnaire or use an existing one, if available. The questionnaire should calculate a score that determines the client's risk category. This will determine your asset allocation.

Once you have set up your process, you need to spend time on it only to rebalance assets when necessary, to change money managers as needed, and to have quarterly performance reviews with clients.

Introduce the Process to Your Prospects

Be proud of this wealth-management process. Let confidence exude from you as you share it with your clients and prospects. Here is how you can present it:

> Mr./Ms. Prospect, I would like to share with you how I intend to invest your assets when you become a client. I will determine with you your long-term objectives and the risk you are willing to accept to reach those objectives through a formal planning process. Once we have determined your objectives and risk tolerance, I will allocate your assets to reflect the proper amount of risk and return. Most investors do not realize that up to 90 percent of an investment portfolio's success is based on the right asset allocation. Once I have determined the proper allocation, I will diversify your equity assets by size and style and your fixed-income assets by maturity. This will give you the right level of diversification to protect your assets and the opportunity for gains in most market environments.
>
> I have spent a great deal of time researching the best professional money managers for each asset type and class. This ensures that your assets will be managed by the best in class. The final step will be to reallocate as needed and monitor the performance of the managers we have selected, and I will review the performance with you quarterly. My job is to be a manager of the managers we have selected. I am confi-

dent that through this process, your long-term objectives will be met and we will limit the risk of your portfolio. I am also confident that over time, this disciplined wealth-management process will outperform your current portfolio.

This is all you need to say about the wealth-management process. The prospect will intuitively know that this process is the right one, and she will be confident that her assets will be well managed when she becomes a client. The key is that the process is more important than the individual investments that are selected. Prospects will be impressed with this process and be drawn to the advisor who has such a well-thought-out and disciplined approach.

You can be absolutely confident that over the long term, your clients' portfolios will perform well because of this wealth-management process. In most cases, this kind of disciplined process will outperform the clients' previous approach. Most affluent investors are more interested in protecting their assets, and they expect reasonable returns, given their risk tolerance. This process produces just that.

The new advisor now has all the tools (except one) for building the foundation that will lead to a million-dollar practice: motivation, the numbers, the overall marketing strategy, how to get appointments, how to take advantage of appointments, how to turn prospects into clients, and how to manage the wealth-management process. The remaining question is: How do I fit all this together and carry out the right tasks day after day? I cover that, time management, in Chapter 9.

Summary

- A new advisor should spend the majority of his time marketing, not managing money.

- Money management can and should be delegated to professional money managers. This saves valuable marketing time, and the investment results will be better in the long run.

- The key elements of the wealth-management process are creating an investment strategy, allocating assets based on client objectives and risk, selecting funds and money managers, diversifying, monitoring performance, and quarterly performance reviews.

- During the planning process, you should set realistic expectations and revisit them periodically. Remind the client of how wealth management works, given her long-term objectives and style.

- There is a place for special products, alternative investments, and special situations, but they should fit into the process by asset class. I recommend that no more than 10 percent of the equity assets be allocated to special situations.

- Take time to research the best-of-the-best managers and funds. Monitor their performance and replace them if significant negative changes take place, but also give them time to meet their performance expectations.

- As a rule of thumb, use mutual funds for portfolios under $400,000. Use separate account managers for ones over $400,000.

- Begin every new client relationship with an investment plan that determines your client's long-term objectives and risk tolerance. Revisit the plan throughout the relationship.

- The new advisor should be able to clearly articulate the wealth-management process to prospective clients.

- It doesn't take much time to set up your wealth-management process; it can be done during your training phase.

- Develop an investment matrix to incorporate the specifics of the wealth-management process as a ready reference.

- The new advisor should be completely confident in his ability to manage money using this wealth-management process.

Time Management for New Financial Advisors

"Time is money" is never more true than in financial services. How you spend your time determines how successful you are. There are so many distractions and so much information in this business that it takes a deep level of motivation and discipline to focus on the right activities. Those advisors who focus on the right activities are well on their way to building a million-dollar business. The right activities are:

- Appointments with new, qualified prospects
- Prospect follow-up calls and meetings
- Prospect drop-bys
- Client calls
- Client appointments

You should spend the majority of your time doing these tasks. It takes both courage and a deep level of motivation to spend time doing them because, to some degree, they expose you to rejection, and rejection is painful. This is especially true for the new advisor, who must, if he wants to succeed, spend the majority of his time making new appointments and following up with prospects—high-rejection-potential activities.

Make a Daily and Weekly Schedule

Building a daily and weekly schedule that puts you in the position of maximizing your marketing time is essential to building the foundation for a million-dollar business. Marketing time is time spent *executing* marketing tasks, not preparing to do so. It is the time you spend executing your marketing plan. The following are four key elements of this schedule.

1. Do the Most Difficult and Most Important Things First

The first step in building the daily and weekly schedule is to recognize that the hardest and most important tasks should be done before anything else. If you do this, you create momentum that sets the pace for the entire day. When you have completed the highest-priority activities, you have a feeling of accomplishment and the knowledge that whatever else happens during the day, you have already done the most important things. For that reason, start the day doing those activities that will result in getting new appointments.

2. Keep a Log

Keep a log of how you spend your time each day. This is an invaluable tool for effective time management. The log will keep you honest because it will show clearly how you are actually spending your time, which may not be how you *think* you are spending it. I recommend that at the end of the day, you record what you did during each hour. You should have spent at least 70 percent of your 7:30 to 5:30 working day marketing.

3. Block Your Time

If you do the same activity for a period of time, you build momentum, you get better at the activity, and the hard activities actually get easier. These periods are called *time blocks*, and they also protect you from interruptions that disrupt your momentum.

One-hour uninterrupted time blocks are ideal. During those time blocks, don't let anything interrupt your activities. Allow no other activity during a time block except the marketing contacts you are making. It takes a lot of discipline not to be distracted from the task at hand, but you must have that discipline and motivation to succeed.

Time blocks work because if all you do during a time block is make marketing contacts with no distractions, you will make a maximum number of contacts and make a maximum number of appointments. Between time blocks, take a break and do other things that need doing.

4. Prepare in Advance

A great deal of preparation is required in order to make time blocking work: You should have, in advance, all the prospects and telephone numbers you are going to contact, you should have written and memorized all scripts, and you should know exactly what you are going to say to the prospects before the time block begins.

A Sample Schedule for the New Advisor

For the new advisor, I recommend that you have three one-hour marketing time blocks, with ten- to fifteen-minute breaks in between. The following is a sample morning schedule for what I am describing:

7:30–8:30	Marketing contacts for new appointments
8:30–8:45	Break
8:45–9:45	Marketing contacts for new appointments
9:45–10:00	Break
10:00–11:00	Marketing contacts for new appointments
11:00–11:30	Callbacks, catch up on administration
11:30–1:00	Appointments, drop-bys, or nonmarketing activities (have lunch at your desk unless you have an appointment scheduled)

In the afternoon, spend the majority of your time following up with prospects, getting more appointments, and going to appointments. Use the same time-blocking principle. The following is a sample afternoon schedule:

1:00–2:00	Prospect follow-up contacts
2:00–2:15	Break
2:15–3:15	Prospect follow-up contacts or marketing calls for new appointments
3:15–4:00	Callbacks, catch up on administration
4:00–5:30	Appointments, drop-bys, or marketing calls for new appointments

In this sample schedule, you are spending at least four hours on marketing to get new appointments, two to three hours on actual appointments, and one hour on prospect follow-up. If you follow this schedule, you will spend between 70 percent and 80 percent of your time on the essential marketing activities. This is using your time effectively.

During an entire day, this schedule should result in your scheduling at least two or three new appointments, going on two new appointments, and making five prospect follow-up contacts. Also, keep in mind that you often need to schedule more than eight appointments in order to see eight new prospects. The appointments that are no-shows or that cancel can often be carried over to the next week to help meet the objective of eight appointments with new prospects that week.

This schedule also gives you one to three hours of time for callbacks, breaks, and other essential but nonmarketing activities. In the evenings, in the early mornings, and perhaps on the weekends, do things such as writing investment proposals, education, administrative work, organizing your day, and marketing preparation. This means that if you are committed to building a million-dollar practice, this job requires sixty hours a week in the early years. While this seems like a big time commitment, it is no more than any successful business owner must put in to launch a business. You are, in effect, starting your own financial services business.

It is impossible to follow this schedule every day, because you will have meetings, training, and a variety of other necessary activities that will require that you be flexible. However, you should make up the marketing activities at another time during that day or on another day.

The bottom line: It is important that you have eight appointments per week with new prospects throughout the first two years of your career to build a million-dollar foundation. These first two years of your career are the time to build, which means spending the majority of your time marketing. This means that you should spend a minimum of forty hours a week making calls to get new appointments, setting new prospect appointments and client appointments, making prospect follow-up calls, and calling clients.

Client Calls

As you convert prospects to clients, you should contact these clients at least once per month. The goal is for you to have fifty client relationships (with a minimum of $100,000 in investable assets) by the end of your second full year. If you contact three clients per day (fifty clients per month), that means spending between one and two hours each day doing that.

I recommend that you allocate up to two one-hour time blocks to client calls, between 9:00 A.M. and 11:00 A.M. This should replace some of the marketing calls for new appointments when you have enough clients. However, during their first year, most advisors will not have enough clients to spend more than one hour on client contact, which means that you will require only one one-hour time block for this. During the second year, you will be more effective at getting new appointments, and it will take you less time to make the necessary eight appointments—by then, you will have established networks and referrals from existing clients, which makes getting appointments easier.

Fridays

If you keep the schedule I have recommended on Monday through Thursday, then in many cases, you will have scheduled eight new appointments and all prospect follow-up calls. This means that you can use Friday as a catch-up day. Friday mornings can be an excellent time for actual appointments and drop-bys.

An Alternative Schedule: Appointments All at Once

Another way to schedule the week is to dedicate one day a week just to appointments.

The advantages of doing this are:

- You get into an "appointment zone," and in many cases, this makes your appointments more effective.

- It provides more flexibility so that you can complete the maximum number of appointments.

- It makes prospect drop-bys easier to incorporate throughout the day between appointments.

- It is more efficient because you minimize the amount of time it takes to actually get to your appointments. If your appointments are spread out among all five days, you must leave your desk, drive to the appointment, and then drive back to the office. If the appointment is a no-show, the travel time is wasted, and the daily schedule is disrupted.

Having all your appointments on one day does require more preparation. I recommend that you plan your appointment-only days in detail and in advance:

- Make only morning or afternoon appointments; do not set specific times. This gives you the flexibility to allow good appointments to go longer if required.

- Schedule the appointments for that day in proximity to one another so that you spend your time in one area. When you call for the appointments, call prospects in a similar geographical area so that the appointments will be closer together.

- Review all your existing prospects to see which ones are in the area so that you can drop by between new appointments.

- Set up a list of drop-bys for existing prospects in the same area.

Thursday is an ideal day for appointments because this gives you Monday, Tuesday, and Wednesday to make the Thursday appointments. It also leaves Friday free to be a flexible, catch-up day.

If an appointment is a no-show, you can go to another appointment and revisit the no-show appointment throughout the day.

Keep an appointment log, including the times you expect to see the new appointments, directions (written in advance), and a list of potential drop-bys. You can have eight new appointments and do four to five drop-bys during a ten-hour appointment day if you are well organized.

Administrative Tasks

Because most new advisors generally do not have good client associate support, you should be prepared to do much of your administrative work yourself. You must be very organized in order to do this. In the earliest stages of your career, you will probably be required to do some of your own basic operations and account-opening tasks, so you will need to learn how.

I recommend the following system for easily organizing your administrative tasks:

1. *Set Your Priorities.* Anything related to servicing your accounts should come before all other administrative tasks.
2. *Assign priority letters.* Assign a priority letter to each task:
   A: Most important, must be done that day
   B: Important, must be done that week
   C: Not important, can be done that month
3. *List and file.* Each week, make a list of your A, B, and C tasks, and put

all the corresponding paperwork in file folders labeled *A*, *B*, and *C*. You or your client associate will work through each of these tasks. Maintain a separate *pending* file folder with *A*, *B*, or *C* written on each *pending* item. This can all be done electronically if that is your preference.

4. *Review and delegate.* Review with your associate the tasks you need to delegate to her or him at least every week—if required, every day. Assign each task, explain the deadline, and give a copy of the corresponding paperwork to your associate. When you meet with your client associate, review the pending tasks to determine the status of those tasks.

It is ideal to have these meetings once a week, but you might need to have a daily meeting occasionally. If you don't assign a task to your client associate, you should do the task yourself, according to its priority, during nonmarketing time blocks. If Fridays are a flexible day, then this is an ideal time to catch up on the B and C items.

Telephone Coverage

Telephone coverage can be a challenge, and using voicemail effectively can help, especially during marketing time blocks when sales support is not available. Incoming callers generally accept reaching voicemail, but be sure to check your voicemail between marketing time blocks so that you can return phone calls in a timely fashion.

The new advisor should consider developing a "buddy" relationship with another new advisor: Each buddy can cover the other's phones (if you lack sales support) if the two of you alternate marketing time blocks. If you alternate appointment days, your buddy can also cover your phone when you are on appointments.

Scheduling for experienced advisors was covered in Chapter 6.

Preparation Training

The training period between when you are hired and when you begin production is the ideal time to determine which market action plans you will use and to develop them. Collect all the names for these initial market action plans and do all the prequalification research. Practice and memorize the appointment scripts, the objections responses, and the appointment questions. Additionally, develop your wealth-management process, build a presentation for the second appointment, set up your prospecting follow-up contact process, and learn the basics of operations and opening new accounts. If you use this training time to set up your practice, then you will have a head start—all you will have to focus on from day one is the execution of your marketing plans.

Summary

- To build a million-dollar practice, it is essential that you use good time management from the beginning of your career.

- Spend the majority of your time every day on the right activities: calling for new appointments, doing drop-bys, having new appointments, making prospect follow-up calls, and calling and seeing clients.

- Do the marketing activities first every day.

- One-hour time blocks are a key time-management technique.

- You must prepare in order to make marketing time blocking work. A marketing time block is for the *execution* of the plan, not its preparation.

- The new advisor should have three one-hour marketing time blocks before noon every day, and at least two one-hour marketing time blocks in the afternoon (includes appointments).

- If you follow the sample schedule, you should get, daily, two to three new appointment commitments, two appointments that you go on, five prospect follow-up calls, two to three client contacts, and several drop-bys.

- The new advisor should spend 70 percent to 80 percent of his time each day on marketing activities. There should be at least forty hours per week on these activities.

- You will keep yourself honest about how you really spend your time if you keep a time log every day.

- If you follow the sample schedule, Friday can be more flexible a catch-up day. Friday morning is ideal for drop-bys.

- Having one day per week dedicated to appointments can be very effective. You must organize the day well for it to work. You can do eight new appointments and five–ten drop-bys (five minutes each) in one appointment day. Thursday is an ideal appointment day.

- Sometimes the new advisor must take care of her own administrative and operational activities. The new advisor must have an organized way to handle administrative items in a timely manner.

- Drop-bys are an invaluable marketing technique, but the new advisor must be very organized to fit them into a busy schedule.

- The preproduction period is an ideal time to set the stage for execution once the new advisor gets his production number.

As a new advisor, you now have all the elements you need to build the foundation for a million-dollar practice. If you follow all the steps I have outlined in this first section of the book, you will have done everything you need to do to be ready for the next step on your way to the million-dollar level. That next step is to balance clients and prospects as your client list grows. The experienced advisor needs to understand this balance as well. We will look at this issue in Chapter 10.

PART 2

Taking It to the Next Level: Building a Million-Dollar Practice

Balancing Clients and Prospects

uilding the foundation consists of developing one hundred qualified prospects and at least fifty client relationships, all with assets over $100,000. The total assets under management for the foundation should be at least $15–20 million. If you follow the process I outlined in Part 1 of this book, you can build this foundation in two years or less, and you will most likely have spent at least 70 percent of your time marketing during this period.

It is important for the advisor who has built the right foundation to reflect with pride on the accomplishment of having developed one hundred qualified prospects and fifty client relationships with $100,000 or more. Very few advisors ever reach one hundred qualified prospects, and that achievement alone is golden.

Once you have built the foundation for a million-dollar practice, you are ready to take on the next set of activities that will take you there. You now need to shift your focus from primarily marketing to a combination of marketing *and* servicing the clients you already have. If you make this transition effectively, it will be much easier for you to actually reach the $1 million level, and you will reach it more quickly.

This is not as difficult as it may sound. In this chapter, I will outline how to organize yourself to do this.

If You Haven't Built the Foundation, Fill In the Gaps

If you are an experienced advisor and you have not built a foundation of one hundred prospects and fifty relationships over $100,000, you must fill in the gaps. Count all the client relationships over $100,000 that you have, and count all those under $100,000 that have the *potential* to reach

$100,000 within the next twelve months. This is the total number of relationships that meet the requirements for your foundation. I will call these your *qualified relationships* for now.

If you have a length of service of two to five years, then your goal should be to build a pipeline of seventy-five prospects with $150,000 or higher. If you have a length of service of over five years, then your goal should be to have fifty prospects with $250,000 or more. The reason the number of prospects is less for the more experienced advisor is that the minimum qualification level is higher.

Subtract the number of qualified prospects and clients that you have from the recommended foundation numbers, and the difference is the number of prospects and clients you need in order to fill in your foundation properly. To get these relationships, you must make a commitment to spend time marketing. There really isn't any other way.

Having Good Clients Makes Getting More Easier

It is important that you remember that the total number of client and prospect relationships should stay the same—no more than one hundred each. However, over time, the asset minimums of both prospects and clients should increase. To reach a million-dollar practice, you will need at least twenty-five $1 million-plus client relationships, at least seventy-five client relationships that are between $250,000 and $1 million, and at least fifty prospects in the pipeline with a qualification level of $250,000 or higher.

A base of at least fifty qualified client relationships gives you an extraordinary opportunity that you did not have before because you can leverage these relationships to bring in more assets and new clients.

> **Fundamental Truth:**
> Servicing your clients properly will bring in more assets and new clients.

The advisor with at least fifty client relationships can use most of those relationships to help her develop her prospect pipeline. This is leveraging your client relationships, and this leverage doesn't exist until you have built the foundation because you don't have enough clients to make it work. You must still work hard, but your job is easier now; it is easier to build *upon* the foundation than to build the foundation itself.

There are three ways to leverage your client relationships:

1. Bring in the assets your clients hold at other institutions.
2. Acquire new prospects that your clients introduce you to.
3. Broaden the range of products and services that each client uses.

In order to be able to leverage your client relationships, however, you must build rapport with and trust in your clients, and be sure that you are taking care of their needs properly; in other words, you must service your clients well. The best way to do this is to establish a client contact process.

The Client Contact Process

The client contact process involves regular client contacts with specific objectives. It will allow you to get maximum leverage from your current client relationships in order to deepen account penetration, capture more assets, and develop new prospect opportunities.

Frequency

In this process, you should contact each client at least once a month:

- Eight regular monthly contacts
- Three quarterly reviews, face to face if possible (one every three months; the fourth one is the annual review)
- One supersession: an annual review plus planning session, face to face if possible

Objectives

Prepare in advance what you want from each contact with each client, and organize the components of each contact. These components are:

> *Part 1: Connection.* Make a personal connection, talking about the non-business aspects of the client's life.
>
> *Part 2: Review.* Give a brief review of the client's portfolio and, if appropriate, recommendations.
>
> *Part 3: Marketing.* This may include discussions about adding additional

products or services or about investments and assets held elsewhere, or it may be a request for help in marketing to nonclients. (Not all elements will be used in each contact.)

Part 4: Offer of help. End by asking the client how you can help.

Each client contact will be different, and you will not cover all the components every time. The idea is to have a monthly contact and prepare a plan for each call.

The quarterly reviews should include the same four components, but it should expand the portfolio review and make it more formal. The annual supersession should include an expanded portfolio review and a planning session or planning update. If you include these components in your contacts, in most cases you will accomplish the goal of providing great client service, expanding the relationship, discovering assets held elsewhere, and leveraging clients to get new ones. You should also contact each of your fifty to one hundred prospects once a month.

Organize Your Time

If you are to contact each of your fifty to one hundred relationships and fifty to one hundred prospects once a month, then you need to contact at least two to five clients and two to five prospects each day. By the end of your third full year, you should have one hundred client relationships and one hundred prospects and you should contact five clients and five prospects each day. If you have six or more years of service, you should have one hundred client relationships and fifty prospects, and you should contact at least five clients and two prospects per day. If you can contact an average of two clients or prospects per hour, then it takes at least three hours per day to make the necessary contacts.

> **Fundamental Truth:**
> Do the most difficult and most important things first.

Keeping the principle embodied in this Fundamental Truth in mind, I recommend that you make these contacts between 8:30 and 11:30 a.m. or between 9:00 and noon, depending on the time zone you work in. Spend time during the first hour of every working day deciding which clients and prospects to call and determining the content of each call.

There is no more important task for the advisor than contacting her clients and prospects every day, using this schedule.

If you have any time left during the first hour after organizing the prospect and client calls, then work on the highest-priority nonsales tasks. If you do this, you will have contacted five clients and five prospects and completed the highest-priority nonsales tasks by lunchtime every day. You can then spend lunchtime and the afternoon on at least one client and one new prospect appointment (for more senior advisors, one to two new prospect appointments a week is fine), marketing for new appointments, and high-priority administrative tasks. *This is the ideal day for the experienced advisor.*

If you are well organized, your contacts and appointments should take five hours. This should represent 50 percent to 60 percent of your day. Delegate as many of your other tasks as you can to administrative staff. Do your reading and research outside normal office hours.

The result of following this schedule is that you will contact all fifty to one hundred clients and one hundred prospects at least once per month. If you contact them any less often, you will be underservicing both clients and prospects. This is another reason why it is not feasible to have more than one hundred client relationships and one hundred prospects. These numbers should stay the same, but you should consistently upgrade both clients and prospects.

It is challenging to balance marketing and client contact, but it is absolutely achievable. If done right, good client contact can improve your marketing results.

An Example of a Typical Client Monthly Contact

Mr./Ms. Client, this is Joe Advisor. How are you? I hope all is going well with your family. How is your son doing at XYZ University? I am calling to give you a quick review of your portfolio.'' [Expand on this.] ''I also want to recommend that we consider adding a small amount of managed futures to your portfolio.'' [Expand on this.] "We discussed the account you had with ABC Firm, which might be an appropriate source of funds to invest in my managed futures recommendations. While I am talking to you, I also wanted to ask your permission to introduce myself to your CPA—it would be helpful for both of us, I believe, to get to know each other. Is there anything else on your mind you would like to talk about? Anything else I can do to help you at XYZ?

This call should take between fifteen and thirty minutes. Notice that it includes all four components that I mentioned earlier.

If you follow this schedule diligently, you will be a long way toward reaching a million-dollar practice. If you keep this schedule, the following should take place:

- You should add at least $12 million in new assets.
- You should add six new $250,000-plus relationships.
- You should upgrade six current client relationships that are under $250,000 to over $250,000.
- You should increase your business by $100,000 each year.
- You should increase your business as a result of good contact frequency and deeper account penetration.
- You should have excellent retention.
- You should constantly upgrade your prospect pipeline, adding new potential clients to the practice each year.

As you develop more client relationships, you will have less time to spend marketing, as you will need to spend more time servicing clients. This doesn't mean, however, that you slow down growing your business. On the contrary, the more relationships you have, the bigger they are, and the more trust they have in you, the more business you can do. There are four ways to grow your business through your existing client relationships, and Chapter 11 will cover the first of them.

Summary

- It takes a different focus to make a good foundation to a million-dollar practice.
- A good foundation to build on is fifty relationships (with at least $100,000) and one hundred prospects (with at least $100,000). More experienced advisors should have at least fifty prospects.
- The number of client relationships and prospects should not exceed one hundred of each, but should always be upgraded.
- You should leverage existing client relationships to bring in more assets and provide introductions to nonclients.
- Contact each client and each prospect once a month. This should be

done in the mornings. With one hundred prospects and fifty to one hundred client relationships, this means that you should contact five clients and five prospects a day.

- There are four components of each client call:
    Part 1: Connection
    Part 2: Portfolio review
    Part 3: Marketing
    Part 4: Offer of help
- The monthly contacts should include three quarterly reviews and one supersession (annual review and planning session).
- Organize and prepare for each client and prospect contact in advance to get the maximum impact from each call.

Getting More Assets from Existing Clients

The easiest way for an advisor to get more assets is from existing clients. My experience shows that most clients have as many assets somewhere other than with their advisor as they have with him. In some cases these assets may be held in 401(k) or retirement plans, but at some point these assets become available. If you have built a relationship of trust with your client, he will be open to discussing consolidating at least a portion of those assets, provided that you ask. These are the easiest new assets to get because a relationship of trust already exists.

You can expect to achieve up to 50 percent of your new asset goal by bringing in outside assets from existing clients. Let's say that you have one hundred client relationships with a total of $50 million in assets. This $50 million is likely to be only half of these clients' investable assets because they hold another $50 million somewhere else. On average, this is $500,000 per client that may be held elsewhere. If you acquire an average of only $60,000 of this per client per year, you will add $6 million in assets per year. This is half of a $12 million goal.

The more assets you have under management, the more assets there are that are held elsewhere that you can bring in.

The Away-Assets Process

The primary reason that most advisors do not get more assets from existing client relationships is that they do not have a process for discovering those assets, acquiring them, and tracking them.

The process I recommend has these elements:

1. *Discover.* Determine exactly what assets each client has that are held elsewhere.

2. *Acquire.* Have a way to bring in assets that are held elsewhere.

3. *Track.* Keep track of the assets that are held elsewhere and how many of those assets you acquire each year.

The way to use this process is to incorporate it into the overall client contact process that I outlined in the last chapter.

Discovery: The Annual Planning Session

Discovery is the key to making this process work, and the best way to discover these other assets is through an annual planning session, which should be part of your annual review with each client. This planning session can include a formal investment plan, planning questions that you have developed, or a planning update. The planning session can be as detailed or as simple as is appropriate for each client. You should include the following elements:

1. Reverify the client's long-term goals and objectives.
2. Assess or reassess the client's risk tolerance.
3. Review the performance of the portfolio.
4. Review asset allocation and adjust if needed.
5. Review the client's liabilities (margin, mortgage, and business credit).
6. Review the client's protection (life insurance, disability insurance, long-term care insurance).
7. Review the client's estate plan.
8. Evaluate expected assets (sale of business, bonus, inheritance).
9. Discuss assets held elsewhere.
10. Get feedback on service quality.
11. Ask for a referral.

Item 9: Discuss Assets Held Elsewhere

In order to acquire additional assets from existing clients, you must discuss these assets each year at the planning session. This establishes a baseline of just how many other assets the client has. As your client's circumstances change from year to year, she may add more of these assets without your knowing about it if you do not do this.

The best way to position yourself for asking about these assets is to share with the client the role a true wealth manager should have. The following is an example of how you can do this:

> Mr./Ms. Client, if I am doing my job correctly, my relationship with you should go beyond just advising you on the assets you have at XYZ Financial. I see myself as a wealth manager, and in that role, I would like to advise you on all aspects of your financial life. In fact, you would be underutilizing me if you did not allow me to expand our relationship to your entire financial situation. To do all I can for you, it is important that I have an accurate and complete baseline on all your financial assets and update that baseline annually. Clearly I know what you have with me. What I would like to ask (or verify) is what assets you have that are held away from XYZ Financial. By knowing about all of your assets, both here and at other institutions, I can give you the best possible advice about your assets with me. It also gives me the opportunity to provide you with a second opinion on the assets held at other institutions and how to potentially reduce the fees on those assets, and, when applicable, to give you ideas that might enhance the performance of those assets. Would you feel comfortable sharing that information with me?

If you conduct a conversation like this with each client during his annual review, you will discover many other assets held by existing clients. Without doubt, this discovery process is the most important step in acquiring new assets from existing clients. Most advisors have not done this.

Acquisition

Keep a file (a hard-copy file or electronic one) for each client with the details of all the assets held at other institutions, and update this file at least annually as you discover new assets. Develop a specific strategy for bringing in these assets, and put the strategy in each client's file. Examples of elements that strategy might include are:

- Finding ways to reduce fees
- Incorporating these assets into the client's overall plan
- Coming up with ideas for better performance
- Presenting innovative ideas—alternative investments, structured products, annuities

- Simplifying the client's life by having all her assets in one place
- Simplifying paperwork and having one consolidated statement
- Moving company retirement assets

Refer to this file as part of your client contact process: As you contact the client each month, refer to the file and, if appropriate, share ideas on why the client should bring in all or a portion of these assets. The following are some examples of how to do this:

> Mr./Ms. Client, I am glad we had a chance to review your portfolio today. I would like to add to our conversation an idea about holding your IRA accounts at XYZ Financial. At our firm, we charge no account fees for retirement assets over $XXX. If you transferred your assets to me, you would not only save your IRA account fees, but we could include these assets in our overall plan and simplify your paperwork. Would you consider making the transfer?

> • • • • • • • • • • •

> Mr./Ms. Client, I enjoyed visiting with you today. I also wanted to talk about the retirement plan you have with your company. You may not be aware that at a certain age, you can roll over all or a portion of those assets into an IRA rollover account. I am convinced that I can do a better job of managing those assets for you while incorporating those assets into our total plan. Would you be interested in the details of how we could move those assets into an IRA rollover at XYZ Financial?

> • • • • • • • • • • •

> Mr./Ms. Client, I am glad we had a chance to review your portfolio. I would also like to let you know that we have an investment available that I believe would fit with the equity portion of your portfolio. It is a structured investment that is tied to the performance of the S&P 500 index and will have most of the upside, but the principal is guaranteed not to go below what we invest. My suggestion is that we use the money (or a portion of it) you have invested with ABC Firm for this investment. What do you think?

> • • • • • • • • • • •

> Mr./Ms. Client, I feel good about our conversation today regarding your investments. However, there is something I would like to add to your portfolio. Managed futures is an investment that is a noncorrelated asset class, and I would like to add this to the other investments in

your portfolio. Over time, this should add to the performance of your portfolio. My recommendation is that we take a small portion of the assets you have with ABC Firm and invest in the managed futures recommendation that I am making.

• • • • • • • • • • •

The point of all these examples is that during the monthly contact, you should execute the strategy you have developed to bring in all the client's assets. Most affluent investors want their lives simplified, and if you have built a strong relationship and offer a good rationale for consolidating their assets with you over time, they will.

Tracking

The advisor who wants to maximize the opportunity to bring over more assets from existing clients should track the money each client holds at other institutions and track the progress he is making toward bringing it in. I recommend that you use a spreadsheet to keep track of these assets. List each of your one hundred client relationships by name, and beside each name list the assets held elsewhere. Total these assets at the bottom of the column to give you an idea of how big the opportunity is. As you bring this money in, list those amounts in a second column, and list the difference in a third column. This spreadsheet is a good way for you to know at all times how much money your clients are holding at other institutions and how you are doing at acquiring it.

You need to realize that the easiest assets to bring in are those from existing clients. The key to acquiring these assets is discovering how much money each client holds at other institutions during your annual planning session with each client. You can bring in at least $6 million in new assets each year by developing a strategy to do so and using the monthly contact system to execute the strategy. Keep track of where these assets are, how much they are, and the progress you make at bringing them in.

Capturing the assets your clients hold at other institutions is just one of the four ways you can build your business using your existing clients. The second way is to use the trust you have built in them to get new clients. I will cover how to do this in the next chapter.

Summary

- The easiest new money to bring in is money that your existing clients hold at other institutions.

- You can reach at least 50 percent of your annual new asset goal and bring in a minimum of $6 million in new assets by bringing in clients' outside assets.

- Discovery is the key to making this process work, and the best place for discovery is in the annual planning session.

- Create a file for each client on the details of the assets she holds elsewhere.

- Develop a strategy for each client for capturing these assets, and put it in the file.

- Execute the strategy through the monthly contact process.

- Use a spreadsheet to keep track of the total assets held at other institutions and to keep track of the progress you make toward bringing them in.

CHAPTER 12

Leveraging Clients to Get New Ones

The most efficient and effective marketing you can do is to leverage your existing clients to get new ones. This gives experienced advisors a real advantage; however, many experienced advisors miss this opportunity. Once the advisor has built a foundation of fifty to one hundred client relationships (each with investable assets of over $100,000), leveraging existing clients is likely to take the advisor halfway to the goal of having twelve new affluent client relationships of $250,000 each and $12 million in new assets each year.

To be effective in leveraging clients to get new ones, you must be very organized and consistent in your approach. This chapter focuses on four methods to leverage current clients to get new ones:

1. Referrals
2. A CPA and attorney network
3. Speaking opportunities
4. Client events

Referrals

There is no marketing activity that is more effective than a proactive, organized referral process. If you had to engage in only one form of marketing, a proactive referral process should be it. Eighty percent of most advisors' new affluent households come from referrals.

If you are in frequent contact with your clients, have a disciplined wealth-management process, and provide great service, you are in the right position to ask for referrals. As simple as these things are, many advisors do not do them and so do not have satisfied clients. High client satisfaction will occur if you contact clients frequently, have a portfolio performance that is consistent with client goals and expectations, and provide great service. This is the prerequisite for effective referral marketing. As an advisor who is committed to having a million-dollar practice, you should have these client-satisfaction fundamentals in place.

It is important that you ask each client for a favorable introduction at least once a year. Because each relationship is different, you should customize your approach for each client; but in any case, you should show confidence in asking for a referral because you can be valuable to anyone a client may refer to you. The right attitude is not that you are *asking* for something from the client, but that you are *offering* the client the opportunity to help someone she cares about. This concept goes back to providing outstanding client service and working with a manageable number of relationships—each client feels special.

Next, I present several techniques for asking for these referrals.

Planning Session or Quarterly Review

During a planning session or quarterly review, you can handle asking for a referral in two ways: You can informally ask for a referral at some point, or you can provide a written agenda and make "favorable introductions" the last point on the agenda. If you do the latter, it is at this point in the meeting that you bring up the subject of referrals; since it is on the agenda, it cannot be missed. Either approach works well, and the scripts that follow work either way.

Scripts to Use After a Planning Session/Quarterly Review—Informal

> Mr./Ms. Client, I feel good about what we discussed today. I am convinced that this is the right way to do our business. Is there anyone you know who would benefit from this process? As you know, I use a professional approach and would simply offer that person the opportunity to discuss his or her situation.

If the response is, "I cannot think of anyone right now," follow up with a letter thanking the client for the planning session. Enclose a pen, along with a note that says, "I wanted to send you a complimentary pen so that as you think of others, you can write their names down," or:

Mr./Ms. Client, I hope you feel good about our review and the wealth-management process we use. Have you found our process and way of doing business beneficial?

If the answer is yes, you can continue with one of the following:

I am glad you feel that way. A lot of people do not go through this type of process, and it is frustrating for me to realize that there are people who really need our help, but who do not know about what we do. Are you aware of anyone in that situation?

• • • • • • • • • • •

Good, because I would like your help. There are many investors who, if they knew what we did, would be interested in doing business with us. What I would appreciate is knowing if you are aware of anyone who might benefit from our approach. Does anyone come to mind?

• • • • • • • • • • •

Good. As you know, there are investors that we are not working with who would benefit from our approach and who may not be getting the attention or service that they should. Is there anyone you can think of who may be retiring or going through a life-changing event and would benefit from our approach?

The Agenda Technique

Mr./Ms. Client, I hope that you feel this review has been of value to you and that you feel as good about our professional relationship as I do. I believe there are many investors who, if they knew about our wealth-management process, would be interested in working with me (our team). My challenge is finding those people so that I can share our wealth-management process with them. Specifically, I work best with investors who are experiencing changes in their lives; for example, individuals who have recently retired or are about to retire, whose companies have downsized or laid them off, who have moved recently or become divorced, or who have suffered the loss of a spouse. Does anyone come to mind who might be experiencing changes in circumstances that you think I could help?

If the answer is yes, then:

Could you introduce them to me?

If the answer is no or if the client says, "I can't think of anyone right now," then:

> I appreciate your giving it some thought and appreciate your willingness to help. I want to add that throughout this year, I will be offering a number of educational and fun events that are designed to appeal to the interests of my best clients, of which you are certainly one. There are two purposes for these events: One is to show my appreciation for my clients, and the other is to have a nonthreatening way for me to meet new prospective clients. When I invite you, I will ask you to please invite anyone else you think I should meet and who might enjoy the event. Would you be open to that?

Be Specific

One of the techniques to increase the number of referrals is to be specific about what you are looking for. Money in motion (see Chapter 32) is an example of this. Share with your clients examples of money in motion to help them think of potential prospects to refer to you. Note that you can be specific in this same way in any of the scripts or situations I present here.

> Mr./Ms. Client, let me be specific about the kinds of people I can help. People who have recently retired or are about to retire, who are changing jobs or relocating, or who are suffering through the loss of a spouse or a divorce are all people that I know I can help. Do you know anyone who is in any of these circumstances?

Scripts for a Separate Call

> You are one of my best clients, and I enjoy working with you. I would like to build my business with clients like you. Does anyone come to mind (a friend, work associate, or family member) who is similar to you and who would benefit from having a relationship with me at XYZ Financial?

[If you are given a name, keep asking, "Does anyone else come to mind?"]

* * * * * * * * * * * *

Usually when I call you, it is about your investments. Today I am calling about my business. I was thinking that with so much investment uncertainty, there may be some people you could think of who would benefit from my approach. Maybe someone you work with, a neighbor, friend, or relative?

* * * * * * * * * * * *

If the client says no, send a pen to remind him to think of others.

Scripts for Calling Prospects Who Have Been Referred to You

Mr./Ms. Referral, I work with Mr./Ms. Client, and he/she suggested that I call you to share the approach we use at XYZ Financial. May I share with you the process we use that I believe makes us different? Do you have time now, or should we schedule an appointment?

* * * * * * * * * * * *

Mr./Ms. Referral, my name is Joe Advisor, and I am an advisor with XYZ Financial. I was recently going through one of my planning sessions with Mr./Ms. Client, and I asked him/her if he/she could think of anyone who would benefit from the wealth-management approach we use. He/she gave me your name. I take my job very seriously and am proud of the approach we use. I was hoping that I might have the opportunity, either over the phone or face to face, to share with you how our approach benefits my clients, and find out more about your situation. Is that something you would be interested in?

A CPA and Attorney Network

Another excellent technique for leveraging current clients is to ask for introductions to their CPA and/or their estate attorney. According to Thomas Stanley, author of *Millionaire's Mind*, most millionaires find their financial advisor via referrals from their CPA or attorney. This is why you can benefit from a strong network of CPAs and attorneys.

You do not need to have a large number of CPAs or attorneys in your network in order to make it effective. For example, a strong network can be made up of as few as six CPAs and attorneys who consistently refer potential affluent clients; it is certainly advantageous to have more than six, but six is enough to make this plan work. Note, however, that the follow-up and relationship-building time required to have an effective network will limit the number of relationships that you can maintain— most advisors cannot adequately manage more than a total of twelve CPA and attorney referral sources.

The first step is to contact each client once a year, ideally during a quarterly review or annual planning session, and ask if she is satisfied with her current CPA and if she has an estate planning attorney. If the client is satisfied with her current CPA, you should ask for permission to call the CPA for the purpose of getting acquainted; make the same request if she has an estate attorney that she is satisfied with. Explain that you are asking to get acquainted with these people because a good relationship between you and the CPA or attorney can be very helpful, as there is a degree of overlap among you. Once the client gives you permission, call the CPA or attorney and suggest an informal appointment to get to know each other for the client's benefit.

If the client is not satisfied with either his CPA or his attorney, he is an excellent candidate to refer to your existing CPA/attorney network.

Scripts for Contacting the Client about His/Her CPA or Attorney

Mr./Ms. Client, do you have a CPA or estate planning attorney that you are satisfied with? Would you mind if I contact him/her so that I could make sure that he/she has everything that he/she needs from XYZ Financial?

· · · · · · · · · · · ·

Mr./Ms. CPA, this is Joe Advisor from XYZ Financial, and the reason I am calling you is that we have a mutual client. [Give the client's name.] I thought it would make sense for us to get to know each other for the benefit of our mutual client, and I also make it a practice to get to know the top professionals in my market. Would you be available for an appointment where I could find out more about your practice and we could get to know each other better?

· · · · · · · · · · · ·

During the first meeting with the CPA or attorney, do the following:

- Make your primary emphasis understanding the CPA's or attorney's practice, specialization, and experience.

- Discuss your mutual client and how you and the CPA or attorney can work together for the benefit of that client.

- Give a very brief description of your practice.

- Finally, make the CPA or attorney aware that you are developing a small CPA/attorney network where mutual referrals, when appropriate, could be given.

I recommend that if you develop a good initial relationship, you make a follow-up meeting to learn more about each other's practice.

The key to building a successful CPA/attorney network is to regularly contact and educate the CPAs and attorneys in the network. Here are my recommendations on how to do that:

- Meet with each CPA or attorney at least six times per year (ideally, once per month).

- Try to add value each time you visit the CPA or attorney—provide her with information that will help her practice. Your priority is to educate her on areas that are of interest to her and to her clients. This is why it is critical that you understand her practice and the type of clients she has.

    During these visits, provide the CPAs and attorneys with examples of the type of clients you work with and how you help them. It is very important that the CPAs and attorneys know exactly what you do for your clients. This will raise the comfort level the CPA or attorney has with your practice and will make it easier for her to provide referrals.

- Invite the CPAs and attorneys to your office. This can be very helpful in building trust, because it shows them firsthand how your practice works. You can further distinguish your practice in the eyes of the CPAs and attorneys, and further raise their comfort level, by sharing the technology and wealth-management tools you use, and by introducing them to your team members.

- Provide seminars for the CPAs and attorneys where they can get continuing education credits. I also recommend that you schedule fun events after such a seminar (or as stand-alone events) to develop these relationships further. These events could include golf, sporting events, or dinner.

- Contracting, educating, and offering value to the CPAs or attorneys regularly is more important than how many referrals you give them. If you have six total CPAs and attorneys in your network, you should get twelve referrals per year (two from each). If you close 50 percent of these referrals, you should get six new affluent client relationships from your CPA/attorney network each year.

The bottom line is that developing a CPA and attorney network can be one of the most effective marketing techniques you can have. Building this network with existing clients' CPAs and attorneys is the best place to start. Regular follow-through (monthly contact) is required to build the kind of professional and personal relationships that will result in these influencers providing regular referrals. For more information on marketing to CPAs and attorneys, see Chapter 28.

Speaking Opportunities

You can further leverage current clients by finding out what organizations they and their spouses belong to and offering to speak to those organizations. This technique can put you in front of 240 new prospective clients each year.

Most clients and their spouses each belong to at least one organization. Some clients may belong to more than one organization, and some clients may not belong to any, but overall, your pool of fifty to one hundred clients probably has access to at least twenty-five different organizations. If these organizations have an average of twenty members and you get in front of twelve organizations each year, you will reach 240 potential prospects. If you follow up and set appointments with 20 percent of the attendees, this will generate fifty new appointments with qualified prospects, and if 25 percent of the appointments become new clients, this marketing technique alone would generate twelve new client relationships per year.

A key element of this marketing technique is that most organizations are looking for interesting topics and speakers. Your expertise on the current state of the economy and the markets is very interesting to many. Other potential topics could include:

1. How much is needed for retirement
2. The importance of a financial plan
3. The wealth-management process

4. The state of the current market and what is ahead

5. The fundamentals of successful investing

To be effective, you must be very organized and ask each of your fifty to one hundred clients once a year for the opportunity to speak at their organizations; be sure to ask both husband and wife, as they most likely belong to different organizations. In most cases, your client will not be the person in charge of the organization's speakers, but he can put you in touch with the right person. You can ask the client to talk to the program coordinator ahead of time, or you can simply ask for the contact's name and number and call her directly.

Once you have given your talk to a particular organization, offer to speak to this organization at least once a year on a different, relevant topic; that way, you can continue to market through these same organizations each year. As you develop new client relationships, find out what organizations they belong to and offer to speak to those organizations.

The following are examples of how you can introduce this idea to your clients and to organizations:

> Mr./Ms. Client, I enjoy educating investors about XYZ Financial's view on the current investment environment. Are you a member of an organization that would be interested in this kind of talk? Who would be the best person to call about the logistics?

> Mr./Ms. Club Official, I was referred to you by my client [client name]. The reason for my call is that XYZ Financial encourages us, as a service to our communities, to talk to local organizations about the current investment environment. I would enjoy having the opportunity to address your group. Would you be interested?

I recommend that when you speak to the organization, you do not bring any materials to hand out. A much better technique is to pass out response cards requesting information or a follow-up call. This provides an easy way for you to follow up with interested prospects. After the seminar, contact those who filled out response cards and offer them an appointment. The following is a script to do this:

> Mr./Ms. Prospect, this is Joe Advisor, and you attended my recent talk at the ABC organization. I received your request for more information. I

would be happy to mail that information to you, but I wanted to offer you my time to review your current financial situation and provide a second opinion. I would be glad to bring the information you requested to that meeting or mail it to you in advance. Would you be receptive to meeting with me?

Make sure you ask the organization's program coordinator for permission to pass out the response cards. You want to reflect positively on your referring clients, and getting permission is professional and courteous.

Client Events

Inviting clients to events that they are interested in is another way to leverage current clients to meet new ones. The key concept in this marketing technique is to help clients help you. Typically, your clients' best friends are those who like to do the same things they do.

By organizing events around your clients' interests, you are providing your clients with an easy and nonthreatening way to introduce you to their friends who have the same interests. The first step is to survey your best clients to determine what their two favorite outside interests are, such as golf, fly-fishing, wine tasting, fine dining, sporting events, or cooking classes. Educational seminars on topics of interest to particular age groups are another good idea for client events. The next step is to group clients by interests and invite them to these events. The key ingredients for making these events successful are that the events be tied to the clients' interests and that the events be fun and well organized.

You can have between four and twelve events per year, depending on how far you want to take this marketing technique. Ideally, you should invite each local client to an event at least once a year. This will determine the frequency and size of each event: As a guideline for larger events, invite twenty-five clients and guests four times per year; for smaller events, invite eight clients and guests every month.

The leverage for meeting new prospects begins when you invite your client. Tie this invitation to your past requests for referrals. The following is an example of how to do this:

Mr./Ms. Client, this is Joe Advisor, and I am calling to invite you to a golf event I am hosting for my best clients. It will be [provide time, date,

Example Information Request Response Card

(front)

❏ Please send me XYZ Financial's most recent economic update report.

❏ Please send me XYZ Financial's research on the following companies:

_____ , _____ , _____ , _____ , _____

❏ Please send me XYZ Financial's report on fixed-income opportunities.

❏ Please send me XYZ Financial's report on tax law changes and how they affect investments.

❏ I would like to discuss a cost-free financial plan that XYZ Financial offers.

❏ I would be interested in a complimentary follow-up appointment to review my current investment situation.

(back)

Name

_____

Work Address

_____

Work Phone Number

_____

Home Address

_____

Home Phone Number

_____

E-Mail Address

_____

location, and so on]. I really appreciate your being such a good client, and I know you enjoy golf, so I hope you can attend. This event can also be a relaxed way for me to meet prospective clients who like golf. I would really appreciate it if you could invite someone whom you think I should meet. I hope you and a friend can attend this fun event. I will send you several invitations.

Mr. /Ms Client, I want to invite you to a dinner we are hosting at our home later this month. [Give the date.] Can you attend?

If the answer is yes:

I also would like to encourage you to invite a couple that you think we should meet and that might benefit from our wealth-management process. Can you think of anyone who might be interested?

If eighty clients attend events throughout the year, and on average each client brings one friend, then you will meet eighty new people. If you convert 10 percent of the new introductions to clients, then you will acquire eight new clients through this marketing technique.

The best way to follow up with these prospects is to invite them to other events or educational seminars. Over time, a relationship will grow, and offering them a complimentary portfolio review will be part of the natural progression.

Clients will feel good about the event, which helps retention, and they are helping you in an easy, nonthreatening way; the client is simply inviting a friend to an event that you are hosting. Often clients are reluctant to provide referrals directly because they worry that doing so could jeopardize their relationship with their friend if you do not perform well. However, inviting a friend to a fun event is much less of an endorsement; it is up to you and the prospect to build the relationship through the event. If these events are well organized, and if you follow through, you will get new clients. I know advisors who have successfully built their entire marketing efforts around client events.

The most effective way for you to get new clients is to use one or more of these leveraging techniques. Working through existing clients to meet new ones is much more effective than trying to meet new prospects "cold." A new advisor can meet at least 50 percent, and even 100 percent, of his asset and new client goals using these techniques. You must have satisfied clients, be well organized, have good follow-through, and be sensitive to the client relationship to make this marketing technique work; however, if done correctly, this can be the easiest, most enjoyable, and most effective marketing that you can do.

Now you know how to bring a client's assets that are held at other institutions to you, and you know how to use your current clients to acquire new ones. The next technique of growing your business through your clients is how to expand the products and services that your current clients use. Read Chapter 13 to find out how.

Summary

- The most effective and efficient way that an experienced advisor can market is through existing clients.

- At least 50 percent of the annual new asset and new affluent client goal should come from techniques that leverage current clients.

- A proactive referral process is the most effective marketing activity an advisor can engage in.

- To get referrals, the advisor must have satisfied clients, and must ask for referrals. Ask each client for a referral at least once a year.

- Establish a network of six to twelve referring CPAs and attorneys. This is among the most effective marketing techniques an advisor can use. The CPAs and attorneys your clients use are the place to build this network.

- Follow-up and relationship-building activities are the key ingredients for a successful CPA and attorney network (six to twelve contacts per year with each influencer).

- Offering to speak at clients' organizations is time-effective and can get the advisor in front of 240 new prospects per year.

- To be effective with speaking engagements requires good follow-up of the response cards.

- Client event marketing is an ideal way to meet new prospects.

- Invite each client to an event she is interested in and encourage her to invite a friend with a similar interest.

- Event marketing is a nonthreatening way for clients to get you in front of prospects they know.
- Follow up with prospects you meet at client events by inviting them to future events and educational seminars, and culminate by offering them a complimentary portfolio review.

Expanding the Client Relationship

One of the most effective and efficient ways to grow your practice is by doing more business with your existing clients. Most advisors are not organized enough to do this and generally do not expand their relationship with their clients as far as it can go or establish minimums for their clients. This is one of the most important fundamentals of growth.

In addition to bringing in more assets, there are two reasons to expand your client relationships and increase business:

1. The more products and services a client uses, the more business you will do with that client. In my experience, clients who use five or more products and services do *three times* the business of clients who use two or less.

2. Raising the minimums for your clients is an efficient way to grow your business, by working with individuals who can afford what you offer.

Minimums

Each client should generate a minimum level of business in order to stay in your practice. This concept is consistent with the policy in many other professions—for example, a well-established accounting firm will charge a minimum fee no matter how simple the tax return is that it completes; if a client is unwilling to pay that much, the accounting firm will refer him to another firm.

A successful advisor should handle her practice the same way. Each of your clients should generate at least $1,000 a year in business; this minimum amount of business could certainly be higher, but should not be much lower after an advisor has three or more years of experience in the business. Clients who have $1 million or more invested should be generating $10,000 or more per year in business.

Whether the minimum amount is $1,000 or a higher number, you must run your practice like a business. Time is money, and the time you spend with clients who do not generate enough business is time taken away from clients who do.

Adding products and services to your clients' relationships is an ideal way to not only increase your business from each one, but also raise clients' minimums.

Add Products and Services That Don't Compete with the Portfolio

Most advisors have an established process for managing their clients' portfolios. Generally, once you have invested the assets and set up the management of the portfolio, a predictable amount of business is generated. The most obvious way to increase business at that point is to add more assets to the portfolio. This is especially true as fee-based pricing has become more popular. My experience has been that most advisors do a good job of generating business through active portfolio management; the challenge is how to add more business without changing the way the portfolio is being managed.

The way to do this is to add products and services that do not affect the assets in the portfolio. The reason most advisors don't add these products and services is either that they are not organized enough to introduce them on a regular basis or that they are not comfortable enough with these products and services to introduce them.

Typically, these products and services do not compete with the assets that the advisor manages through the wealth-management process. These are add-on products that generally require little or no additional assets, but still add business.

Examples of additional products are:

- Annuities
- Home equity loans
- Life insurance
- Lines of credit
- Long-term care insurance

- Managed futures
- Mortgages

Services by themselves may not directly add business, but they can have a positive impact. Additional services of this type tie a client closer to you and significantly improve retention. These services are hard to unwind and will make a client think twice before leaving. They also make a client more comfortable with you in your role as manager of his entire financial life—this relationship should lead the client to the inevitable conclusion that he should have all his assets with you.

Examples of additional services are:

- Credit cards and/or debit cards
- Direct deposit
- Online access
- Web bill paying

Clients who have over $1 million in assets are your biggest market for additional products and services; not only do they have the greatest need for them, but they also have needs that clients with fewer assets don't have. For example, liability management can be just as important as asset management for very wealthy clients; they are generally more appropriate candidates for alternative investments; and they are more likely to have concentrated stock, so they are more likely to need strategies for dealing with this situation. The more complex strategies and products that your $1 million-plus clients need can generate significantly more business, and these products do not compete with the assets you are managing. This is why your goal should be to get at least $10,000 or more in business from each account of $1 million or more. By introducing these products and strategies, not only are you increasing the opportunity for more business, but you are also showing your clients the value that you add.

Examples of additional products for $1 million-plus clients are:

- Concentrated stock strategies (liquidity, protection)
- Liability management
- Life insurance strategies
- Trust and estate strategies
- Alternative investments

Managed futures and alternative investments should be included in a portfolio only in smaller increments and only if they are consistent with the client's risk tolerance. These investments can be noncorrelated assets that, in small quantities, can decrease risk and add to performance. Annuities are excellent products as well, especially for conservative investors—you can add them to the portfolio or replace existing assets with them to provide a guaranteed future income stream (in most cases). These products can add significant business without the need to make significant changes to the portfolio.

How to Do It: Be Organized and Have the Discussion

In order to be effective in adding these products and services, you need to do two things: You need to be organized, and you need to have the discussion of them with each client.

Be Organized

1. *Make a spreadsheet.* On a spreadsheet, list the products and services that most of your clients do not have across the top. In the first column, make a vertical list of your top fifty to one hundred client relationships (including your $1 million-plus client relationships). Make a second spreadsheet for your $1 million-plus client relationships, and put on it only the special products and services they need as a result of having more money.

2. *Fill it in completely.* If you discuss a product or service with a client, put a checkmark next to the client's name under the product or service that you discussed with her. Make the checkmark whether the client is interested or not, as long as you have mentioned the product or service. If a particular product or service is not appropriate for a particular client, put "N/A" in that cell. The goal is to have a mark (a checkmark or N/A) for every product and service for each client.

3. *Make new spreadsheets each year.* At the end of each year, make two new spreadsheets using the same or different products and services, one for all your client relationships and another for only your $1 million-plus client relationships.

This simple organizing process ensures that you systematically discuss with each client the products and services that are appropriate for that client. This process will work whether or not the client is interested in each of the products and services you share with him; the only thing that counts is that you take the time to ask if he is interested in more information or details on the product you suggest, and that you provide this information. Just exposing your clients to more options and choices expands the products and services they have and will generate more business.

Have the Discussion

You don't need to make a separate contact to discuss these products and services. You can add these discussions to a portfolio review, a monthly contact, or a client call that you are returning. I recommend that you add these discussions to another conversation that you are having with your clients; a good transition phrase is, "By the way, I wanted to share an idea I thought you might be interested in."

One of the real values of this approach is that it makes every client contact more valuable to both you and the client. You can use this simple spreadsheet along with whatever contact system you use. Many contact systems are good at organizing contacts, but few of them provide the content for the contact (see sample scripts below).

If you do this every year, you should add at least 20 basis points of business. For example, if you have $100 million in assets and are generating $600,000 of business from that asset base, then by systematically exposing your clients to additional products and services, you should add a minimum of 20 basis points to your practice per year, increasing your business from $600,000 to $800,000 the first year.

Reassigning Clients

If you have diligently exposed a client to additional products and services over the course of a year, and she is still under your minimum business level, you need to give the account to a newer advisor who is willing to accept a lower minimum. One of the best expressions of this concept that I have heard is that every client deserves to be in someone's "A" book. Giving a low-fee-generating client to a newer advisor ensures that the client is in someone else's A book and is being well served; as you do this, you are helping another advisor upgrade his client pipeline and his own minimums.

The following script shows how you might handle reassigning a client because she is not meeting your minimum business level:

Advisor: Mr./Ms. Client, this is Joe Advisor from XYZ Financial, and the reason I am calling you is that I am going to reassign your account to another advisor. The reason for my decision is that I do not feel that I can provide you with the level of service you are entitled to, and I want to assign you to someone I trust who has the time to give you better service.

Client: I do not want to be reassigned. I am fine with your service. Can I stay with you?

Advisor: Since you have asked, I will tell you that to provide the level of service my clients should expect, I have a minimum level of annual business of $1,000. Since you have not done that much business with me in the past, I assume that you will not be willing to do it this year. But if you are interested in staying with me, I would be glad to discuss some pricing options and some additional products and services that would benefit you and would generate a minimum level of business. Would you be interested in discussing these?

Example Scripts for Expanding the Client Relationship

IRAs: General Query

Your objective here is to transfer IRA assets held somewhere else.

Mr./Ms. Client, I was reviewing your account and wanted to ask you about your retirement assets. Do you have any retirement accounts held outside of XYZ Financial?

If the answer is no, then:

Then all your retirement assets [if the client has any] are with XYZ Financial? I appreciate your confidence in us, and I will continue to do my best in managing them for you.

If the answer is yes, then:

It would help me to do a better job of allocating your assets if I knew where these retirement assets are and how they are invested. Could you provide me with the specifics? Would you mind sending me a copy of your most recent statement?

IRAs: Beneficiary

Your objective is again to transfer IRA assets held somewhere else.

Mr./Ms. Client, the beneficiary designation on your retirement assets can have some important tax considerations. I would like to have a chance to review with you your beneficiary designations on your XYZ Financial account [if applicable] and to do the same on any retirement accounts that you have outside XYZ Financial. When would be a convenient time to discuss this? I would suggest sending me in advance your statements and plan documents on those accounts that are not with XYZ Financial so that I can review them before our appointment.

Business Financial Services

Mr./Ms. Client, I am calling you because I realize that you are a business owner, and I have never talked to you about your banking relationships. We have a very competitive offering that pays an attractive rate on cash balances with low fees and no compensating balances, with an attractive credit line if you choose to use it. Would you like to know the details?

If the answer is no, then:

Thanks for your time. If the need does arise, let me know.

If the answer is yes, then provide specifics or offer to arrange an appointment where this offering can be discussed.

Annuities

Mr./Ms. Client, with the volatility we have experienced in the equity markets, many of my clients have reexamined their risk tolerance, and in many cases they are looking for more conservative investments. One idea I would like to share with you is a variable annuity. It grows tax deferred, can be diversified, and will give you most of the upside of an equity portfolio, but the downside risk is limited to a positive _____ a year. Would you like the details?

If the answer is no, then:

Thank you for your time. If your interests change, I can provide the details anytime.

If yes, then give the specifics of a particular variable annuity.

401(k)

Mr./Ms. Client, do you currently participate in a 401(k) plan?

If the answer is yes, then:

You may not realize it, but under current tax law, you may be able to transfer all or a portion of your 401(k) to an IRA rollover account. The benefits include my being able to allocate the assets in keeping with your investment plan and reallocate them as the market dictates. Further, it would streamline your reporting and give you an open platform to invest your assets in. As long as the rollover is over $ _____, there would be no fees on this account at XYZ Financial. With your permission, I can review your plan documents to see if you are eligible for this option. Are you interested?

Mortgages

Mr./Ms. Client, I am sure you are aware of the record volume of home refinancing occurring because of the current interest-rate environment. XYZ Financial has some attractive mortgage products and very attractive rates. Would you be interested in the details?

If the answer is no, then:

Thanks for your time. Let me know if your interest changes.

If the answer is yes, then provide the details of offerings and rates.

Life Insurance

Mr./Ms. Client, I find that many of my clients have older life insurance contracts (ten years or more) that can be replaced at a lower cost.

The cost is lower because life expectancy is increasing. If you would send me a copy of your policy and share how much it costs, I will do a complimentary review to see if I can save you money.

Home Equity Line of Credit

Mr./Ms. Client, many of my clients have taken advantage of our home equity line, which enables them to have access to their home equity to provide additional liquidity. This is a relatively low-cost way to access additional credit. Is this something you would like to know more about?

Long-Term Care Insurance

Mr./Ms. Client, I have found that many of my clients have concerns about the rising costs of long-term health care. A sobering fact is that 60 percent of people who reach age sixty-five will need long-term health care at some point in their lives. Presently, the insurance to protect you and your heirs is relatively inexpensive. It may also be something you should consider for your parents. Would you like to learn the details?

Managed Futures

Mr./Ms. Client, with the volatility we have experienced in the equity markets, I would like to share an idea with you that over time could lower the risk and increase the return of your portfolio. The idea is to add a small percentage of managed futures to your portfolio. Managed futures are not correlated to the equity markets and generally move in the opposite direction. These investments help to offset risk, as they tend to do well during uncertain times. Managed futures are professionally managed and diversified. Would you be interested in more details?

Examples of Scripts for $1 Million-Plus Clients

Concentrated Stock

Mr./Ms. Client, several of my clients who, like you, have had a successful career with a public company have been granted restricted stock and/or stock options. Would that apply to you?

If the answer is yes, then:

As you may know, you have alternatives in how you receive the options/stock, but all of them have tax implications. I would like to have the opportunity to review your restricted shares and stock options, and share with you our thoughts on what your best alternatives would be. Additionally, in some cases we can provide some liquidity and protection options for your restricted shares before they are released. Would you be interested in this kind of review?

Lending

Mr./Ms. Client, I have found that many of my clients who, like you, have significant net worth have unique lending needs. We can provide potential solutions for effective liability management. How do you currently handle your lending needs? [If appropriate] I would like to meet with you to discuss what we could offer you at XYZ.

Trust and Estate Planning

Mr./Ms. Client, most of my clients who have a net worth similar to yours have spent time developing a long-term estate and trust plan. What kind of trust and estate planning have you done? We would be glad to give you a complimentary review, and to update your plan as it relates to your trust and estate issues. Would you mind sending me a copy of your trust [if one exists] so that we can do a preliminary review to see if a follow-up meeting would be appropriate?

Alternative Investments

Mr./Ms. Client, several of my clients who, like you, have significant net worth have expressed an interest in private equity investments. A private equity investment can complement your existing portfolio, and, while the risks are greater, there are opportunities for significant upside potential. Private equities are companies that you can invest in before they are public. It takes the kind of net worth that you have to even qualify for these investments. If you are interested, I would suggest that you consider a small percentage of your portfolio for private equities. Would you like to know the details of some current offerings?

Expanding your business with existing clients takes discipline, organization, and a willingness to go beyond the comfort range that most advisors have. As much work as it is, it is still less work than getting new clients. We now have three ways to use your clients to build your business: leveraging clients to get new ones, bringing in clients' assets held at other institutions, and broadening your relationship with your clients. We will now look at the fourth way to use clients to grow your business.

Summary

- The more products and services a client is exposed to, the more business he will do.

- Clients who use five or more products and services generate three times as much business as clients who use two or less.

- Clients who have $1 million or more in assets have the greatest need for additional products and services.

- The best way to be sure to expose all your clients to appropriate products and services is to use annual spreadsheets, one for all clients and an expanded one for those over $1 million in assets.

- Mark the spreadsheets with a checkmark if the product or service has been discussed, or with N/A if the product or service is not appropriate or if the client already has the product or service. At the end of the year, all products and services should be checked or marked N/A for each client. Start a new list every year.

- If you complete the checklist each year for each relationship, you can add 20 basis points or more to your total practice.

- You can make your discussions of additional products and services an add-on to your monthly contacts with clients.

- You should have a minimum level of business that each client does of at least $1,000 per year, except $1 million-plus relationships, which should generate $10,000 per year.

Your Natural Market

f you organize your clients by age, occupation, or outside interests, you will see that they cluster into groups. For example, say that a large portion of your clients are retirees over sixty-five, golfers, and business owners. You can then combine these groupings—combinations might be retirees over sixty-five who like golf, or business owners between fifty and sixty who fly-fish. Or it may be that a large portion of your clients have different occupations but like golf, or a high percentage are in a certain age group but have different occupations and interests. The combinations can be endless.

These similarities among your clients—alone or in combination— represent your natural affinities, or your *natural market*, and can provide a significant marketing opportunity because people (advisors, in this case) tend to market better to people they are more comfortable with. These natural groupings show where you are more comfortable, and where you have been more successful in your past marketing.

Every advisor has a natural market, and focusing on this market is one of the best marketing opportunities you have, but most advisors have never taken the time to determine what their natural market is or how to leverage it.

How the Natural Market Works

The theory behind this approach is that clients associate with other people whom they work with, those who have similar interests, and those who are of a similar age: "Birds of a feather flock together." There are three primary benefits to this approach.

- It is a way to have contact with your clients in a format that is fun for, and valuable to, those clients.

- It gives clients a way to socialize with and offer value to their friends.
- It allows you to meet prospects in a nonthreatening way.

Through natural marketing, you make it easier for your clients to introduce you to their friends—your prospects. Natural marketing is nonthreatening because it is generally easier for a client to invite a friend to a fun event or to a seminar than to make a referral. The client feels less of a commitment than when making a referral because a referral puts a client in the position of endorsing the advisor—the client fears that if the advisor loses her friend's money, her friend will blame her. With natural marketing, the client is making an introduction by extending an invitation to an event, not by giving an endorsement.

How to Develop a Natural Marketing Plan

Step 1: Organize Your Clients

Organize your top fifty to one hundred relationships:

- By age range (in ten-year increments)
- By occupation
- By outside interests
- By the source of the account (how you acquired the account)

This analysis is the basis for the natural marketing plan. Start your plan with the two largest occupations, age ranges, and outside interests (two groups in each of these three categories equals six groups in all). For example, say that your analysis shows that:

- About 60 percent of your clients are retirees and business owners.
- About 80 percent of your clients are either between fifty and sixty or over seventy years old.
- About 75 percent of your clients are golfers or enjoy fly-fishing.

Step 2: Make Lists

Once you have done the analysis, list the clients in each of these six groups. These lists are the foundation of the natural marketing plan.

Step 3: Organize Events and Seminars

Once you have analyzed your clients and made your lists, organize events and seminars for those clients with similar age ranges and interests. Later in this chapter are examples of how to use natural marketing techniques for occupations, age ranges, and outside interests.

Step 4: Follow Up

You must follow up with new prospects that you acquire through these events and seminars. You should call each new prospect following the seminar or event and either invite him to another event or seminar or, if appropriate, ask him if he would feel comfortable meeting with you to discuss his specific situation.

How to Create Your Groupings

Same Occupations Natural Market: Referrals

People from the same occupation have strong connections and valuable information:

- People in a particular occupation have a good idea of the best way to market to others in that occupation.

- People in a particular occupation know others in their field and have a good idea of how qualified those people are (income, stock incentives, position, seniority, and so on).

- People in a particular occupation are aware of money in motion within their own firm and elsewhere in the industry—who is retiring, who has been transferred, who the new senior managers are, who the movers and shakers are, and other such information.

The best way to leverage the occupations groupings in your natural market is to ask for referrals from the clients in those occupations. Here is a sample script that demonstrates how you can ask a client for introductions to others in her occupation:

Mr./Ms. Client, I have recently analyzed my business and determined that the majority of my clients do what you do. [State the occupation.] It is clear to me that I work well with people in this occupation, and I wanted to ask your help: Is there anyone whom you work with or know in your industry that I should be talking to? Examples might be someone who has done very well in your business, someone who is retiring or relocating to this area, or someone who has had a significant event occur in his or her life. If so, would you feel comfortable providing me with an introduction?

Same Age Ranges Natural Market: Seminars

Clients who are of a similar age are usually at a similar place in the investment cycle. The investment cycle does not apply to all investors of the same age in the same way, but age is typically an important factor in determining an investor's financial needs. For example:

- Investors in the forty to fifty age range are most interested in funding their children's college education, setting up retirement plans, and perhaps purchasing a vacation home.
- Investors in the fifty to sixty age range are focused on having enough money to retire.
- Investors in the sixty to seventy age range are focused on travel and estate planning, and on not outliving their retirement assets.

Most people are friends with other people of a similar age. This is because they often share interests and family circumstances. The best way to capitalize on similar age ranges is to organize educational seminars that are of value to clients in a particular age range. When you offer educational seminars for particular age ranges, not only are you providing a valuable service to clients, but you are also giving them an opportunity to invite a friend of a similar age with similar interests—a prospective client. This is an excellent way to meet prospects. Be sure to ask your clients to bring a friend of similar age to the seminar.

Here are some examples of seminars you can offer that focus on the needs of people within a particular age range:

- Seminars on 529 plans for forty- to fifty-year-olds who are concerned with funding their children's educations.
- Preretirement issues seminars for fifty- to sixty-year-olds, covering how much money they need to retire, net unrealized appreciation, accelerated savings strategies, and other such information.
- Seminars on topics such as estate planning, gifting strategies, and staying ahead of inflation for sixty- to seventy-year-olds.

Here are two scripts you can use to invite clients to such events:

Mr./Ms. Client, I wanted to invite you to a seminar that, based on your investment circumstances, I thought you would be interested in. The topic of the seminar is _____, and the date and time is _____. Would you be interested in attending?

If the answer is yes, then:

Is there anyone else you think I should meet who might be interested in this seminar? If so, I would encourage you to please invite that person. Does anyone come to mind?

Mr./Ms. Client: The reason for my call is to invite you to a seminar that I am conducting on [relevant topic to appropriate age group]. In the past, I have found this topic to be very interesting and relevant to clients and prospects who are at a similar stage in their investment cycle. Would you be interested in attending?

If the answer is yes, then:

Good. Is there anyone else you think I should meet who might be interested in attending? It is a nonthreatening way for me to meet prospective clients who might have an interest in this seminar topic.

Same Outside Interests Natural Market

Your clients are likely to have friends who share similar outside interests—people like to be around other people who enjoy doing the same things. By classifying clients by their outside interests, you can organize events that appeal to these interests. Examples include golf, fly-fishing, fine dining, wine tasting, cooking, and travel.

The best way to leverage your clients' interest groupings is to organize fun events. These events focused on clients' outside interests provide an excellent opportunity to meet new prospects. Invite clients to events they are interested in, and ask them to invite a friend who shares the same interest. Your clients will appreciate being invited to an event they are interested in, and you will have a nonthreatening way to meet prospective clients.

A Marketing Board of Directors

Once you have grouped your best clients by occupation, age range, and outside interests, you can ask their help in finding prospects in those same groups. The idea is to create a "marketing board of directors," made up of clients who fall into a particular category, that will help you find and market more effectively to people in those occupations, age ranges, and interests.

The ideas I have presented so far focus on offering events that appeal to people with the same occupation, age range, or interest. Now, you are asking people in these groups for advice on marketing to others in the same group. There are no better counselors than these people for telling you the best marketing technique to reach a certain group of people. What you want to do is ask, "What advice can you give me on how to market effectively to people in the same field/age range/interest group as you?" Here is an example of it:

> Mr./Ms. Client, in reviewing my clients, I realized that most of them have the same occupation as you do. I wanted to ask your advice: I want to attract more clients like you, so what advice can you give me on how to approach individuals who do what you do?

Use Your Groupings to Uncover Your Best Marketing Activities

You can determine what marketing activities have been most successful for you with these groups by analyzing how you acquired your current clients. This is good information on which to base your future marketing efforts. For example, if you discover that your greatest source of clients and prospects is seminars, then this indicates that your primary marketing activity should be seminars. If you take the time to do this analysis, you can spend the majority of your marketing time doing those activities that produce the best results. In addition, if you want to develop a market niche(s) beyond your clients, your natural market is the best place to start. You have developed the expertise and experience necessary to market effectively to this particular niche.

Natural Marketing for Prospects

The same principles of natural marketing that apply to clients can also apply to prospects. If you categorize your prospects by age, occupation, and outside interest, you can invite prospects to attend events and educational seminars. Another benefit of this is that a new advisor with few clients can use natural marketing techniques before she has an established client base. By including existing prospects in the natural marketing process, you double the number of affluent clients and prospects you can build relationships with, and at the same time, you create goodwill.

In Chapter 7, I covered gathering information on the interests and details of your prospects. Now you will use that information. Organize them the same way I described for organizing your clients. Then list prospects by age range, occupation, outside interest, and source.

If you are organizing a client event around golf, invite existing prospects who like to golf to the event. Do the same with educational seminars that are appropriate for both clients and prospects in a particular age range. By including prospects, you can double the attendance at seminars and events and further develop your relationship with your prospects.

You can even take this a step further by asking each prospect to bring a friend who shares a similar interest. You can also call prospects and ask for suggestions on marketing to other prospects in similar occupations, and you can ask prospects who else they know in their occupation that you should be talking to.

Natural marketing is one of the most effective and efficient ways to leverage clients and prospects for the purpose of finding new prospects. It is simply a method of organizing clients and prospects by age, occupation, outside interests, and source. This provides opportunities to recognize good clients, and to help them help you in an easy, nonthreatening way. This is what effective marketing is all about.

I have talked about getting new clients and getting more from your existing ones. But if you don't hold on to your clients, you will be in trouble. I'll cover that next.

Summary

- Natural marketing is simply the classification of clients and prospects by age, occupation, outside interests, and how you acquired the client or prospect (the "source").

- Natural marketing gives you an opportunity to help your clients help you by introducing you to new prospects with common interests, age ranges, and occupations.

- Asking for referrals to others who share the same occupation is an effective natural marketing technique for clients and prospects with similar occupations.

- Educational seminars are the most effective natural marketing avenue for clients and prospects in similar age groups.

- Fun events are the most effective natural marketing avenues for clients and prospects with similar outside interests.

- A marketing board of directors is an effective natural marketing technique for getting marketing ideas from clients and prospects with similar occupations, age ranges, and interests.

- Organizing clients and prospects by source is the best way to determine what kind of marketing you do most effectively, and to determine how to spend the majority of your marketing time.

- Natural marketing techniques can work as well with prospects as they do with clients.

- Inviting a friend to a fun event or a seminar is an easier way for most clients to introduce prospective clients to their advisor than a direct referral.

- You must follow up with prospects you acquire through events and seminars. Schedule an appointment with them as soon as possible after the event or seminar.

CHAPTER 15

Client Retention

Retention is just as important as acquiring clients. My experience has shown that most advisors who are actively marketing meet their goals for bringing in new accounts, but when they take into consideration the relationships they lose, their net gain can be low. A strong acquisition strategy without a strong retention strategy is like trying to fill a bucket that has a hole in the bottom.

Client retention doesn't just depend on you, the advisor. It depends on your client associate, too—the client associate can play an invaluable role in your client-retention strategy. The client associate carries out many of the client-service tasks not only in conjunction with, but also independently of, the advisor. However, most client associates are so busy reacting that they seldom have the time to be proactive. To remedy this, you must take responsibility for expanding the role of your client associate.

I recommend that you apply the client-retention strategy that I am about to outline to your client relationships with $250,000 in assets or more, or to client relationships with the *potential* for reaching that level. These are the relationships that you must keep.

The Right Number of Client Relationships

Good client service is built on a single, essential point: a manageable number of client relationships. If you have too many client relationships, it is very difficult to provide the level of service required to keep your clients. You determine how many client relationships this is by assessing how frequently you need to contact your clients in order to keep them satisfied.

You need to contact every client at least once a month. This is twelve contacts per year. Four of these contacts should be quarterly reviews, and one of those quarterly reviews should be a supersession for annual planning.

If you have more than one hundred client relationships, you will not have time to provide this level of contact frequency and still have time to market. In the case of an experienced team, I recommend that the senior advisors limit themselves to fifty relationships.

> **Fundamental Truth:**
>
> You grow your business by raising the level of minimum assets, not by increasing the number of relationships.

The most affluent households—$1 million plus—require more frequent contact, better service, and more time spent each time you contact them. As an example, I worked with an advisor who limited the client relationships he worked with to clients with $100 million or more. In his case, this was between ten and twenty total relationships. This small number of relationships required so much time that this advisor spent more time working with his clients than any advisor I have worked with. He spent the majority of this time on activities that went beyond the investment side of the relationship; he served as a "family office" for his clients and worked in all aspects of their lives, including recreation and advising on outside business interests. During each of the four years I worked with this advisor, he did over $10 million per year in gross production. The higher the affluence of a client, the higher the service required for retention of that client.

In the end, you must make a choice about how to run your practice. The model I describe in this book is to work with fewer, but more affluent, client relationships. In this model, each relationship requires more time, which limits the number of relationships you can work with. Remember that to do $1 million in business, you need only seventy-five relationships with assets between $250,000 and $1 million and twenty-five relationships with assets of $1 million or more.

The number of client relationships you have has a significant effect on your client associate, too. The client associate should make each client and prospect feel like she is getting Ritz-Carlton service, and for the client associate to provide this level of service, he must have a manageable number of relationships. The time that a client associate spends with smaller, less affluent relationships is time that he can no longer spend serving more affluent relationships. Advisors often underestimate how much time it takes a client associate to answer calls and service smaller relationships.

Five Factors That Drive Retention

Once you have ensured that you have the time to provide good service to your clients (by limiting their number), you need to focus on the factors that then drive retention:

1. Portfolio performance consistent with client goals and expectations
2. Effective problem resolution
3. Frequent, proactive client contact
4. A broad relationship
5. Ensuring that the new-relationship experience is positive

Client retention is in your hands because you can control all these factors. Furthermore, this is not difficult to do.

Portfolio Performance That Is Consistent with the Client's Goals and Expectations

There are two sides to performance: what the client expects and how her assets perform. If these two factors are mismatched and the client expects better performance than she is getting, there is a problem.

Expectations

If a client's assets are performing as the client expects, or better, the client will be very satisfied. If you educate your client about the kind of performance he can expect, given his goals and risk tolerance, then his expectations are likely to be in line with the long-term performance he will get. Educating clients is key to setting their expectations.

Performance

The keys to better portfolio performance are allocation, diversification, and a disciplined investment process. If you manage these components wisely, the long-term results will be good. Over the long term, a conservative approach with the right allocation will outperform a less disciplined, aggressive investment approach.

Effective Problem Resolution

Operational problems are inevitable, and the majority of clients understand this. The key to good client retention is not to have zero operational problems, but to quickly resolve the problems that occur. *How many* operational problems there are is a much smaller factor in client satisfaction than *how well* these problems are resolved.

Problem resolution is one of the most important service initiatives a client associate can focus on. Ideally, every problem is resolved quickly; however, in the real world, this is not always the case. The client associate should hold herself accountable for excellent problem resolution with each client. I recommend that client associates grade themselves on how they resolve each client's problems, with a goal of having an A for each client relationship.

Communication is the key to effective problem resolution. You must communicate to the client associate that she must acknowledge all operational problems that occur with clients, and make resolving them her highest priority. If the client associate gets frustrated during the course of solving a problem, then step in to help.

When the problem is resolved, the client associate should communicate this to the client right away. If the resolution is being delayed, the client associate should be communicating with the client regularly to let him know what the status of the problem is and when it will be resolved. Most clients will accept a delay as long as they know that the problem is being attended to, and as long as they have an idea of when the problem will be resolved.

Frequent, Proactive Client Contact

Steps for the Advisor

Clients want to hear from you. I cannot overemphasize the importance of this. Clients want to feel that you care, and that you are paying attention to them and their assets. There is so much competition for affluent clients that if they do not feel appreciated, it is easy for them to transfer their assets to someone who *will* appreciate them.

You should make a minimum of one proactive contact per month with each client. A proactive contact is one that you initiate; reacting to a client's call to you doesn't count. One contact per month is twelve per year. Three of these twelve contacts should be quarterly reviews, and one of them should be an annual planning or review session—a supersession. Contact more often than once a month is fine, but once a month is ideal. This schedule limits the number of total relationships you can have to about one hundred (five contacts per day).

There are a number of other contacts you can make with your clients that can have a very positive impact on retention. These contacts supplement, but do not replace, the monthly advisor contact. Following are some ideas:

- Send your clients mailings with personal notes attached.
- Have your associate contact the client.
- Provide client events or seminars. Using natural marketing techniques, organize your clients by interests and age. By organizing events and seminars focused on your clients' interests and age groups, you can provide fun events and interesting, relevant seminars for your clients. Holding these kinds of events and seminars is an excellent way to demonstrate to your clients how much you appreciate them.
- Send a client two movie tickets for her birthday. The client will feel good about the fact that you not only remembered her birthday, but also sent her a gift. Movie tickets are a nice night out, and your client will think of you during and after it. The goodwill this creates is greater than the dollars you spend for the tickets.
- Have your manager call the client, thank the client for his business, and offer him access to her if needed. Involving a full-time manager can go a long way in making clients feel important. E-mail the client's name and number to your manager, and ask her to make a goodwill call. Because of the manager's time limitations, I recommend that you ask your manager to call only your best clients—those with at least $1 million-plus.

Steps for the Client Associate

Providing outstanding, proactive service is as important as any job the client associate can do. Outstanding service involves asking clients if they have any service needs before they call and ask. I recommend that the client associate call each client at least once a year and ask if the client has any service issues. This gives the client the feeling that both the advisor and the client associate really care about providing great service. Here is an example of a client associate script for doing this:

> Mr./Ms. Client, you are one of our best clients, and we are committed to providing you with outstanding service. I am calling to see if there is anything we can do to better serve you, and to see if there are any service issues that we can help you with.

A Broad Relationship

Clients who use five or more products and services have a near-perfect retention rate. This makes sense, since the more products and services a client uses, the more tied in she is to the advisor and the firm. This is a vote of confidence by the client.

Steps for the Advisor

You must be organized and keep track of which products and services you have introduced to your clients. In most cases, the more the client is exposed to appropriate products and services, the more likely he is to use them. If a client is going to refinance his home or use a credit card, why shouldn't it be through his trusted advisor? If you have a competitive product, all you have to do is ask your client for the business. If you commit to this and expose your clients to a broad range of products and services, you are likely to increase your business by 20 basis points and achieve a very high retention rate.

Let me be clear about what counts as a different product or service. The primary investments that a client has count as one product: "investments." Some examples of additional products are annuities, estate planning, insurance, lending, mortgages, and managed futures. Some examples of additional services are banking, credit cards, direct deposit, Web bill paying, and online statements.

Steps for the Client Associate

It is appropriate for the client associate to talk to a client about services that the client could use. Some examples of these services include credit or debit cards, banking services, direct deposit, online statements, and Web bill paying.

All services may not be applicable to all clients, but most are. In the course of conversations with clients throughout the year, the client associate could ask the client if she would be interested in the services the client associate believes would be applicable. Here's an example of how the client associate might position these services with a client:

> Mr./Ms. Client, I appreciate your question regarding last month's statement, and hopefully I have answered it. While we are talking, I thought I might mention the ability to get your statements online at your home. Many other clients enjoy having that feature, and I wanted to offer it to you. Would you like to know the details?

As the client associate gets to know the client, he will know the best time to introduce a service and what services are most appropriate for that particular client. This should not be a hard sell. It should simply be the offering of a service that could make the client's life easier. By organizing the client associate to make these calls, the advisor will be adding great leverage to her own time. The client associate will be improving retention by adding those services, and the advisor does not have to spend her time offering them. Remember, the goal is for each client to have five or more products and services. Why not use your client associate to help you reach that goal with each client?

The same principles apply to the $1 million-plus relationships. The client associate should call these clients and offer the same services as he does for the other clients, but he can offer additional services to the $1 million-plus relationships. The $1 million-plus services could include a life insurance review, lending opportunities, and trust and estate reviews. The client associate can set up the contacts for the advisor by asking the $1 million-plus clients (in the course of servicing these accounts) if they would be interested in a review of these services. This can set the stage for the advisor to follow through if the client is interested.

The client associate can be organized to do this with a checklist and scripts written by the advisor. Set up the checklist as a spreadsheet, with the clients' names in the first column and the list of services in the subsequent columns across the top of the spreadsheet. The client associate should place a checkmark next to the client's name under each service offered to the client. If the service is not applicable to that particular client, the client associate should write "N/A" under that service. The client associate fills in each blank whether or not the client is interested, as long as the client associate offered that service. The objective is for the client associate to have placed a checkmark or N/A under every service next to each client's name.

I recommend that the advisor write scripts for the client associate as conversation starters to introduce the services. The scripts should be attached to the checklist.

Ensuring That the New-Relationship Experience Is Positive

The new-relationship experience is very important because it is the client's first experience with the advisor's firm. It sets the perception that the new client has, which, in turn, colors many of the experiences that the client has with the firm later on. A good first experience subsequently encourages positive perceptions.

The client associate and the advisor together should develop a checklist of all the things that need to be done to make the first experience a good one. One of these new-account tasks should be a letter from the client associate introducing himself to the new client and offering himself as the person who will be responsible for the service side of the relationship. The client associate should follow up the letter with a personal call doing the same. The client associate should also call the client right after her first statement arrives and review the statement with the client so that she is comfortable reading it. These things will ensure that the new-account experience will be positive.

Create a spreadsheet that organizes the client associate to ensure that the new-relationship experience is a good one. Put the new client's name in the first column, and list the tasks to be completed in the subsequent columns across the spreadsheet. As the client associate completes the tasks, he should place a checkmark on the row for that client under each task. Each new client should have a checkmark under each task within ninety days of opening the new account.

Scripts for the Client Associate

The following are scripts that a client associate can use with clients to expand the services these clients use. This section also includes an example of a welcome letter and welcome call that the client associate should use with new clients within thirty days of opening the account.

Welcome Call

Mr./Ms. Client, I am calling to introduce myself and thank you for your business. Do you have any questions regarding your account that I may assist you with? I will call you when you receive your first statement to go over that with you. In the meantime, if you have any questions, you can call me at [client associate's direct line].

Thank-You Letter

Dear Mr./Ms. Client:

Thank you for choosing [advisor's name] to help you reach your financial planning goals.

I am writing to introduce myself to you as part of [advisor's name]'s support staff. I am your primary service contact. In addition to [advisor's name]'s financial advice, I am here to assist you with any service requests and questions you may have.

Please do not hesitate to call me directly if any questions should arise. We take great pride in servicing our clients and look forward to a continuing relationship with you.

> Sincerely,
> [Client associate's name]
> [Address]

Banking Service

Mr./Ms. Client, I am calling to inform you of a service we are offering to our best clients to better serve their banking needs. If you add our banking service, you will have the convenience of managing all of your financial needs in one place. In addition, you will have access to XYZ Financial Web bill paying, a simple and convenient alternative to the hassle of writing checks and stuffing envelopes, at no cost to you. Would you like details on setting up the account?

Direct Deposit

Mr./Ms. Client, I am calling to see if you were aware of our direct deposit service at XYZ Financial. Receiving your benefits or paycheck can be easier and more convenient when you use the direct deposit service for your accounts. With direct deposit, your paychecks [or social security and other types of benefits] are deposited automatically into your account on each payroll/benefit date. That means no more worrying about stolen checks or checks lost in the mail, and no more waiting in bank lines to deposit payments. I would be happy to assist you with the enrollment if you are interested in this service.

Web Bill Paying

Mr./Ms. Client, I am calling to see if you are currently using our Web bill-paying service. Web bill paying allows you to pay bills electronically to anyone, anywhere and anytime.

529 Plans

Mr./Ms. Client, helping families plan financially for the college education of their children or grandchildren is an important part of our job. The government has a tax-advantaged program designed to help families provide funding for their children's education. Would you be interested in the details on setting up this type of account?

Online Services

Mr./Ms. Client, I am calling to see if you would be interested in using the XYZ Financial online service. This service will connect you to your accounts and give you the tools to track your accounts. By accessing your accounts through this online service, you can see your account balances and other relevant account information. Would you be interested in receiving more information on this?

Credit Card Services

Mr./Ms. Client, I am calling to inform you of a service we are offering our clients. We now offer credit cards from XYZ Financial with low rates and generous credit lines. Would you be interested in receiving more information?

Client Scripts for the Client Associate for $1 Million-Plus Clients

Estate Planning

Mr./Ms. Client, do you have a current will or living trust to avoid excess probate tax? If not, may I suggest that you meet with your advisor to make sure you have taken advantage of all the tax laws to ensure your beneficiaries get everything they are entitled to? I would be happy to set that meeting up for you if you are interested.

Life Insurance

Mr./Ms. Client, we have found that many of our clients who have older life insurance policies can replace them for a lower cost. If you send us a copy of your policy and premiums, we can do a complimentary review to see if we can get you a lower price for the same coverage. Would you be interested?

A good client retention strategy is not complicated, but it requires attention. The core drivers of retention are good investment performance consistent with the client's goals, frequent contact (at least monthly), good problem resolution, a good breadth of products and services (with a goal of five or more), and a positive new-account experience. The client associate is key to good retention, and she can take proactive steps that can make a very positive difference in client retention.

Experienced advisors have a lot to do in order to retain clients, and must also make time to market. It may seem overwhelming. I will explain how to do it all, by managing your time effectively, in Chapter 16.

Summary

- Your client relationships need to be limited to one hundred for client retention to work.
- A good client-retention strategy is as important as a client-acquisition strategy.
- The client associate can play a critical role in the client-retention strategy.
- The recommended client-retention strategy should be limited to those clients who have $250,000 or more (or have the potential to reach this level), not to exceed one hundred relationships.
- Five factors drive retention:
  1. Portfolio performance that is consistent with the client's goals and expectations
  2. Effective problem resolution
  3. Frequent, proactive client contact

4. A broad relationship
5. Ensuring that the new-account experience is positive

- Client events and seminars focused on client interests and age are excellent ways to show appreciation and help with retention.

CHAPTER 16

Time Management and the Client Associate

How an advisor spends her time will determine how likely it is that the advisor will become a $1 million-plus advisor. Time is all an advisor has, and how you use that time and your energy determines your success. You have only a limited amount of energy; how many hours you work each day is less important than how many of those hours are productive. The advisor who is committed to a million-dollar practice must devote his high-energy hours to the right activities, or else the opportunity for that day is lost.

Fundamentals of Time Management

You need to balance client contact, marketing time, and administrative time every day. To be effective, you must be organized and follow the three fundamentals of time management:

1. Prioritize
2. Delegate
3. Block your time

If you follow these fundamentals, you can get everything done that is necessary to build a million- or multimillion-dollar business.

Prioritize

There are two levels of prioritizing. The first level is your daily priorities—the tasks that you deem most important to do each day. The second level is your overall priorities—the general areas of activity that are the most important.

> **Fundamental Truth:**
> **Do the most difficult and most important things first.**

Prioritizing daily tasks ensures that you perform the most important activities first, while your energy is high. Resist the temptation to spend high-energy hours on administrative tasks, reading, research, or preparation. Those tasks are easier but not as important as time spent developing relationships with affluent clients and prospects.

1. Your first priority needs to be monthly contact with clients.
2. Your close second priority should be following up with existing prospects and getting in front of new ones.
3. Your third priority should be doing the one or two highest-priority administrative tasks daily that cannot be delegated.

Return calls and do lower-priority administrative tasks at the end of the day, when you have spent much of your daily energy. You must constantly prioritize, and you should always spend the high-energy early hours of the day on the high-priority tasks so that no matter what comes up, these tasks are always done first.

Your First Priority Needs to Be Monthly Contact with Clients.

Spending time contacting clients is your number one task. Every client survey I have ever seen shows that client satisfaction is tied to regular contact by the advisor. If you limit your number of client relationships to one hundred, and you are committed to contacting each client at least once a month, then you need to contact five clients each day; if each call lasts about thirty minutes, then you need to commit approximately three hours each day to client contact. Some of these client contacts could last fifteen minutes, and some could last an hour or more if they involve an annual review or planning session. Three of these monthly contacts should be a quarterly review (in person, if convenient), and one should be a yearly planning supersession (also in person, whenever possible).

The bottom line is that you need to spend three hours a day in order to provide the service level that one hundred clients require. Contacting your clients less than once a month is not enough, and more than once a month can be too much—a contact once a month is just about right.

Your Close Second Priority Should Be Following Up with Existing Prospects and Getting in Front of New Ones.

You must spend time marketing every day if you expect to achieve a million-dollar or multimillion-dollar practice. If you are not committed to a disciplined marketing process, there is very little chance that you will build a million-dollar practice. The most successful multimillion-dollar advisors whom I have worked with have all had at least one thing in common: They never stop marketing.

For an experienced advisor, marketing can take many forms. Some examples of very effective marketing techniques that I have observed in million- and multimillion-dollar advisors are golfing at private clubs, fly-fishing, hunting, charity work, network groups (their own), nonprofit boards, center-of-influence networks, client events, and client referrals. This is not an exhaustive list, but it is a sample of the way many of the successful multimillion-dollar advisors I have worked with market every day.

I recommend that you market from one to five hours, or more, every day by contacting prospective clients. The most successful advisor I have ever worked with ($10 million-plus per year) marketed many hours every day. The bottom line is that you must build marketing time into every day.

Your Third Priority Should Be Doing the One or Two Highest-Priority Administrative Tasks Daily That Cannot Be Delegated.

Even though you should spend most of your high-energy time each day on client and prospect contact, you need to spend time on administrative tasks in order to build and maintain a million-dollar practice. Problems that require your personal attention will come up and must be dealt with effectively and efficiently. If you prioritize properly, you should be able to personally handle ten high-priority administrative items per week. If there are more than ten that you need to handle, chances are that you are not delegating properly.

Examples of administrative items that you cannot delegate include resolving an operational problem that the client associate cannot, putting together an important client or prospect presentation, following up on an unresolved client problem, preparing a presentation for a meeting with a CPA or a client seminar, and preparing for a top-client portfolio review.

You should do at least two of these high-priority administrative tasks each day, and you should schedule thirty minutes to one hour daily to work on these issues.

Delegate

You must try to delegate everything that is not involved with building client relationships and with being in front of affluent clients and prospects. While you need to *oversee* portfolio management, client reviews, and high-priority administrative tasks, you do not have to *do* each task. Your priority should be to establish processes and follow-through checks, not to actually do these tasks. Think of yourself as a Broadway actor, focusing on the audience and the performance, and not spending time on the scenery, the music, and the makeup; for a great performance, the actor must give those tasks to someone else so that she can focus her attention on the performance. The advisor must do the same thing. Relationship building and marketing are the hardest things to delegate, but try to delegate everything else.

Block Your Time

Time blocking is focusing on one task for a block of time. You should set up one-hour time blocks for each high-priority task. During a time block, only do one type of task—for example, client contact, prospect contact, appointments, or administrative tasks. When you are doing only one task, you get into a rhythm, and you get better within the time block as you repeat the task. An advisor is much better off contacting two or three clients in one hour than contacting a single client, then doing an administrative task, and then making a prospect call. Mixing up different activities can be both distracting and inefficient.

The Role of the Client Associate

The work flow between the advisor and the client associate is critical to successful time management. The experienced advisor who is committed to growing his business must delegate most of the administrative and operational tasks to his client associate. This means that the client associate has four main areas of responsibility:

1. General administrative and operational duties

2. Client-service tasks

3. Screening calls

4. Preparing and customizing templates and template libraries

This can be daunting if the advisor does not help the client associate by being very organized himself.

General Administrative and Operational Duties

Delegate to the client associate everything except those things that you absolutely must do yourself; delegate everything that is not involved with building client relationships and with being in front of affluent clients and prospects. Avoid giving your client associate piles of tasks to do because she will have no idea what she should work on first. Prioritize the work you give her by attaching a note to each task explaining what needs to be done, and be sure to include all corresponding paperwork. Prioritize all tasks with a 1, 2, or 3:

1. The task needs to be done that day.

2. The task needs to be done that week.

3. The task needs to be done that month.

Keep a copy of the tasks you have delegated and indicate the date you delegated them. Keep these copies of the tasks in a pending file. Each day, when you meet with your client associate, review the pending file and check the status of each item. This process helps the client associate prioritize what is most important to the advisor and also holds the client associate accountable to a date for completion. If the client associate is accountable, he will either work hard to meet the deadline or explain to the advisor why he cannot meet the deadline. I recommend that you assign tasks and review the pending file with your client associate once a day, as early in the day as possible. This meeting should not take more than thirty minutes. This keeps the advisor from interrupting the client associate throughout the day. This system can be set up electronically if the advisor prefers.

Client-Service Tasks

The client associate can help the advisor not only with administrative tasks but with providing the outstanding service that affluent clients expect. Most client associates do not have time to be proactive with service and instead react to problems as they arise; this is merely a lack of organization. If the advisor wants her client associate to take service to the next level, she must help organize the assistant to do so. The client associate has four areas where he can take service to a very high level: the new-relationship experience, expanding the services that clients use, outstanding problem resolution, and proactive service.

Screening Calls

The client associate should screen calls for the advisor whenever possible. Clients should be trained to know that the advisor will not pick up the phone as soon as they call, but will always call back within a reasonable time. I have never worked with a professional in any industry who took my call whenever I called him. My expectation and those of clients should be that unless it is a market-related event, the advisor will call back by the end of the business day. This system allows you to call back after you have made the proactive client and prospect calls and appointments or between them. A sample client associate script for screening calls may be as follows:

> I am sorry, Mr./Ms. Client, Joe Advisor is [on the line, meeting with a client, away from the office]. Is there anything I can help you with?

If the answer is yes, get the details. If it is no, then say:

> I will ask Joe to call you after his meeting(s). Is this afternoon okay?

Note that the client associate should always ask if she can be of service. In many cases, the advisor doesn't need to call the client back because the client associate can handle the problem. Also, the client associate has given the advisor the freedom to call back in the afternoon when it is most convenient for him. This allows you to call back after you have finished your calls to clients and prospects.

Preparing and Customizing Presentations and Presentation Libraries

For the most part, you can prepare client and prospect presentations and reviews well in advance of the meeting. With the help of your client associate, you can prepare a menu of different presentations on different topics and hold these presentations in a presentation template library so that, with minimum customization, they can be ready for presentation in a short period of time. The key to making this work is for you and your client associate to take the time in the beginning to set up the presentation template library.

The same principles hold for quarterly and annual client reviews. The format of the reviews, the agendas, the performance data, and the planning information can all be prepared in advance. Like presentations, these reviews can be set up in advance; then, with minimal customization, they can be made ready just minutes before the review. The advisor must commit to setting up the format and to training the client associate how to customize it in order to make this process work.

Rewarding Your Client Associate

A good client associate can be an invaluable asset to the experienced advisor in building a million- or multimillion-dollar practice. It is very important that you reward your client associate so that he feels like an appreciated member of your team. This reward should be in the form of both recognition and compensation. Recognition is easy to give but often is not given enough. Look for every opportunity to recognize your client associate's good work. Compliments go a long way, but so do flowers, movie tickets, and nice cards. These are easy things for you to give and will add greatly to the client associate's morale and good feelings about the job.

An outstanding client associate deserves outstanding pay. Unfortunately, the industry does not pay client associates well, and it is up to the advisor to supplement her associate's pay. Many advisors pay their client associates a percentage of their business; others give them a bonus at the end of the year. How you pay is less important than the fact that you are willing to pay extra for outstanding work.

Good recognition and compensation will keep a good client associate loyal for many years, providing the advisor with the support required to build a million-dollar business.

Sample Schedule

Taking into account the time-management fundamentals and the activities that the advisor must do every day to build a million-dollar practice, I would recommend the following daily schedule as a guideline:

7:30–8:00	Meet with your client associate (assign tasks, review pending items)
8:00–8:30	Do one or two nondelegatable, highest-priority administrative tasks
8:30–11:30	Five client contacts and two to five prospect follow-up contacts
11:30–1:00	Client/prospect appointment or administrative catch-up
1:00–3:00	Marketing to new prospects
3:00–4:00	Return calls, answer e-mails, and plan the next day
4:00–5:30	Client/prospect appointments or administrative catch-up

This schedule should start one hour later for Eastern time zones.

If you follow this schedule every day, then every day you will achieve the following:

Five client contacts	2 hours
Two to five prospect follow-ups	1 hour
One client appointment	1 hour
One prospect or client appointment	1 hour
One client associate meeting	1 half-hour
Two high-priority administrative tasks	1 half-hour
All calls returned	1 half-hour
Miscellaneous	1 half-hour
New prospects contacted	2 hours
Total	9 hours (this includes lunch)

Following this schedule results in the following use of your time:

Client and prospect contact	33 percent	3 hours
Client and prospect appointments	22 percent	2 hours
Marketing time	12–25 percent	2 hours
Administrative time	22 percent	2 hours

Thus, 70 to 75 percent of your time is spent on client and prospect contact and on marketing activities. Only about 25 percent of your time is spent on administrative activities. Reading, research, and presentation preparation should be done outside the normal nine-hour day. Note that if you want to reduce your working day to eight hours, you should reduce marketing time from two hours to one, but you should recognize that by reducing your marketing time, you will delay reaching the million- or multimillion-dollar business level; you can still do it, but it will just take longer.

Also note that you may not be able to follow this schedule perfectly in a normal day. Unexpected events may occur that will make it impossible. But the principle of time blocking high-priority activities and doing them first is very important for those advisors who are motivated to build a million-dollar business.

How an advisor spends his time will define his success in this business. Good time management is the critical difference between the advisors who achieve a million-dollar practice and those who do not. Prioritizing how you spend your time, delegating, blocking your time, and using your client associate effectively are all essential ingredients required to build a million-dollar business.

Time management is about productivity, and an important tool for increasing productivity is being part of a team. Chapter 17 looks at how teams work and how and if you should form or join a team.

Summary

- Good time management will determine whether or not an advisor will be able to build a million-dollar practice.

- Spending the majority of your time building relationships with clients and prospects is required for a million-dollar practice.

- Time-management fundamentals are delegating, prioritization, and time blocking.

- Advisors must organize a good work-flow process between themselves and their client associate.

- Strong recognition and good compensation are required to motivate and keep a good client associate long term.

CHAPTER 17

Teams

Teams have proliferated in financial services over the past five years, and for good reason: Advisors who work in a team generally do better than those who work on their own. Many financial services firms have over 50 percent of their advisors in teams. The team structure works well in financial services in large part because of the productivity and client-service (retention) improvements they afford. While being on a team is not a prerequisite for having a million-dollar practice, being on a good team can increase the probability of reaching $1 million and reduce the time it takes to reach it.

Advantages of Teams

Deeper Expertise

Teams often specialize so that each team member can be an expert in something without needing to be an expert in everything. This specialization can be in a particular product area, marketing, portfolio management, presentations, or some other element.

Better Client Service

Clients appreciate their advisor being part of a team because they feel that with a team, there is always someone there to take care of them who is familiar with their situation. This gives clients a sense of continuity should something happen to their advisor.

Deeper Motivation

Team motivation can be very powerful. Teams that have regular meetings where every team member is held accountable for his tasks and his results are teams that work harder. Many advisors feel a higher level of accountability to other team members than they do to themselves; this improves motivation, but also improves productivity because each person's results are transparent.

Better Ideas

Financial services can be a competitive business, and advisors can be very protective of their best practices and reluctant to share them with potential competitors, even within the same firm. Sharing ideas among and getting input from all members of the team is invaluable.

Pooling of Resources

There are many ways to enhance productivity, but many of them are expensive, such as hiring a fully paid assistant, upgrading technology, and purchasing marketing resources. A team can share in these extra expenses. Resource decisions are much easier to make when the team members share the costs.

Better Penetration

Better account penetration can occur, especially when one or more of the advisors on a team has a mature business. I have seen several examples of two senior advisors joining together and finding opportunities in each other's business that would not have been discovered otherwise. Better account penetration also can result when a senior advisor turns over her inactive or smaller accounts to a junior partner—in many cases, the junior partner will find new assets and generate more business just because he is paying more attention to these relationships. An example of this is when a new advisor joins a senior advisor and completes a financial plan for every account assigned to him; the junior partner often finds a significant number of new assets as a result. Another example is a team in which a partner brings a particular expertise to the team and uncovers opportunities that an advisor without that kind of expertise could never find.

Pitfalls of Teams

There Must Be a Good Fit

While the benefits of being on a team are numerous, the team will work only if there is a good fit between team members. In a team that has a good fit, the phrase "One plus one equals three" is true. Too often, however, advisors join or form a team as a way to increase productivity without thinking about team fit or synergy. Teams don't automatically increase productivity; if the fit is not good or synergy doesn't take place, teaming can actually hurt productivity: "One plus one equals one." It takes time to put a team together, to have team meetings, to measure results, and so on. If productivity is not higher, then all of this is a waste of time.

Hiding Behind the Efforts of Others

I have seen situations where a team did less business than the advisors had done on their own. This generally occurs when one of the team members hides behind administrative duties, relying on the other team members to do the work. This is why accountability is so important.

Types of Teams

The majority of successful teams that I have observed fall into one or more of these general categories:

1. Specialization
2. Inside and outside
3. Vertical (or superstar)
4. Junior and senior

Specialization

In this kind of team, each member brings an area of specialization or expertise that is different from those of the other team members. When the team works with clients and prospects, different team members are brought in as their expertise is needed. Examples of such areas of expertise are insurance and estate planning, retirement planning, investment planning, liabilities, and corporate services. These teams generally do well because the value of each team member is apparent, and each can be paid based on the additional products and services that she provides to clients. This structure also gives the team the opportunity to differentiate itself because of its depth and its wide range of expertise.

Inside and Outside

In this structure, there is an outside advisor, who is primarily responsible for marketing and building new relationships, and an inside advisor, who manages the portfolios and handles the administrative and operational aspects of the team. The outside advisor can sell the inside advisor's expertise. If the senior advisor has very strong marketing and relationship skills, he will be the outside advisor—the outside (senior) advisor describes the wealth-management process, while the inside (junior) advisor implements the strategy and supports the outside (senior) advisor. In other cases, a junior partner will be the outside partner, marketing the experience and skills of the senior partner. The senior inside partner is brought in after the first appointment. The advantage of this partnership is that marketing, portfolio management, and organization can require different skill sets, and by consolidating them through a partnership, great synergy can occur.

Vertical

The vertical structure is sometimes described as the "superstar" structure. This type of team is completely centered around one very successful advisor. This advisor has it all—she is a great marketer and has a strong wealth-management process, and all she needs is administrative support to handle the details of the practice. All business goes through the superstar, and that person pays to have the high-quality support she needs to support her productivity. Some of the most productive teams I have ever worked with are organized in this fashion. This structure allows great talent to flourish by enabling the superstar to spend all her time doing what she does best without being distracted by the daily operational, administrative, or money-management aspects of the business.

Junior and Senior

The junior and senior team structure is essentially a succession-plan structure: The senior advisor wants to ensure that when he retires, the practice will remain intact and the clients will be managed by the junior partner. These partnerships can go on for years, with the junior partner apprenticing, in effect, to eventually take over the business. Often the junior partner's split eventually increases to 50–50, and in some cases it grows to majority ownership. This team structure can provide high levels of commitment for two reasons: First, since the senior partner typically selects the junior partner, the senior partner has real commitment to the junior partner's success; and second, the junior partner is committed to the partnership long-term because of the big payoff when the senior partner retires. The clients appreciate the orderly succession plan, and the senior partner can stay in practice longer because she can spend less time at it while the clients are being well serviced by her successor. (A senior advisor looking for a junior advisor to help her bring in new assets or generate more business from her smaller accounts should, in most cases, look for a new advisor with proven marketing and business skills, not an unproven advisor who might look good on paper but does not have the results or the experience.)

Blends

The four categories of teams are not always pure, and in some cases there are combinations and blends of more than one category within one team. The purpose of outlining these four is to give you examples of how successful teams can be structured, and to encourage you to think through which arrangement will suit you best.

Forming and Strengthening a Successful Team

There are two parts to the life of a team: forming it and strengthening it after it has been formed. When you form a team (or explore joining one), you need to:

- Assess your weaknesses and strengths
- Ensure that there is a good fit
- Try it out first
- Have a plan for dissolution
- Be definite about fair compensation

Strengthening a team that has already been formed requires a different set of activities:

- Align values
- Promote commitment
- Promote good communication
- Build in measurement and accountability

Forming a Team

Assess Your Weaknesses and Strengths

There are advisors who would like to be part of a team but do not know where to start. The place to start is to do an honest assessment of your strengths and weaknesses. Your strengths are what you can offer a team, and your weaknesses are what you need from a team—often teams form so that one member's strengths fill in another member's weaknesses. An example of this might be two advisors, one who has excellent organizational skills, portfolio management experience, and the ability to generate business, and another who has excellent marketing skills but who might not have the time or interest to manage the assets or to provide the required service once the prospect is brought in.

Ensure That There Is a Good Fit

Fit is more important than which type of team you form or join. The best fit among team members occurs when:

- The advisors' values are aligned.
- The advisors' goals are similar.
- There is a high level of commitment of time and energy.
- There is willingness to be accountable.
- There is a high level of professional respect.
- The members' skills complement each other.

This list is not all-inclusive, but it outlines the characteristics of the best teams that I have observed. Many teams may have some combination of these elements, and I have not found that any one of them is more responsible for a team's success than the others.

Try It Out First

Joining or forming a team is like a professional marriage and should be taken just as seriously. Start by forming a "situational team." A situational team is one in which the advisors come together to undertake a particular marketing activity and split the business that comes from it. This allows team members to professionally "date" before they form a team, to determine whether forming a permanent team is appropriate. Some examples of this are:

- Putting on a joint seminar.
- Inviting an advisor with a particular expertise to help close a prospect.
- A junior advisor inviting a senior advisor with strong presentation skills and experience to close a prospect.
- A senior advisor identifying a talented new advisor who may be a potential partner, and offering him all her resources, with the understanding that the junior advisor will include the senior advisor in most of his prospecting and split the new business 50–50. The case for this approach is that the new advisor will bring in more business with the senior advisor's help than he could on his own, and the senior advisor will be exposed to more opportunities than she would have on her own.

Have a Plan for Dissolution

A team needs to determine in advance what will happen if the team dissolves. The breakup of a team can be very emotional, and the breakup is not the time to make decisions about who gets what.

Be Definite About Fair Compensation

Team compensation should start with all members receiving what they originally brought to the team. For example, if an $800,000 senior advisor joins with an advisor doing $200,000, the combined business should be split 80–20 as a baseline. However, all new business above that baseline could be split differently. In this example, whichever advisor brings in the new business should have fees split in his favor. The same is true for the advisor who adds secondary products and services to an existing client of another team member. A variation of these ideas is two advisors who team and split the business initially based on what each brought to the partnership, then split all new business 50–50 no matter who is responsible for it—the idea is that over time, each advisor will get an equal share of the business.

How to Strengthen a Team Once It Has Been Formed

Once you join or form a team, you need to strengthen it. There have been many books written about building teamwork, but there are basic elements I have seen that make the most difference.

Align Values

Sharing similar values will strengthen a team. Examples of values include work ethic, shared vision and goals, compensation of support staff, communication, and investment philosophy.

Promote Commitment

The best teams are those whose members are committed to the growth of the team, with each member being willing to commit a lot of energy to the team's success.

Promote Good Communication

Good communication is essential to a team's success. As in any relationship, good communication overcomes most problems. The team should encourage communication by all team members and provide opportunities for team members to share their opinions on how to make the team better. One of the greatest benefits of a team is the ideas and creativity that can result when the team members are all motivated to improve the team. All team members should have the opportunity to review and give input regarding all aspects of the team's activities.

Build In Measurement and Accountability

Every team member should be held accountable for her responsibilities, and team meetings should be held to review accountability. These meetings motivate all the members to excel, so that they can proudly share their results at team meetings.

In the long run, working toward parity is best. If the split is not even, there should be an incentive for all team members to get an equal share as the team's business grows. There are endless split combinations possible.

Examples of Successful Teams

The first example was a vertical team where the senior advisor was a superstar and built a team that supported him. All the business that the team generated went through the senior advisor. He paid the other team members based on what he perceived their value to the team's business to be. The senior advisor spent 100 percent of his time building new relationships and maintaining relationships with his most affluent clients.

He was involved extensively in high-profile community activities and, as a result, was considered one of the "movers and shakers" of the city in which he was based. He had deep relationships with many CEOs of public companies and was an advisor to many of the entrepreneurs in this market. His team was built to support these relationships. The team had a process for investing money and providing very high levels of service to these affluent relationships. The most affluent clients were assigned to a team member who was primarily responsible for servicing them. The senior advisor seldom discussed specific investments with his clients; he delegated the wealth-management process to his team. His role evolved into being a family office for the most affluent investors in this marketplace. This team generated in excess of $10 million in business per year.

Another example was a combination of a junior and senior team and an inside and outside team. The senior advisor had been in business for thirty years and specialized in portfolio management. A second partner had been added to the team to help develop relationships that the senior partner did not have time for. The second partner was primarily involved in client relationships and portfolio management. Five years later, the team added two junior advisors who had a proven marketing process and results, with the intention of using their marketing expertise to get the senior advisors in front of new prospects. The senior advisors had the investment expertise but needed someone to market their expertise, which the junior advisors could do effectively. The team also added a new member to develop her own smaller accounts. Not only has this team's business grown, but there is a strong succession plan for when the senior advisor retires. This team generates $3 million in business per year.

Another example involves two senior advisors, one of whom specializes in portfolio management and one of whom specializes in marketing. The portfolio manager has the credentials, expertise, and experience to put him among the best in his market. He is a good investment manager and has excellent presentation skills. The marketing advisor spends 100 percent of her time finding opportunities for the other partner to be in front of new affluent prospects worth $5 million or more. The marketing advisor looks for other advisors in the firm who might need the team's expertise, spends a good deal of time working with influencers who can refer business to the team, and markets the team's world-class wealth-management process to different distribution channels and individuals. This team also has a business manager who has the responsibility for providing first-class customer service and for handling all administrative and operational aspects of the team. This team generates $3 million in business per year, and since its formation, its business has grown at 25 percent per year.

Another example is a team with two senior advisors who had two different skill sets. One of the senior advisors had a very conservative practice with a large asset base and a relatively low velocity rate on his assets. The other partner had fewer assets, but a higher velocity rate. The partner with the higher velocity rate was an idea machine and was always coming up with new ideas for his clients. The high-velocity advisor found ways that the other advisor had never thought of to do more business with the combined book. The more conservative advisor provided a level of experience and expertise in lower-risk investments that the other advisor did not have. The result of this partnership was a velocity increase for the consolidated books and an overall growth rate of over 20 percent per year. This team does $2.5 million in business per year.

Still another example involves a senior advisor and a junior advisor. The senior advisor has a mature practice, but is still highly motivated to grow. He brought in a junior advisor whom he had known for a long time and in whom he had a great deal of confidence. The junior advisor spends 80 percent of his time marketing for the team and 20 percent of his time working with the senior advisor's smaller accounts. The senior advisor continues to work with his largest relationships and spends 20 percent of his time supporting the junior advisor's marketing efforts and doing joint marketing activities with him. A third advisor works with the smallest accounts and sets up the presentation and seminar logistics for the team, which is its primary marketing method. Not only has the senior advisor's business grown as a result of adding the two junior advisors, but an excellent succession plan is in place. This team does $1 million in business per year.

A further example involves a senior advisor and a junior advisor. The senior advisor is a good portfolio manager and an excellent marketer. The junior advisor has had some success in marketing, but she enjoys the analytical and client relationship aspects of the business. The senior advisor trained the junior advisor to run the portfolios and support his marketing efforts. The senior advisor now spends the majority of his time marketing to his target market of $5 million-plus investors. The junior advisor runs the portfolio, looks for money-in-motion leads to give to the senior advisor, and helps the senior advisor prepare for presentations and meetings held with prospects. This team generates over $1 million in business a year.

Advisors who are part of a good team are more productive than those who are sole practitioners. This observation is validated by the testimony of members of productive teams; these advisors can be zealots in support of the team concept. However, as productive as a good team can be, there are many factors that must come together to make a team successful. It is not an easy process and it requires a high level of ongoing commitment, but the results are well worth the time and effort. Being a member of a productive team with shared goals and values is as good as it gets in financial services.

As I have said all along, at least a quarter of your one hundred relationships need to be $1 million-plus. These clients are difficult to get because everyone wants them. But you *can* get them if you understand how they think, which is what I will discuss in Chapter 18.

Summary

- Advisors who are members of a team generally are more productive than those who are sole practitioners.
- The key to a successful team is having a good fit and shared values among the team members.
- There are four broad categories of teams:
  1. Specialization
  2. Inside and outside
  3. Vertical (or superstar)
  4. Junior and senior
- Situational teaming has many advantages. It allows an inexperienced advisor to leverage the expertise, resources, and experience of a senior advisor. It also gives the potential team the opportunity to work together before formalizing a partnership.
- Teaming can be beneficial in allowing better penetration of accounts through added expertise, different perspectives, and better development of smaller accounts. This can lead to a higher velocity rate for a mature practice.

- Fair team compensation is essential for a productive team. All members of the team need to feel that they are fairly compensated for their work and that they have the opportunity to grow as the team grows.

- In looking for potential team members, an advisor should do an honest assessment of his own strengths and weaknesses and look for other team members who could benefit from his strengths and help with his weaknesses.

- All team members must be accountable and have a forum for regular communication.

CHAPTER 18

What Millionaires Need

Building a business with clients who have $1 million or more in investable assets is essential to building a million-dollar practice.

This market segment epitomizes the low-percentage/high-payoff dynamic of financial services marketing. This dynamic means that the advisor does not need many $1 million-plus client relationships to have a successful practice, but it can be very challenging to get these clients. Remember that it takes only twenty-five $1 million-plus client relationships to build a million-dollar practice. You should have million-dollar client relationships, but why are they so hard to get?

- This is the most competitive market segment—it is the target of all financial services companies, as well as many other companies.

- Traditional marketing techniques do not work with this segment.

- Almost every $1 million-plus prospective client already has an advisor, and that advisor is going to work hard to keep that client.

- What you have to do to win million-dollar clients is beyond what many advisors know how, or may be willing, to do.

As challenging as building a practice with $1 million-plus client relationships can be, there is plenty of opportunity to do so. Every year, approximately 15 percent of $1 million-plus investors switch financial providers. If there are 10,000 millionaires in your market, this means that every year, 1,500 of them will switch advisors. Remember, you need only four of these investors each year. If you want to increase your success in acquiring new million-dollar clients, you have to understand how these clients think.

The Millionaire Market Does Not Respond to Traditional Marketing

So many companies want the business of millionaires that they are bombarded with every kind of marketing imaginable, and they tune it out. The $1 million-plus market has become desensitized to cold calls at home, seminars, dinner invitations, and mailers. These are successful, busy individuals whose time is too valuable for them to be enticed to a seminar by a free dinner. In most cases, people in this market will not even open the envelope from a mailing. Telemarketing to them *at home* is also a complete waste of time because the majority of them are on the "Do Not Call" list, and those who are not are trying to figure out how to get on it. The only exception to this is the retiree market. You can have some measure of success if you identify retirees who have $1 million or more, particularly in older neighborhoods, who might be called less and are not on the DNC list, and invite them to an age-appropriate seminar. While cold-calling millionaires at home is not effective, contacting them at work can be, as long as you have researched each contact in advance to determine how you can provide value to that individual. You must understand this if you are going to effectively acquire $1 million-plus clients.

Reach Them Through Someone Else

If a millionaire is not satisfied with her current advisor, she has many friends and other advisors that she trusts who can introduce her to a proven financial advisor. A millionaire does not need to look at an advisor who is unknown. In many cases, the millionaire client may not actually be dissatisfied with her current advisor but is open to alternatives; in fact, this is likely to be the case.

The most effective way to market to millionaires is through referrals from other clients, networking, personal contacts, or referrals from the millionaire's other advisors (such as CPAs, attorneys, Realtors, and business brokers). The objective is to get the opportunity to meet millionaires through someone else.

To be effective in marketing to millionaires, you should include at least these three marketing ideas:

- An organized, proactive referral process from existing clients (see Chapter 12)

- Access through influencers—the client's advisors, such as CPAs and attorneys (see Chapter 12)

- Exposure to millionaires through their outside interests—organizations, social events, or outside activities (see Chapters 11 and 14)

Thomas Stanley says in *A Millionaire's Mind* that the majority of America's millionaires are business owners (32 percent), corporate executives (16 percent), attorneys (10 percent), and physicians (9 percent). These are the niche markets you should focus on (Chapters 25, 26, and 27).

These strategies are not the only way to get in front of the millionaire market, but in most cases, they are the most effective.

Prove That You Are Better

Once you meet with the millionaire investor and go through the fact-finding process, you must be able to prove that the investor would be better off with you. You must be able to demonstrate that you will serve his needs better; you must prove yourself through your actions, not your words. It takes patience and time, but the reward is worth it—remember that it takes only twenty-five $1 million-plus client relationships to build a million-dollar practice.

Most, if not all, of the things you must do to prove yourself to a millionaire prospect and make her a client are also things you must continue to do to keep her as a client. In other words, master the methods for acquiring $1 million-plus clients, and you will have mastered the things that will retain them. These are:

Demonstrated professionalism, expertise, and confidence

Very high levels of service

A well-thought-out wealth-management process that you can explain articulately and clearly and execute

Demonstrated Professionalism, Expertise, and Confidence

Professionalism and expertise are among the qualities that millionaires want most. This expertise can be shown by an industry-accepted professional designation like CFP or CIMA. This distinguishes you as an advisor from most others and is a concrete example to the affluent investor of your commitment to your professionalism and expertise. These designations and credentials are not required, but they add to your credibility.

One of the most compelling marketing statements you can make to a prospective million-dollar client regarding your expertise is:

> Mr./Ms. Client, I have made a real commitment to my professionalism and expertise by studying for and passing my Certified Financial Planning Examination. In making a comparison between me and your current advisor, I would ask you to ask him or her if he or she has made the same commitment.

Generally, the more money an investor has, the more sophisticated he is. The days of "salesmanship" and "product selling" are over. These tactics have given the financial services industry a black eye, and million-dollar investors are wary of advisors who appear to be salespeople. Professionalism and expertise are the most valuable commodities today. Million-dollar clients are attracted to advisors who take the time to understand their situation and what is important to them, and have the expertise to provide solutions to meet their goals.

Very High Levels of Service

If you want to attract millionaire clients and keep them, you need to provide consistently superior service. Millionaires are "spoiled" in many ways because they are so sought after—people in this market are used to receiving excellent service in all aspects of their life. They know the difference between good service and outstanding service, and they expect the best. The advisor who wants to build a million-dollar practice must have a very high-level service process:

- Work with only a limited number of clients.
- Contact your clients at least monthly.
- Resolve client problems quickly through your client associate.
- Make sure each client is satisfied by having your client associate provide "high touch" and proactive service.

Newer advisors with scant client associate coverage may need to take on these tasks themselves, staying close to their million-dollar clients and ensuring that their needs are being taken care of.

Millionaire clients expect to develop a relationship with their advisor. The advisor needs to look at these clients as more than just clients and be willing to commit time to developing these relationships. Being attuned to the client's personal life can be just as important as understanding her investments.

The best advisors commit to building personal relationships with their clients by spending time on outside activities in which the advisor and the client may have a mutual interest (golf, fly-fishing, hunting, or cooking, for example); by meeting the client's children; by attending important life events like marriages, funerals, and visits to the hospital; and by going to dinner.

The most successful advisors I have worked with provide a "family office" to their very best clients. These advisors are trusted counselors in every area of the client's life, not just all financial matters. They have proven providers of almost every kind that they can refer their clients to. This offers wonderful networking opportunities as well. The advisor who is committed to working with millionaire clients must understand that the relationship is as important as the investments.

A Well-Thought-Out Wealth-Management Process

Having a proven, well-thought-out wealth-management process that is tailored to the individual's financial needs and goals is a valued commodity to most millionaire clients.

However, to attract and keep the millionaire market, not only must you have a well-thought-out wealth-management process, *but you must be able to explain it articulately and clearly.*

Millionaire investors expect leadership from you. They expect you to have so much experience and expertise in this process that you exude confidence. By nature, investing has an uncertain outcome, but the successful advisor who has built a process that minimizes risk while providing competitive returns is very appealing to this market. The more convinced you are that your process of investing money is the right one, the more attractive you will be to the millionaire prospect. The most successful advisors I have worked with are those who were most confident about their wealth-management process.

Millionaire investors are interested in five key financial areas. If your wealth-management process meets their goals in these areas, you are likely to attract and keep millionaire clients. The areas are:

1. Preservation of assets and reasonable returns
2. Competitive management fees
3. A long-term financial plan
4. Performance monitoring
5. A simplified financial life

Preservation of Assets and Reasonable Returns

If you want to attract and retain clients in this market segment, you need to have a wealth-management process built around these clients' conservative investing style. The majority of millionaires have made their money already, and their highest priority is to preserve it while having reasonable growth. Many millionaires are in their late fifties and sixties and do not have time to rebuild their portfolios—they want to keep what they have and stay ahead of inflation.

Their portfolios need to have the correct asset allocation for their level of risk tolerance, and must be well diversified and conservative. You must meet with these clients regularly (at least quarterly) to review the performance of their portfolio, to remind them of their investment objectives, and to remind them of what a reasonable return is, given their risk tolerance.

To put these concepts in perspective, I remember a quote from a $4 million advisor. This advisor had approximately twenty-five relationships that totaled $500 million in assets. He would say, "I'm really a closet indexer who provides extraordinary service to my clients." He meant that his clients had already made their fortunes, and they were coming to him to provide reasonable growth without subjecting their portfolios to much risk.

It is appropriate to allocate a small percentage of the portfolio to a more aggressive position. Examples of this may include private equity, hedge funds, and managed futures. Generally, these investments are well diversified and can add growth to the portfolio by being noncorrelated assets. The key concept in making this work is allocating only a small percentage of the portfolio to these more aggressive investments.

Competitive Management Fees

The $1 million-plus market is very competitive, and while the lowest-cost provider will not always win, the millionaire client needs to feel that she is getting a good value.

Since the measure of a portfolio's performance takes into account the fees to manage it, management fees can significantly diminish performance. It is hard to consistently generate double-digit returns if you are managing a large portfolio conservatively. Keeping this in mind, every 100 basis points makes a difference, and to achieve acceptable performance, you have to price the management of the investments competitively. In today's environment, it would be hard to justify charging a $1 million-plus relationship more than 1.5 percent for a blended portfolio; 1 percent or less would be more in line.

The key to generating more business from these relationships is to add extra products and services. By broadening the relationship through liability products, insurance products, estate planning, and trust services, you can increase the business these relationships generate without adding to the cost of the portfolio management. These are all areas of the millionaire's financial life that must be addressed. The advisor who recognizes the importance of these needs, develops an expertise in these areas, and incorporates that expertise into his practice will be going a long way toward attracting and retaining the $1 million-plus market segment.

Planning and Wealth Management

The planning and wealth-management process is also an important priority for the $1 million-plus client. Relating an investment strategy to an overall plan is especially important to this segment. It is essential that you take the time to really understand your clients' objectives and emotions as they relate to their investments.

Issues like retirement objectives, real estate purchases, estate planning, risk tolerance, insurance, lending needs, and charitable inclinations are all key factors in developing the kind of business relationship that is required for this segment. The more time you spend on these areas, the better. Studies show that for many millionaires, how the liability side of the balance sheet is managed is more important than the asset side, and estate planning and insurance are also important to this affluent segment; tax minimization and transfer of assets can be achieved with good estate and insurance planning.

You can differentiate yourself by addressing these areas through the financial plan. Most advisors do not spend enough time up front in the long-term planning process—advisors who do will differentiate themselves in a positive way.

Performance Monitoring

In addition to the plan, you should make monitoring performance periodically (at least quarterly) a high priority. In most cases, the client's satisfaction is related more to being on track with the long-term plan than to absolute return. Periodically reminding clients of performance as it relates to risk and the long-term plan will have a positive impact on satisfaction and retention.

A Simplified Financial Life

Another reason to use a thorough planning process is the millionaire's need to simplify her life. If a millionaire client trusts that you have all the products and services she needs, she will be inclined to simplify her life by working with you as her only advisor. The key to making this happen is to work with the millionaire to develop a detailed plan for reaching her financial and related objectives. The advisor who "owns" the plan will "own" the client. Millionaires tend to be time-starved, and if they can consolidate their mortgage, insurance, banking, and estate planning needs with one trusted advisor who has incorporated all these needs into a long-term plan, why wouldn't they? Having multiple providers all working independently of one another does not make sense. By providing a long-term plan and being the single provider, not only is the advisor building a practice that will attract the millionaire market, he is also building in incremental revenues beyond the fees charged for investment management.

The Over $10 Million Market

Clients and prospects who have over $10 million in assets require a specialization that the advisor must commit to if he wants to attract these clients and prospects. While the millionaire client requires a high level of service, the decamillionaire requires extraordinary service. Most advisors who specialize in this market must limit their total number of relationships to between twenty-five and fifty. A "high touch" is required, with frequent contact and exceptional administrative and operational service.

You must offer very competitive pricing. This does not mean giving away the business, but the pricing must be competitive for the value received. This market recognizes and appreciates the value of performance and service, and is willing to pay for it as long as the price is in a competitive range. You need to have a high level of expertise in trust and estate planning, concentrated stock strategies, alternative investments, and high-level portfolio management. A professional designation, while not required, especially appeals to this group. These people want to work with the very best in the industry.

The bottom line with this market is that it requires specialization and experience with its needs. This cannot be done part time—if you cannot commit to building your business around the decamillionaire, you are better off partnering with another advisor who can. You may have the contact and the relationship, but not the specialization; in that case, you should situationally team with someone who is committed exclusively to this market (this is a form of subcontracting). Properly managed, the amount of business that a decamillionaire can generate is enough to split and still be very profitable.

In my experience, if an advisor who doesn't specialize in decamillionaires acquires one, in many cases the relationship will eventually be lost. This is the most competitive market in financial services, and if the advisor does not have this specialization, it will be only a matter of time before someone who does will make inroads into the relationship and lure the account away. This is a highly specialized market with very specific requirements. Do not try to beat the specialists if you are not one yourself; rather, join them through situational partnering. The $10 million-plus market is very lucrative and is a very competitive market segment, but if the advisor understands what appeals to this market and builds his practice around these needs, then he will be able to attract and retain the $10 million-plus market. This market requires extra work and a longer lead time, but the advisor needs to add only one or two new $10 million-plus relationships a year to build a million-dollar practice over a reasonable time.

If you follow these strategies and have at least twenty-five $1 million-plus relationships, you will eventually reach a million-dollar practice. But that is not the end of the road. What comes after that? Read Chapter 19 to find out.

Summary

- This market is desensitized to the traditional marketing techniques of mailings, cold calls at home, and seminars.

- Referrals are the most effective marketing approach with millionaires. Referrals from existing clients or influencers (CPAs and attorneys), network sources, personal relationships, and outside activities are the best way to acquire new $1 million-plus clients.

- Service rules. The expectation of service is very high with this group. You must be committed to outstanding service to attract and retain this group.

- The planning and wealth-management process has high appeal to the $1 million-plus segment.

- Professional credentials are important to this segment.

- A conservative investment approach is better than an aggressive approach with this segment.

- Performance and fees are important because of the competition that exists for this segment.

- Insurance, estate planning, and lending are important priorities for this market and provide opportunities for add-on business.

- The advisor must provide strong leadership to the millionaire market. This leadership should be the result of expertise and experience and a well-thought-out wealth-management process.

- Investing in personal relationships should be a high priority for advisors who have $1 million-plus clients.

- Specialization is the key to building a practice that will attract and retain decamillionaires.

CHAPTER 19

Beyond a Million-Dollar Practice

Achieving a million-dollar practice in financial services is the standard of success that most advisors measure themselves against. Less than 1 percent of all registered representatives ever build a million-dollar practice. However, once you have reached the million-dollar level and have taken the appropriate amount of time to celebrate, the obvious question is: What's next? The answer should be another question: What does it take to become a *multi*million-dollar producer?

In my more than twenty years as a manager, I have worked with fifteen advisors who built a multimillion-dollar practice. Of the fifteen, there were seven who stood out as best practitioners because they built these practices on their own and had no special situation or circumstances. Each of these seven advisors produced over $3 million in business and managed an average of over $1 billion in assets, with an average length of service of twenty years. This translates into at least $50 million in new assets per year. One of these seven stands out in particular as being extraordinary in his practice management and subsequently his results. This advisor produced over $10 million in business in each of the four years that I worked with him; in his biggest year, he did $15 million in business.

As challenging as this may appear, these concepts and processes will result in a multimillion-dollar practice no matter where you are located. These advisors' approach and style in building a multimillion-dollar practice varied, but there were also many common traits and characteristics that all seven of them had. This chapter is about those common traits and characteristics.

For most advisors, building a multimillion-dollar business is uncharted territory, as there are so few people in the industry who ever achieve this level. Those who do are generally too busy and too competitive to share their practices. I believe that the common traits and practices of these advisors can serve as a road map for those who aspire to build a multimillion-dollar practice. I will cover two areas:

Business practices of the multimillion-dollar advisor

Personal traits of the multimillion-dollar advisor

Business Practices of the Multimillion-Dollar Advisor

If I had to summarize what it takes to build a multimillion-dollar practice, I would say that it takes everything that is required to build a million-dollar practice, but more of it and done better. All the principles I have already covered in this book apply, except that the energy and execution need to be at a higher level. This deeper commitment is manifested in six areas:

1. Bigger relationships
2. Extraordinary service
3. Stronger relationship focus
4. A team business structure
5. Willingness to invest in one's own practice
6. Stronger marketing focus

Bigger Relationships

What separates multimillion-dollar advisors from million-dollar advisors is primarily the size of the relationships that multimillion-dollar advisors work with: They work with wealthier individuals. A multimillion-dollar advisor should have between fifty and one hundred relationships, with each of these relationships having a minimum of $1 million invested with the advisor.

In order to reach the multimillion-dollar level, your goal should be to add $50 million in assets each year. You can reach a multimillion-dollar practice and not add assets at this rate, but the $50 million per year is the pace you should strive to reach.

Extraordinary Service

When the majority of your client relationships are $1 million-plus, there is little room for error. The bigger the client, the higher the expectations. These clients are the target of every financial services firm and are prospected constantly. Outstanding marketing brings these clients in, and outstanding service keeps them. Superb service is a prerequisite for adding a net $50 million in assets per year—it is so much easier to grow your assets if you are not losing clients.

Extraordinary service takes outstanding service to the next level. Both you and your client associate must take the time and make the commitment to provide this level of service. Multimillion-dollar clients are the most sought-after segment of the financial services market; the competition for these clients is fierce, and they are being recruited every day. They must receive high-touch, extraordinary service, or they will move to competitors who will provide it.

In many ways, service becomes the differentiating point among advisors. In most cases, performance is a commodity; in a well-diversified, properly allocated portfolio, the differences in returns will be minimal. The bottom line is how the client feels about his financial services experience. All the principles I covered in Chapter 15 apply; the difference is that both the advisor and the client associate must take the time and make the commitment to contact clients more frequently, be more proactive with service calls, and have a flawless problem-resolution process. This requires more time and, as a result, fewer relationships.

Having fewer relationships will not hinder you if the relationships you have are all over $1 million. An example is an advisor who does $4 million in business with thirty total relationships, none of which has under $10 million in assets. Another example is an advisor who consistently did over $10 million in annual business who worked only with clients with over $100 million in assets—he had only ten to twenty relationships that he worked with directly. Having a small number of relationships does not mean that you will do a multimillion-dollar business, but having a small number of very wealthy relationships does.

Every market in the United States has enough million-dollar households that you will never run out of million-dollar prospects to contact. Good advisors will always get more than their fair share of these prospects if they put themselves in front of them. The number of million-dollar households in the United States is growing so quickly that the number you acquire this year will be replaced by at least that many new ones next year.

Stronger Relationship Focus

Multimillion-dollar advisors recognize that relationships with affluent clients and prospects are their number one priority. They realize that relationship building is all that counts, and this shows in how they allocate their time—they do the things that their best clients and prospects do. They even build their personal lives around their clients' interests—that is often how they meet their clients. Some examples:

- One advisor acquired a billion-dollar relationship through Ducks Unlimited and a common interest in bird hunting.

- Another advisor developed the majority of his relationships through a prestigious country club he belongs to—he played golf every Friday with a rotating, regular group of four foursomes consisting of some of the wealthiest investors in his market (they all eventually did business with him, although it took time).

- Another advisor plays chess with his largest relationship every week. The advisor had never played chess before he met this client, but he has become very good at it.

- Another advisor had a number of clients and prospects who had their own airplane. In order to be in the same circle, he bought a plane before he had a pilot's license—it wasn't long before he had his license and was inviting clients and prospects to fly with him, instead of his prospects and clients inviting him to fly with them.

- One advisor hosts intimate, first-class dinners at his home every month and sometimes every week, with fine food and wine; there are typically eight or fewer guests, usually two client couples and two prospective client couples, along with his wife and himself.

These shared interests draw clients, prospects, and advisors together in ways that allow them to simply enjoy spending time with each other. These advisors enjoy spending time with clients and prospects—they do not consider this work, they consider it fun. They have developed excellent interpersonal skills, are good listeners, and focus on the needs of their clients and prospects, rather than their own.

Multimillion-dollar advisors are with their clients and prospects all the time; they delegate everything else to their team. These advisors are aware of the outstanding-service issues and have built a wealth-management process that requires only a small percentage of their time. They delegate these tasks to high-quality, well-trained members of their team so that they can spend the majority of their time with clients and developing relationships with new ones.

A Team Business Structure

The multimillion-dollar advisor's team plays a critical role in her success. Every multimillion-dollar advisor I have worked with has had a strong team behind her to support her business. All of these multimillion-dollar teams are vertically organized behind the multimillion-dollar advisor: The multimillion-dollar advisor is the "superstar," and the role of the team is to support her efforts. I cannot think of one example of a multimillion-dollar advisor who belongs to a team of equal partners. These advisors build their teams around themselves vertically to support their talent.

The multimillion-dollar advisor is primarily responsible for setting up the wealth-management process, but once it is set up, she spends the majority of her time on the marketing and relationship side of the business. The team handles all the administrative elements, the client service, and the mechanics of investments. This enables the superstar to spend her time doing what she does best—finding new affluent prospects and building stronger relationships with existing clients.

The majority of these multimillion-dollar teams have very loyal, long-term team members. The advisor recognizes the value of effective team members and provides a high level of recognition and compensation. One advisor I know of pays his senior team member (who does not have an advisor number) $1 million each year (the advisor makes over $5 million). It is not uncommon for these multimillion-dollar advisors to have the same team members for ten years or more.

Sometimes these advisors have junior advisors who have a smaller percentage of the practice. In most cases, this is a succession-planning team blended with the superstar structure—the multimillion-dollar advisor is grooming a younger advisor to eventually take over the practice when the senior advisor retires.

Willingness to Invest in One's Own Practice

These advisors never wait for the firm to give them money. They do what they need to do to make their plan work. If they need another team member, they pay for it themselves. If they need an airplane, they buy one and pay for the fuel themselves. Their client events are always first class and cost a lot of money, but they pay for the events whether or not the firm reimburses them. They look at this as reinvesting retained earnings in their practice.

Stronger Marketing Focus

The multimillion-dollar advisors whom I have worked with market all the time. They market and think about marketing more than advisors who don't do their level of business. They have learned that consistent marketing is the key to consistent growth, and they have developed marketing activities and processes that work for them. These marketing activities do not generally involve the traditional marketing techniques of cold calling, seminars, and mailings. The majority of the marketing activities used by multimillion-dollar advisors are of the following seven types:

1. Influencers and client referrals
2. Internal marketing (situational partnering)
3. Client and prospect entertaining
4. Membership marketing
5. Philanthropic marketing
6. Pathing
7. Rolodex marketing

Influencers and Client Referrals

Multimillion-dollar advisors all have a network of influencers (CPAs and attorneys) who refer clients to them and have a systematic process for getting referrals from clients. This is a necessity, since the majority of $1 million-plus investors get their financial advisors either through another advisor or an influencer, or from their friends (who are also $1 million-plus investors). Multimillion-dollar advisors are especially good at getting referrals from clients and influencers.

To reach the multimillion-dollar level, you must have outstanding service, good relationship skills, and a successful wealth-management process. All these elements together produce a very favorable experience for most clients, which means that they are very willing, almost eager, to give you referrals. Also, multimillion-dollar advisors are leaders and are confident of what they offer; they believe that they are the best, and they have no hesitation about asking clients to refer prospective clients to them.

Internal Marketing (Situational Partnering)

Multimillion-dollar advisors have a high level of expertise and experience. They have confidence in themselves, and they market themselves internally within their firm—many advisors have gaps in their own skill set that the multimillion-dollar advisor can fill. This can be especially true of less experienced advisors, who can uncover prospects but lack the ability to close them. Leveraging the contacts and efforts of other advisors can put the multimillion-dollar advisor in front of many more qualified prospects than he could find on his own. This is very profitable, even if they split the business. I know multimillion-dollar advisors who have grown their business by as much as 20 percent per year through an organized internal marketing process.

Client and Prospect Entertaining

Client entertaining is something that all multimillion-dollar advisors do. The types of entertaining they do can be very different, but what they have in common is that they all do it. In many cases, their clients have become their friends, so this kind of entertaining comes naturally and can be fun. Of course, they encourage their clients' friends to join them. These client entertainment events are small and intimate, so that maximum relationship leverage takes place. Because friends of affluent clients are generally also affluent, it is not necessary to have many prospects present for the marketing to be successful. These events not only provide great introduction opportunities for prospects, but also serve as excellent retention tools for existing clients. Examples of these events include fine dining at the advisor's home, hunting trips (often out of state or out of the country), golf outings, ski trips, fishing trips, spa trips, and shared vacations.

Membership Marketing

Several of the multimillion-dollar advisors I have worked with use memberships at high-profile country clubs as a very effective client acquisition platform. These advisors do not openly prospect at the club but become very involved in its leadership. The more involved they become, the more $1 million-plus prospects they meet, and they soon became part of the fabric of the club.

Golfing is another catalyst for further developing relationships and meeting new people at the club. These advisors attend all the major events and in many ways build their social life around the country club. This is a relationship business, and being involved with a country club that has affluent members gives an advisor a perfect opportunity to meet and develop relationships with affluent prospects. Business inevitably follows.

Philanthropic Marketing

The most successful advisor I have ever worked with, a decamillion-dollar advisor, was a leader in the most important high-profile philanthropic organizations in his marketplace. As a board member of these organizations, he had the opportunity to meet and develop relationships with the other board members, who were inevitably $1 million-plus investors. This required a major time commitment on his part, but the quality of the prospects he worked with was high, and over time he acquired a good number of his best clients through his philanthropic involvement. If anyone asked the leaders of this community who was a leader in financial services, his name would inevitably come up. His reputation validated the effectiveness of this strategy.

Pathing

Pathing is a marketing technique that I have seen several multimillion-dollar advisors use:

1. The advisor identifies key prospects to do business with.
2. By doing some research, the advisor finds out where his target prospects live and which social, philanthropic, and professional organizations they belong to.
3. The advisor determines what people he knows who belong to one or more of the same organizations.
4. The advisor asks one of these people if she would feel comfortable introducing the prospect to him through some activity that they would have a common interest in. This might be meeting over lunch, playing golf, having dinner, or going to a sporting event.

5. Once the introduction is made and the advisor and prospect have spent some time together, the advisor takes the next step on his own to further develop the relationship with this prospect, which often means inviting the prospect to another activity or event.

Rolodex Marketing

For the multimillion-dollar advisor, Rolodex marketing is a combination of many of the other marketing techniques. Being involved in a high-profile country club, taking a leadership role in philanthropic organizations, being involved in social networks, developing a network with influencers—these all lead to meeting affluent investors.

Many of these relationships are interconnected, and that is when it all comes together—many times the people who are board members of philanthropic organizations also are business leaders, are members of the same country club, and run in the same social circles. These individuals become the core of the advisor's business; they refer other affluent prospects to the advisor, and the circle continues to widen. Those referred know the advisor by reputation and are drawn to him. These interconnections lead to deeper relationships because of common interests and involvement.

The multimillion-dollar advisor becomes part of this group and emerges as one of the community leaders. It takes years to develop this kind of reputation and build these relationships, but once all the pieces come together, a multimillion-dollar practice will result.

Personal Traits of the Multimillion-Dollar Advisor

All the multimillion-dollar advisors I work with share certain qualities.

Deep Motivation

These advisors are all high achievers and goal oriented. The word *overachiever* fits every one of them. They are driven to achieve beyond the money they make—once they have reached a certain level of income, it is all about the achievement; each one of these advisors can tell you where he ranks nationally within his firm. They have as much passion for their achievement as they do for financial rewards. They value being part of the inner circle of top advisors, and they value being recognized by their senior management.

This high level of motivation is what fuels them to continue to market *no matter how successful they become* or how many years they have been in the business.

Process-Oriented

These multimillion-dollar advisors are also very organized—they have developed a process for every aspect of their business. They have a process for wealth management, for client meetings, for presentations. They set up these processes, and their team implements them; the team can generate high-quality marketing presentations literally in minutes. The advisor develops the processes and the business, and the team does the rest.

Client Leadership

These advisors all provide strong leadership to their clients. They are very confident of their ability to serve their clients and make them money. They believe strongly that their process for investing money is the best, and that conviction comes across to their clients and prospects. Affluent clients and prospects expect their advisor to know what she is doing, and these multimillion-dollar advisors never hesitate and are always convinced that they can do a better job than anyone else anywhere.

Clear Personal Goals

Every multimillion-dollar advisor I have worked with has a clear vision of what his long-term goals are and how he is going to reach them. These advisors may fine-tune this vision or even change it, but they always have a vision and a plan. They can clearly articulate their market strategy, their business plan, their goals, their service model, their team strategy, and what support they need from management. The visions may vary from advisor to advisor, but they all have a vision, and it is crystal clear.

The Numbers for a Multimillion-Dollar Practice

Only 5 to 10 percent of advisors who are in the business three years or more ever achieve a million-dollar practice, and less than 1 percent ever achieve a multimillion-dollar practice. It takes relentless marketing; a highly organized, process-based business; a strong team; outstanding relationship-building skills; and a very high drive to achieve. For the advisor who is committed to achieving a multimillion-dollar practice, there is a high price to pay, but the rewards in terms of recognition and compensation are more than worth the effort for the select few who reach this level of business.

In order to reach the multimillion-dollar level, you should strive to bring in $50 million in new assets each year. This means bringing in twelve new $1 million-plus relationships each year (includes upgrades). This is not as difficult as it sounds; remember that the average advisor doing $3 million in business has approximately one hundred $1 million-plus relationships.

In order to bring in this $50 million, you should realize that you can reach approximately 25 percent of that goal by bringing in new assets from existing clients. These are the easiest assets to bring in because you already have a trusting relationship with your clients.

Client surveys have consistently shown that most clients have between 50 and 100 percent of their total assets held somewhere other than the institution with which they have their primary relationship. If you have $100 million in assets under management, then your clients probably have at least another $50 million held outside your firm. If you can bring in 25 percent of the assets held elsewhere in a year, you will acquire $12 million in new assets from your existing clients. This is 25 percent of your goal of $50 million per year. You can bring in another 25 percent ($12 million) through a proactive referral program (please see Chapter 12, "Leveraging Clients to Get New Ones"); building a strong CPA network can lead to $12 million in referrals, or another 25 percent; and finally, you can get the remaining 25 percent of these assets ($12 million) through philanthropic and social organizations, natural marketing, and networking.

To reach the multimillion-dollar level, remember above all that it is the size of your relationships that matters, not the number. All the techniques and strategies that we have already covered apply to the advisor who wants to reach this level; he just needs to take these techniques and strategies to a higher level, and draw on an even deeper level of motivation.

We have now covered all the elements of building the foundation for a million-dollar practice, what to do with that foundation to actually build that practice, and what to do to go beyond a million-dollar practice. In

Part 3, I'll present some of the market action plans you can use to build your million- and multimillion-dollar practice.

Summary

- The principles for building a multimillion-dollar practice are the same as those for building a million-dollar practice; they just have to be executed more often and better.

- The key in financial services is the size of each relationship. The more affluent your client relationships are, the more business you generate.

- High-quality service is essential. You must have or build a strong service model.

- The highest priority of multimillion-dollar advisors is building relationships.

- A multimillion-dollar practice entails marketing relentlessly.

- All multimillion-dollar advisors I have worked with have a team. These teams are structured vertically, and members of the team have a high degree of loyalty.

- The personal characteristics that multimillion-dollar advisors have in common are an achievement orientation, a highly organized and pro-cessed-based practice, strong leadership, deep motivation, and a clear vision for their business.

- Multimillion-dollar advisors are willing to invest in their own busi-ness. They do what they need to do to make their plan work. They look at this as retained earnings to grow their practice.

- The majority of the marketing activities used by multimillion-dollar advisors are of the following seven types: influencers and client refer-rals, internal marketing (situational partnering), client and prospect entertaining, membership marketing, philanthropic marketing, pa-thing, and Rolodex marketing.

- If you have a goal of increasing your assets by $50 million per year, you can meet this goal by bringing in assets your clients hold at other institutions; through a proactive referral program; by building a strong CPA network; and through philanthropic and social organiza-tions, natural marketing, and networking.

- You need to have between fifty and one hundred $1 million-plus clients for a multimillion-dollar practice; you should continue to upgrade these clients, and you should not have more than one hundred relationships in total.

Market Action Plans

CHAPTER 20

Seminars

Many organizations and individuals want an expert to explain and interpret the opportunities available in today's market. You can position yourself as that expert if you are proactive in contacting these organizations and groups. Seminars may be one of the most effective market action plan techniques you can use because, done properly, they set you up as being a teacher and authority rather than a salesperson, and this means that you will get follow-up appointments more easily than with almost any other marketing technique.

Key Success Factors

In order to make any seminar work, you must address all three of the following key success factors:

1. *Be knowledgeable, and select an appropriate topic.* The topic that you select can vary—the subject is not as important as your being knowledgeable and getting in front of the right audience. In order to come across as an authority, you must know your subject very well, which means that you need to put in enough time up front to learn your subject.

2. *Prepare.* Prepare not only your talk or class or presentation, but your target market for that seminar, your contact list, and your contact process. See the individual seminar approaches later in the chapter for specifics.

3. *Follow up.* Your follow-up will determine the ultimate success of your efforts:

   • From the beginning of the seminar, prepare the follow-up. Explain to the people in your audience that rather than giving them information that they may not be interested in, you would like them to indicate after the seminar what follow-up information they would like from you. Pass out response cards in advance (see model in Chapter 12), and collect them after the seminar. The same applies to the classes you give. An example of a response card is provided later in this chapter.

- Always call the prospect and offer to personally deliver the material she requested, by appointment.

Five Markets for Seminars

Here are five groups or markets that you can target with seminars:

1. Ready-made audiences
2. Qualified baby boomers
3. Business owners
4. Companies
5. Retirees

Ready-Made Audiences

As I mentioned, one of the three keys to successful seminars is getting the right audience. The easiest way to get in front of an audience of affluent investors is to approach ready-made audiences. Ready-made audiences are groups of people who already belong to an organization that has regular meetings. Examples of these organizations are business clubs and nonprofit organizations, churches and synagogues, YMCAs/YWCAs, and retirement communities.

Topics for these ready-made audiences could include:

1. The wealth-management process—how to do it right
2. XYZ Financial's view on the current investment environment
3. Tax law changes and how they can affect your investments
4. The pitfalls of investing and how to avoid them
5. Investment basics—the importance of the fundamentals
6. The big three: taxes, inflation, fees, and how to reduce their impact

The following are six particularly good ready-made audiences.

Business Clubs and Nonprofit Organizations

Go to the local chamber of commerce and get a list of all the organizations that are in that chamber's region, such as Rotary, Kiwanis, business clubs, garden clubs, and other such organizations. Be sure to get the name of the contact person for each organization (it should be listed with the organization). Call the contact person and offer to do a seminar for his organization at a time convenient to him. Give the contact person a list of topics that you could present, but also be open to any investment topics that the contact person might want to suggest. Generally, clubs that meet regularly are always looking for interesting speakers at their meetings, and they should be receptive to your offer if you are flexible on your topic.

Churches and Synagogues in Affluent Areas

Most of these churches or synagogues have men's or women's clubs that meet regularly, and these also need interesting programs. Contact the church or synagogue office and find out the contact person for the organizations within the church.

Your Best Prospects' and Clients' Organizations

Ask your best prospects and clients which organizations they belong to and call these organizations with an offer to speak. This is especially effective in the adopt-a-town market action plan (see Chapter 24)—being endorsed or invited by an existing member gives you instant credibility. It's also an excellent way to raise community awareness of your presence.

YMCA/YWCA Classes

Contact the local YMCAs or YWCAs in the affluent communities in your market and offer to do a series of classes (usually not more than four) on the basics of investing. The YMCAs/YWCAs offer many classes and are always looking for interesting topics for their members. Conducting one-hour classes is a small time commitment that will get you in front of a group of interested, and often affluent, investors. The same technique can be applied to community colleges offering adult education programs.

Local Businesses

Contact the HR directors at larger companies in your market and offer to do preretirement seminars. This should be positioned as a "free benefit" that the company can offer its employees who are retiring within the next five years. Assure the HR contact that your presentations will be generic and not product-specific, and offer to provide her with a preview of your seminar. In the seminar, be sure to cover the importance of developing a long-term plan, the basics of successful investing, how to determine the amount needed to retire, and how investment needs change after retirement.

Alumni Meetings

Contact the universities and business colleges in your area. Offer to do a seminar through their alumni office on charitable giving, focusing on charitable remainder trusts and charitable lead trusts as they relate to the college.

Qualified Baby Boomers

In this approach, you target forty- to sixty-year-olds with household income over $100,000. There are three ways to find these individuals:

1. Find which zip codes or counties they live in from the U.S. Census Bureau (www.census.gov).
2. Purchase lists of these individuals from a direct marketing firm or list broker.
3. Drive through affluent neighborhoods that are family-oriented, with lots of children, and write down street names. Use a cross-reference phone directory to get the names of the residents (see the appendix).

Once you have developed a mailing list, send the invitations to the seminar. You should expect a 1 percent response rate—for example, 8,000 invitations should result in 80 households responding. I recommend that you confirm and qualify each RSVP.

The following are some points to keep in mind for the seminar invitation you will send out:

*   Offer a choice of dates (e.g., Tuesday or Thursday evening, or Saturday morning).
*   Offer a topic that is relevant to the audience (research the demographics of the audience if needed).
*   List bullet points of what the seminar will cover.
*   Include a response card with not only your contact information but also the offer of a complimentary consultation.
*   Enclose four complimentary tickets to the seminar, two for the guest you are sending the invitation to and two for his friends who have similar demographics and interests.

- Include dinner at a well-known and popular restaurant; it does not have to be expensive, but it should have a private dining room.

The seminar itself should take seventy-five to eighty minutes, and the most effective title is something similar to "Planning for Your Retirement Lifestyle." I recommend that you start the seminar by explaining the importance of planning and of setting up the right wealth-management process; during the remainder of the seminar, focus on the IRA rollover, how it works, and why it is a good idea. End with fifteen to twenty minutes on related retirement issues. It is often good to have an estate planning attorney contribute to the presentation.

After the seminar, hand out a confidential follow-up questionnaire that asks for the attendees' home and work addresses and phone numbers, their projected retirement date, and permission to call them and follow up.

Follow up right after the seminar with those who have given you permission to call. When you call, offer to have two free appointments with them:

Appointment 1: Data gathering

Appointment 2: Presenting the plan and the wealth-management process

You can expect that 75 percent of those who make reservations to attend the seminar will actually attend, 70 percent of the seminar attendees will agree to a follow-up appointment, and 50 percent of those appointments will become clients within twelve months. I know one team that, by using this approach, brought in over twenty clients, each with over $250,000 in assets over an eighteen-month period of time.

Business Owners

This concept has been successful with business owners, but the same idea could apply to a number of different market segments as long as the topic is of high interest to that particular group. Seminar titles for business owners that have the highest response rate are "Retirement Seminar for Business Owners" and "Selling Your Business."

Most of the local business journals and community papers will run a brief announcement or small article on the seminar if you are persistent and sell them on its value to their readers. You can expect such an announcement or article to generate several calls and attendees.

The best market for the seminar is owners of businesses that have annual sales of between $1 million and $10 million. You can develop this list yourself or purchase one. Begin calling the names on this list four to six weeks before the seminar. An example of the script follows.

Invitation Scripts

Mr./Ms. Business Owner, this is Joe Advisor with XYZ Financial. The reason I am calling is to invite you to a seminar educating business owners like yourself about the different retirement plan options that are available to you. You might discover more tax-efficient, lower-cost options than you presently have. The seminar will be at ABC Restaurant, and dinner will be included. The date and time are [give date and time]. Would you be interested in attending?

• • • • • • • • • • •

This is Joe Advisor with XYZ Financial, and the reason for my call is to invite you to a retirement seminar for business owners. We will be featuring our retirement plan specialist and a local CPA, who will discuss ways you could possibly reduce your taxes and the cost of your retirement plan. The seminar will take place at [give time and date and location], and dinner will be served. Would you be interested in attending?

Screener Script

I am calling Mr./Ms. Business Owner to show him/her how to save money on his/her retirement plan.

• • • • • • • • • • •

Before you reach the owner of the business directly, you will often reach a screener or voicemail, but if you use the scripts I have given in those cases as well, you will get callbacks.

The Numbers

Let's say that your goal is eighteen to twenty follow-up appointments with prospects as the result of your seminar.

- Approximately 90 percent of those who attend a seminar will agree to a follow-up appointment. This means that you must have approximately twenty people actually attend the seminar.

- Two-thirds of those who say they will attend will actually attend. This means that you need to have thirty confirmations.

- About half of those who express interest will confirm that they are attending. You need to have sixty people express interest.

- Approximately 15 percent of the people you talk to will express interest in the seminar, so you need to talk to 400 people.

- You should expect to reach a third of the people you call. This means you need to have 1,200 to 1,500 people on your call list.

- If you do one two-hour time block per day, it will take you about a month to set up a seminar that results in eighteen to twenty follow-up appointments with new prospects. This is an excellent call-to-appointment and hours-to-appointment ratio. Clearly, persistence is the key to the marketing plan's success.

Notice that in these numbers, sixty people expressed interest, but only twenty of them showed up. The forty people who expressed interest but didn't attend are just as important as the twenty who came. Follow up with them after the seminar.

If a business owner was interested or took any time on the call, send a written invitation along with a brochure on general retirement options. Follow up this mailer with a call to make sure that she received the invitation and brochure, and make another verbal invitation to attend the seminar.

Once you have sent out the invitations, follow up with a call to confirm that the prospect is attending. You should also suggest he invite a friend who might also be interested in the subject matter.

Hold the seminar at a well-known, but not necessarily the most expensive, restaurant. I recommend that you start cocktails no later than 6:00 P.M. and dinner at 6:45 P.M. Start the seminar when dinner starts. An example of the seminar dinner schedule follows:

- Fifteen minutes for a local CPA to discuss different types of retirement plans and the tax benefits of each.

- Fifteen minutes for the financial advisor to share how her firm can help business owners. Also, provide a brief description of your wealth-management process.

- Fifteen minutes for the retirement specialist to cover case studies and give an overview of the kinds of retirement plans available.

- Fifteen minutes of questions and answers. Allow extra time if any speaker runs over.
- At 7:45 P.M., gather door prize cards and/or response cards. Attendees will usually stay and mix for at least another hour.

The day after the seminar, call all the attendees and follow up with each one based on his door prize card or response card. The objective is to schedule an appointment where you will hand-deliver the material the attendee requested and discuss his particular situation. Do the same follow-up with those who did not attend but expressed interest (the other forty, whom I mentioned earlier).

Companies

This approach involves making a strong connection with a local company and providing seminars regularly to its employees. Because you are focusing on a single company, it is important to develop an expertise in the company's benefits and retirement plans. These seminars are not connected with the HR department and are held off-site.

The keys to success here are maintaining the consistency of the seminars, setting the dates in advance, and ensuring good attendance at each seminar. Your objective with these seminars is to show that you are an expert: Educate, don't sell.

Logistics

To begin, you need at least one personal contact within the company, and ideally several (although if you follow the approach I outline here, you will eventually get them). These contacts can be clients, prospects, friends, or individuals whom you know through them. From your contacts, find out the names of employees who have received awards, have relocated to the area, or have retired. Invite these prospects to the seminar. The ideal prospects for these seminars are those who have between $500,000 and $3 million to invest. Ideally, the seminar will attract prospects who work for the same company, who are retiring at about the same time, and who are in the same geographic area.

I recommend that your seminar cover such topics as "Life After ABC Company," "Net Unrealized Appreciation," or "Pros and Cons of Existing Retirements Plans—What They Could Mean to You." Focus most of the seminar topics on retirement plans. You might also include outside experts to discuss stock options or estate planning.

To have the most impact, present these seminars every six weeks over a one- to two-year period. The best times for these seminars are Tuesday, Wednesday, and Thursday evenings. Invite all the contacts you have in that company, as well as current clients and prospects and past seminar attendees. E-mailing the invitation to prospective attendees generally produces good results—e-mailing is a quick, fast-response, low-cost way to invite people. Each seminar you give will provide you with more names for your mailing list, and once you have given a number of seminars, you will have built a critical mass of prospects: For larger companies, you could have an e-mail mailing list of up to 500 people to whom you can send invitations. The key to good attendance is building the e-mail list; constantly add to the list with the objective of building it to over 100 names. The people on the list will get used to hearing from you, and eventually, word of mouth will spread about you through the company, and it will become easier to add to the list. Constantly upgrade your e-mail invitation list.

Limit the total cost of the seminar to under $500 by offering it at a nice, but not extravagant, hotel, such as one of the suite-type hotels. It is sufficient to provide soft drinks (no alcohol) and cheese trays. Arrive an hour in advance of the seminar to prepare and to meet and greet guests. Also plan to stay after the seminar, which is when you are likely to make the best connections.

As the RSVPs begin to arrive, do some research up front to find out as much as you can about each attendee's situation, especially the date she plans to retire, if you can. It is important to confirm positive RSVPs the day before the seminar.

This process should generate an average of fifteen attendees for each seminar. At the beginning of the seminar, hand out a package about your team; also include a questionnaire that asks the following:

- The date the attendee is likely to retire
- The names of other groups that he thinks might be interested in your seminars
- Names of his friends that you should invite to future seminars
- Topics that he would be interested in for future seminars

  The questionnaire should also:

- Offer a complimentary retirement analysis and consultation.

- Include a calendar of future seminars.
- Ask for feedback on the seminar (an evaluation form).

Set up the follow-up by having a call to action at the end of the seminar. Position yourself as a resource who can educate. Offer a free retirement analysis. Encourage attendees to agree to a follow-up meeting—it is okay to mention that the price of admission to the seminar is accepting a follow-up call. Another way to set up follow-up contact is to mention that a large-group question-and-answer session on these topics can be uncomfortable, and as a result, you will follow up individually to get feedback and answer questions.

Follow Up

The follow-up is the most important part of this process. Generally half of the attendees will agree to a follow-up meeting. If an attendee did not answer all the questions on the questionnaire, call him to get the missing information. If he does not want a meeting, you should still make the follow-up call to get feedback on the seminar with the idea of making a connection (this should be done very softly). Try to follow up with every attendee, if you can.

Over time, approximately 25 percent of attendees will agree to follow-up appointments right away, and approximately another 25 percent should agree to an appointment within twelve months of a seminar. If you have an average of fifteen attendees and you hold eight seminars a year, you should have about one hundred attendees a year; if half of them agree to appointments and if half of these appointments lead to clients, then this process should produce approximately twenty to twenty-five new clients per year.

Retirees

Generally, retirees have the time to attend seminars and are very interested in investment topics, but they prefer to know the advisor before having an appointment with her. Seminars meet all these needs and are very effective with this group. One of the most effective prospecting calls you can make is to call retirees and personally invite them to a seminar tailored to their interests, with a free meal included. In order to stimulate interest, it is key that you make obvious the value that the seminar will have for them. Follow up the call with a written invitation and then a reminder the day before the seminar. Another effective technique with retirees is to contact the recreational directors of retirement communities and assisted living communities (not nursing homes), and offer to provide seminars or a series of classes on investment topics that would be of interest to their residents. (Refer to Chapter 31 for more ideas and information.)

Scripts

Seminars for Clubs or Similar Organizations

Mr./Ms. Prospect, my name is Joe Advisor, and the reason for my call is that XYZ Financial encourages us to serve the community by providing timely informational talks, and I thought you might be interested in having me give one of these talks at one of your club's meetings. Examples of these talks include ____, and they generally take twenty to thirty minutes. I can also tailor a talk to your group's needs if you would prefer a different subject. Is this something you would be interested in?

Seminars for YMCA/YWCA/Adult Education

Mr./Ms. Program Director, my name is Joe Advisor, and I'm a financial advisor at XYZ Financial. The reason for my call is that I want to offer to do a series of four classes that covers the basics of investments. We have had good feedback from our past classes, and we wondered if you would have an interest in reviewing our course outline and considering us for your program.

Seminar Follow-Up

Mr./Ms. Prospect, this is Joe Advisor from XYZ Financial. I enjoyed meeting you and talking to your group about investments last week. I am following up on your response card, and I want you to know I have prepared all the information that you requested. I also want to offer to bring it to you personally, as I will be in your area next Thursday. I thought that if I could get a chance to talk with you about your specific situation, I could provide some valuable free advice that could help you, given the volatile investment environment we are in. Would you be available next Thursday for me to spend a few minutes and bring by the information you requested?

CHAPTER 21

Event Marketing

I n this market action plan, I cover some of the most fun and effective marketing activities you can carry out: prospect events. Here are the six types that we will talk about:

1. Big event
2. Client appreciation event
3. Client appreciation dinner
4. Client advisory board
5. Lunch roundtable
6. Unique events

Almost all of these events depend on your having some clients (and even some prospects and influencers) who are "raving fans" of yours—clients who are especially appreciative of your hard work, expertise, and skill.

Big Event

Organize at least one "big" event (for twenty or more people) every quarter. The purpose is to meet large numbers of affluent prospects in a social setting populated by your raving-fan clients and influencers, who know what you do and talk about you in glowing terms.

Examples of a big event are a golf tournament, an art exhibit, a party at your house, or a private screening at a movie theater for clients and prospects and their families; let the interests of your best clients and influencers determine the kind of event you put on (this means that you need to know the interests of your clients and influencers).

Invite your most raving-fan clients to this big event and ask each of them to bring someone like them. This will lead to a client-prospect mix of approximately 50–50. In addition to clients, also invite your most appreciative influencers and encourage them to bring their own clients to the event as well. And invite any prospects in your pipeline that you think would appreciate the event.

If possible, make sure that each seating of a foursome (or whatever arrangement you use) has a raving-fan client or influencer in it, and that the members of the foursome share interests and backgrounds.

If you discuss business at all, do so only in a very general way; instead, ask questions and listen to what the prospects' issues might be that you could help with.

An Example: A Golf Tournament

A good example of a big event is an annual client and prospect golf tournament (I recommend a scramble format). Hold the tournament at a well-known, highly regarded course, and plan it months in advance to ensure that the right people are there. It is possible to have more than one hundred people participate, but even with that many, be sure that each foursome is a mix of raving-fan clients and prospects.

Sell raffle tickets and mulligans in advance for a local charity. Provide drinks and food, and have pictures taken on the course. At the end of the round, provide lunch and give awards; have the sponsored charity present so that it can thank the financial advisor and his guests. The combination of goodwill, a well-organized golf tournament, good food, and the sponsorship of a worthwhile charity is a perfect way to set the stage for building relationships with affluent prospects.

Right after the event, send thank-you notes and call (to get feedback only). Follow the thank-you mailing with a call to each prospect one week later, either asking for an appointment or inviting the prospect to the next event (see the next paragraph), whichever you feel is more appropriate. Continue to invite, communicate, and share a broad information base with each prospect at least once per month.

Follow-Up Small Event

After a big event, the next step is to invite these prospects to an intimate event, which should not exceed twelve people, including the financial advisor and several raving-fan clients or influencers. Examples of these intimate events are a golf foursome at a prestigious course, a cooking class, a wine-tasting dinner, a fly-fishing excursion, a sporting event, and a nice dinner out. An example of how you can bring up business during the dinner out is to ask the question, "What are you most concerned about in the market today?" This topic can provide conversation for hours. The object is to build a relationship with the prospect—you must have a strong relationship with her before she can become a client. With some prospects, this can occur after one big and one intimate event; with others, it may take one big and five or six smaller events. One team I know that uses this plan arranges twenty to thirty small events a year. These events should be organized and scheduled far in advance to better facilitate the process. Because of the time and expense involved, I also recommend that your targeted prospects have a minimum of $250,000 in investable assets.

Scripts

Invitation

Mr./Ms. Client, I want to invite you to a special exhibit at the Art Center next Wednesday night. It features _____ artist, and we will supply hors d'oeuvres and cocktails. Would you like to attend? The purpose of this event is not only to thank you as a client, but also to give me an opportunity to meet prospective clients who are just like you. Can you think of someone who might fit with us who is like you whom you could bring?

Follow-Up

Mr./Ms. Prospect, I really enjoyed getting to meet you at the Art Center last week, and I wanted to get some feedback on the event. What did you think? I also want to invite you to [dinner/golf/sporting event] next week with several other people that I know you would enjoy being with. Would you be interested?

· · · · · · · · · · ·

Mr./Ms Prospect, As we have gotten to know each other, I've heard you mention several times concerns you've had over your [business/investments/taxes/other problems], and I wanted to invite you to my office to give you some ideas that might help solve some of the issues you've mentioned and, at the very least, will provide a free second opinion on your investment position. I would also like to have the opportunity to share with you our approach and introduce you to the rest of our staff.

Client Appreciation Event

A client appreciation event is a fun event that is focused on the interests of your best clients; these events should be held monthly. The size of the event is generally four foursomes. Golfing is a natural venue for the event, but it could also involve fly-fishing, clay shooting, wine tasting, or cooking. Invite your best clients and influencers and ask each of them to bring a friend, neighbor, or business associate who would enjoy the event. An excellent source of names is a client who is receptive to providing referrals.

In the case of a golf event, start with registration and follow with a one-hour lesson with the local professionals on chipping, sand shots, putting, and so on. After the lesson, have lunch and give a presentation on a general subject that would have a wide appeal to attendees, with the speaker being the sponsor of the event. The presentation should take no more than thirty minutes and should be followed by five or six five-minute presentations on your approach to the business or some other relevant business topic; you can do these yourself, or you can have members of your team do them. End the meeting by thanking the attendees and by telling them that one of the purposes of the event is to grow your clientele; mention that you could bring value and good performance to new relationships and would appreciate their referrals. Follow the presentation with golf and an awards ceremony.

Client Appreciation Dinner

The premise behind this dinner is to leverage the goodwill that you have with your best clients. In every experienced financial advisor's business, there are clients who are especially pleased with the job being done for them. This event channels that goodwill toward introductions to other affluent investors that the raving-fan client knows. You should hold one of these dinners every other month.

Arrange a nice evening at a well-known, high-quality (but not necessarily expensive) restaurant. Italian restaurants are good choices because they often have high-quality food at a reasonable price. The evening should include not only a good meal but some form of entertainment: for example, a wine tasting, a cooking class, or a magician.

Once you set up the evening, invite up to three clients. Tell them in advance that the purpose of the event is to thank them for being your best clients and to provide an easy and fun way for them to introduce you to their affluent friends who might be interested in your approach to investing. Be clear with your clients that before the evening ends, you will politely ask their guests if you can call them, so that they can let their guests know of this in advance.

I recommend that you get a private room and meet your guests at the bar area. Once the guests have arrived, move to the private room, make introductions, and start with hors d'oeuvres and any entertainment you have planned. Make sure that people are seated strategically (use a name card at each place setting) so that you and your team members are seated next to your clients' guests. After the entertainment, welcome your guests and state the purpose of the dinner: to thank your best clients, to meet prospective clients, and to have fun. Dinner should be from a preset menu to keep costs down. After dinner and before they leave, ask the guests directly if you can call them and follow through; an ideal time is when they are thanking you for dinner.

A variation is to also invite a raving-fan client whom you believe may be a center of influence or a future referral source without asking him to bring a guest. The purpose is to show him what the event is like, setting up for inviting him and a guest to a future event.

Ideally, you should schedule six of these events per year. The average financial advisor has fifteen to twenty raving-fan affluent clients; if three different clients (and spouses) attend each event and invite one guest and spouse each, and if you invite each client only once a year, then you can acquire approximately twenty prospects each year. If half become clients, this would be ten new clients per year.

The cost of these events is approximately $100 per individual attending, with the total cost per event being approximately $1,500. Six of these events per year would require a marketing budget of $9,000.

Scripts

Invitation

> Mr./Ms. Client, hopefully you are happy with the performance and service we have provided you. I certainly appreciate having you as a cli-

ent, and I want to invite you to a special dinner we are having on [date/time/place]. I would also appreciate your bringing someone you know who would be interested in how we handle investments. We don't spend a lot of time on marketing, and this is an opportunity for us to meet some qualified prospective clients. I hope to get future business from this event and will ask your guests if I can follow up with them. I would appreciate if you would mention that to your guest and put in a good word for me. Are you interested in attending with a guest? Of course, spouses are invited.

Positioning the Follow-Up at the Dinner

The purpose of our special event tonight is to thank our favorite clients, and to give us the opportunity to meet some potential clients. We are proud of the service and performance we provide, and we would like to have the opportunity to follow up tonight's dinner with our guests by sharing with them what we think is a unique and special approach to financial services. Thank you for allowing us to show our appreciation and to get to know you better. Enjoy your dinner, and let's have fun.

Personal Follow-Up at the Dinner

Mr./Ms. Guest, I would appreciate having the opportunity to give you a follow-up call and spend some time sharing with you our approach to investing and how we could help you. Would you be open to a follow-up call? (*or*, Would it be all right if I follow up tonight with a call to share with you in more detail what I believe is our unique approach?)

Client Advisory Board

This board makes your best clients and centers of influence a part of your acquisition process. Identify your top clients who are also potential centers of influence. Typically you should identify eight to ten clients, but it is also okay to include referral sources that are not clients—limit these to two or three. Send these clients and other referral sources an invitation to become a member of your client advisory board, and invite them to dinner. Send the invitation two to three weeks in advance of the event, and hold these events twice a year. Have someone on your team make a follow-up call within four days of sending the invitation. In the follow-up call, verify the client's interest in attending and give a brief description of what the client advisory board is about. Make a second follow-up call several days before the dinner as a final reminder.

Hold the dinner in a private room, with a small bar set up in advance for cocktails before dinner. Have cocktails for approximately thirty minutes. Before dinner starts, thank the clients for attending and for agreeing to be part of your advisory board, and introduce your branch manager. The branch manager should make a short presentation endorsing you and setting up the referral process. The sponsor of the dinner (a strategic partner) should also welcome the clients, mention that she is a strategic partner of yours, and endorse you. Having the branch manager attend is not a necessity, but it is a nice addition if the manager is willing—a positive endorsement gives you credibility. After these introductory remarks, begin the process of asking for feedback from the clients. Questions and topics to stimulate the conversation may include:

- What are we doing well?
- What could we do better?
- How can we improve our service?
- Share marketing material and get feedback on it.
- Share marketing ideas; get suggestions for growing the business.
- What could our firm do better?

This should end up being an open discussion, with the clients doing most of the talking. It should be informal, not a presentation.

During the course of the dinner meeting, pass out a questionnaire and explain that you will follow up with each client within a week to discuss the questions in more detail. Within a week of the dinner, call each client (or, even better, meet with him) to review the questionnaire, solicit referral names, and discuss next steps. This will result in referrals, excellent feedback, and stronger relationships. The day after the event, send a personal handwritten thank-you to each participant.

I recommend that you invite this same group to at least two of these advisory group dinners per year. It is not necessary to have your branch manager involved after the initial meeting of each group.

Script for Following Up on the Invitation

Hi, this is [name] calling from [team/office name] at XYZ Financial. I just wanted to call and follow up on the invitation we sent you last week regarding our client advisory board and see if you can come.

If the answer is yes, then:

As I mentioned in the invitation, our team is putting together a group of a few of our best clients, whose opinions we respect, to use as a sounding board. As we continue to improve our wealth-management process, we plan to use the group to help us understand how to market our practice more effectively and how to deliver additional client services. In addition, we would like your input on ideas for finding and developing prospects.

Client Advisory Board Questionnaire

Put this questionnaire in a folder with marketing material personalized for each participant at the dinner.

1. When you think of our team, what words come into your mind?
2. When you think of XYZ Financial, what words come to mind?
3. Why do you do business with us, and what do you value the most in your relationship with us?
4. What are some suggestions you have for how to improve our marketing of ourselves?
5. How could this relationship be improved for you?
6. Are there individuals, groups, or associations that you feel we should be meeting with?
7. We have enclosed our most recent marketing brochure, and we would appreciate any comments or feedback as to its impact.
8. Please share with us anything else you would like to provide.

Follow-Up Agenda After Client Advisory Dinner

Your objective is to obtain one-on-one follow-up meetings with all participants; contact them within a week to set up these meetings.

Script for Follow-Up Face-to-Face Meeting

First, I want to thank you again for meeting with me and serving on my board of directors. I want to let you know how much respect I have for you, and I/we really value your opinion. As we discussed during the meeting, I am at a point in my career where I an ready to take my business to the next level.

Then ask open-ended questions like the following:

- Did you have a chance to review the questionnaire and marketing piece that I sent with you when you left our meeting? (This refers to the client advisory board questionnaire.)

- How do you think this marketing piece positions my team/me?

- Would you make adjustments?

- Are there any additional services that you think are missing?

- Are there services I offer that you were not aware of but might need?

- What suggestions do you have for me for using this piece?

- Are there groups, associations, or individuals you know that I should be speaking to or targeting?

- If you were putting together a board of directors of five successful business owners who were colleagues of yours, and who could help you take your business to the next level, whom would you choose? Are those people I should be talking to? How would you recommend that I get in touch with them?

Remember to let the client talk—you are only facilitating the discussion. You should be talking 5 percent of the time and listening 95 percent of the time.

Lunch Roundtable

Invite six clients to a lunch roundtable seminar. Tailor the topic to the interests of this particular client group or choose a topic of general interest, such as your firm's view of the current market. Ask each client to bring a nonclient guest who would also be interested in the seminar. Typically, six clients and two or three prospects will attend.

I recommend that you put on the same seminar every month—this gives you the opportunity to invite new prospects every month to a seminar that has already been organized. This is a nonthreatening way for clients to introduce you to people whom they think you should know. It also gives you the chance to get referrals without directly asking for them.

Alternatively, you can send out a schedule of three or four lunch roundtables to selected clients, allowing them to choose which ones they want to attend.

Many clients and prospects prefer lunch seminars because they take less time and avoid conflicts with family commitments. Schedule these lunch roundtables from 11:30 A.M. to 1:00 P.M.

Lunch roundtables are an inexpensive way to educate clients, increasing the opportunity to do more business with them and add value to the existing relationship. It also provides an excellent opportunity to meet new prospects that clients bring, and to advance the prospecting process with current prospects by inviting them to a seminar on a topic that they are interested in.

Unique Events

This idea emphasizes creative follow-through to get an individual appointment with the prospect. You should plan these events once a quarter or once a month. The event itself is unique and has the objective of providing a different and memorable experience. One of your most successful events could be a group discussion with a local author that will appeal to your prospective clients. Developing such an event can be as simple as contacting a local bookstore and getting a list of local authors from the bookstore staff, then contacting one of these authors and asking her to do a talk on her book (and maybe slant the discussion to the interests of those attending, if necessary). This makes for a unique event that has a high level of appeal and good prospect attendance. Other examples of unique events are art shows (local artists), wine tastings (with wine experts), and beer tastings. Be creative!

During these events, set up the follow-through by finding out as much as you can about the prospect. If you can find out what beer or wine the prospect likes best, you should call and offer to personally deliver it to the prospect. Similarly, you could offer to bring a signed copy of a book if an author has spoken at one of these events. The objective of the follow-up is to get an appointment with the prospect so that you can show how you are different from the "stereotype broker" and show your unique wealth-management process.

Find the invitees for these events by scanning the newspapers for "movers and shakers;" by visiting city offices and finding the value and sale transactions for expensive homes, then identifying the "nicest" neighborhoods and cross-referencing these with the White Pages or www .whitepages.com. Once you have your list of invitees, you might do a Google search to find out as much as you can about each one before you contact her.

A Script for Follow-Up to a Unique Event

Mr./Ms. Prospect, this is Joe Advisor at XYZ Financial. I enjoyed meeting you at a recent event, and I hope you enjoyed it too. At the event, I briefly mentioned our wealth-management process. I want to follow up and share our process in more detail. I also want to give you a memento from our seminar. May I schedule an appointment to deliver the memento and discuss our investing process?

CHAPTER 22

Networking

There are seven ways described in this chapter that you can participate in networks to grow your business:

1. Join a networking club.
2. Network within an occupation.
3. Use prospect pathing.
4. Join special-interest or charitable organizations.
5. Build your own networking group.
6. Network with the contacts you already have.
7. Network with new acquaintances.

The most important ingredient for success in networking, no matter how you do it, is to have the right mindset: Your highest priority should be to help other professionals get business. If you find business for others, they will find business for you.

Join a Networking Club

One way to build or expand your core networking group is to join a networking club. These clubs can generally be found in the business section of the newspaper where the calendar of weekly business events is posted. Joining a networking club is only the beginning—you should assume a leadership position immediately. As a leader, you will be respected by the group, and you will have the opportunity to move the group in the right direction. The best networking groups generally are smaller but are made up of high-quality people who are committed to helping one another. Ideally the group should meet weekly, and members should ask one another for a profile of the clients they would like. Examples of this are:

- "I'm looking for individuals who are retiring or changing jobs."

- "I'm looking for women who were recently divorced, are in the process of getting a divorce, or were recently widowed."

Don't assume that your fellow networkers know what you are looking for. The more specific you are, the more likely you are to get referrals.

As a leader of this group, you should lead by example and be relentless in your search for potential business for your fellow networkers. Examples of finding business for fellow networkers are:

- Listening for people who have aches and pains, for a chiropractor
- Asking your boss to do printing with a fellow networker, (printer)
- Asking clients and friends their summer plans (travel agent)
- Asking clients and friends if they are happy with their CPA (CPA)
- Asking clients and friends if they have a will and a trust, for a trust attorney
- Asking your boss if he needs an event planner or caterer for entertaining, for an event planner or caterer

The key is that you be capable of and committed to providing network opportunities for the members of your group. They should reciprocate or you should ask them to leave the group.

Network Within an Occupation

To network within an occupation, identify an individual in a targeted occupation and approach that person separately from your network group. An example of this would be a divorce attorney (she can provide you with money-in-motion opportunities). Call a divorce attorney, praise her reputation, mention your need for someone like her to help your clients and prospective clients, and then invite her to lunch or breakfast to get acquainted. The key to being a good networker is being a great listener: Ask about how this person does business, her philosophy, and which CPAs she uses (another potential client source).

At the same time, you must come across as a confident, intelligent professional. This is best accomplished by asking intelligent questions. After you've spent the first part of the meeting asking about the other person, she will ask about you, and that gives you an opportunity to showcase your practice, and how you could add value for her clients.

The follow-up to these meetings is critical: Stay in touch. Provide timely information, keeping your name in front of this person.

Use Prospect Pathing

Prospect pathing uses the six degrees of separation rule. This rule states that you can meet anyone in the world you want to through six people. Identify your best potential prospects, finding out all you can about them and finding common links with people you know who can help you meet them. This marketing technique is prospect pathing.

The more organized you are in this process, the more success you will have. Start with the target prospect, then research where he lives and which social and philanthropic organizations he belongs to. Identify someone you know who has a common link with the prospect that would help you. Explain the common link that this person has with your target prospect, and ask her help in getting an introduction.

Join Special-Interest or Charitable Organizations

The first step in this marketing plan is to identify what organizations to join:

- Identify the prospects you would like to do business with and determine what organizations they belong to, or ask your prospects what organizations they belong to.

- Decide what charitable causes or special-interest organizations you are interested in.

As an example, if you have an interest in flying, you could look at the local private airport's Web site for information; you would probably find clubs or organizations that meet at the airport. By joining one of these organizations, you will become an "insider" and a contributor to that organization. As other members come to know your background, you will find business opportunities.

The same principle applies to charities that you have a personal interest in. By joining these organizations and offering your services, you will find others with similar commitments. As you contribute your time and expertise to these organizations, you will gain members' respect, and as they come to know what you do, they will ultimately do business with you. Remember: The majority of affluent investors get their advisors through referrals. Networking proactively creates referrals.

Be sure that you are passionate about whatever organizations you join. If you do not give enough time and energy to make an impact, you will not build the kind of relationships that can ultimately become clients. You should expect that it will take at least six months to a year after you become actively involved in an organization before any new clients are generated.

Once you decide what organizations you want to belong to, volunteer to help those organizations. Volunteer for everything you can in every organization you belong to, and work hard at everything you do for these organizations. Developing a reputation as a hard worker is key to this marketing strategy. If you are willing to work hard, you will quickly be asked to assume more responsibilities and will be given leadership positions quickly. This kind of marketing takes a great deal of time, and in the beginning it may require working many nights and weekends.

As you gain more responsibility and move into leadership positions, you will begin to get to know other leaders within the organizations. In most cases, these people are your prospects. The key is to build relationships with these prospects as you work with them, without asking for their business. You want to avoid, at all costs, getting a reputation for using the organization to solicit business. You will earn your business by working with your prospects on a cause that both of you have a passion for. The prospect will give you a reason to move into a business conversation as you get to know him—he might mention a mortgage or an educational or investment issue, and that will give you an opportunity to give him help. The key to this technique is to listen and understand your prospect's business and professional life.

As your reputation builds within the organization you belong to, it will also build outside the organization. With a good reputation, you will be invited to belong to other organizations within your community; this, in turn, will lead to more opportunities to meet new prospects as you emerge as a leader in those organizations.

Belonging to several organizations is important in order to get the critical mass to make this market action plan work. If you are committed to networking as a market action plan, then your goal should be to belong to two to three different organizations. This should translate into at least one event or meeting per week.

Build Your Own Networking Group

The first step in this market action plan is to write out a list of occupations that you believe can potentially give you business. Next to that list, write another list of those occupations that you believe you could give business to. There should be an overlap between the two lists; this overlap is the basis for your networking group. Examples of this overlap could be CPAs, Realtors (specialists in corporate relocations), business brokers, mortgage brokers, chiropractors, insurance agents, and recruiters.

Once you have determined the occupations that should form your networking group, you need to determine the names of the people you will use in each occupation. You want high-quality professionals who are good but not necessarily the best (the best don't need you to get business). Use every contact you have to identify these individuals. Once you have identified the individuals you want to use, contact them and invite them to join your networking group.

The networking group should start small but can grow over time to as many as forty people, with no competitors allowed. This networking group becomes your "super-Rolodex" that can add value to your clients and prospects. The people invited to the networking group must provide goods and services that you know your clients and prospects will need. An example: If a daughter of one of your clients is getting married, you could refer a florist and a caterer. Another possibility is to focus on the needs of business owners; owners could be served by commercial Realtors, telecommunications professionals, temporary agencies, attorneys, and other such professionals.

Individual members should represent diverse businesses. Aim for a diverse membership with regard to gender, race, age, and background. Aim for clusters of people who can take referrals as a single group, such as a caterer, a florist, a photographer, and a travel agent—they can all take a referral for a wedding. Invite potential new members to come to one of the meetings to see if there is a good fit. Have fun together to keep it interesting. Plan social events on weekends that include spouses and children.

In asking the networking group for what you are looking for, you must be very specific. Examples could include:

- "I'm looking for someone you know who will retire next year."

- "I'm looking for someone who has been with the same company for ten years and who is changing jobs."

Another way to help generate referrals from your group is to tell a story about a specific client whom you helped, describing how you solved that client's problem, then ask the group members if they know someone who may be in a similar situation. You must teach people what you do and how you help people so that they can send you referrals. This will not happen if you just ask for referrals without being specific about the type of people you are looking for and the circumstances that you can help with. It is important before you call the referral that she is expecting your call and that you have identified a specific need you can help with.

If there is a member of your group who is not providing referrals, send him a letter asking if this is a training issue or if the networking group is not the right fit for him.

The following is an example of the format of a very successful networking group:

- The networking group meets once a week from seven to eight-thirty in the morning. It costs $300 annually to belong, which pays for the cost of breakfasts throughout the year. The meetings are very structured, with a set schedule.

- Each meeting starts with fifteen minutes of social interaction, followed by members dividing into groups of four to each table; everyone chooses a card when she arrives, and that determines which group she sits with.

- During the next fifteen minutes, members tell their tablemates about what they do.

- At each meeting, one member is featured, and that member addresses the entire group and talks about his background, his expertise, and what he is looking for.

- The meeting concludes by announcing the speaker for the following week.

Script

> Mr./Ms. Businessperson, my name is Joe Advisor, and I'm a financial advisor at XYZ Financial. The reason for my call is that I'm the president of a small but very good networking group in this area. We are looking for a [occupation] to be a part of our group. We have identified you as one of the best [occupation] and wanted to invite you to our next meeting. We are serious about helping one another, and I'm sure we can provide some referrals to you. Would you be interested?

Network with the Contacts You Already Have

Make a list of all the personal and business contacts you have. Notice that most of these contacts fall into the same industry. This is the market you will then pursue. As an example, if most of your contacts are in the technology industry, than that should be the market you focus on. One advisor who brought in $100 million of new assets in his first two years was able to identify a combination of 1,600 personal and business contacts.

Once you identify your contacts, get in touch with them and invite them to meet with you. The script for this can be as simple as:

> Mr./Ms. Contact, this is Joe Advisor. I have recently joined XYZ Financial, and I wanted to have the opportunity to reconnect with you. I would like to get updated on your situation and share with you what I am doing. Could I buy you a cup of coffee some morning next week? What works for you?

During the appointment, get an update on your past contacts situation and share your wealth-management approach to the business. An example of what you can say is:

> What I do is very deep, customized planning. I go deeply into my clients' needs, including estate planning, retirement, future income needs, education planning, and liability management.

If the contact objects that he already has an advisor, then you should reply with the following:

Has your advisor developed a deep, comprehensive plan with you?

or,

When was the last time you did a deep, customized financial plan?

This approach to planning will separate you from the majority of your competitors and give you the opportunity to share with your past contacts how you are different from their current advisor. Also, estate attorneys and business brokers are excellent sources for referrals—if any of these are in your contact list, be sure to let them know how your planning approach is different.

Network with New Acquaintances

The key here is to meet new people, either individually or in a meeting of people you don't know. Some good sources of meetings are:

1. Newspaper listings of large meetings or conventions
2. Professional association meetings
3. Chamber of commerce meetings

Once you are face to face with a new acquaintance, start with an "icebreaker" conversation that is nonthreatening and not business-related. It can be as simple as a conversation about the weather, sports, or current events:

> "What a beautiful day; have you heard how long this great weather is going to last?"
>
> "Boy, the traffic coming downtown today was terrible. Did you run into any of it?"
>
> "How about [local sports team]? What do you think their prospects are?"

These are just examples; the possibilities for small talk are endless. The key is to make these general, nonthreatening, icebreaker conversations.

The next step is to ask potential prospects what they do or whom they work for. Examples of this step are:

> "Where do you work?"

"Whom do you work for?"

"What kind of business are you in?"

This takes the discussion to the person's occupation, which sets up the potential networking opportunity.

Once the potential networker answers that question, then the door is open to get more specific. Questions may include:

"How long have you been doing what you are doing?"

"How long have you been in the business?"

"How is business going? Are you having a good year?"

"Are you accepting new clients?"

"What kind of clients are you looking for?"

The next step is to briefly describe what you do (they most likely will ask you) and with whom you work, and that you are meeting affluent people every day. Also mention that you are always looking for new people to network with; ask the person if she would be interested in meeting for coffee in the next week to discuss each other's business in more detail. Either offer a potential date and time immediately, or ask for her card and offer to call in the next few days to set up the meeting.

If the potential networker agrees to the follow-up meeting, a simple structure should be followed (at the meeting): Ask the potential networker more detailed questions about her business. Example topics include:

- The person's ideal target client
- The specifics of her firm, business, and offerings
- What makes her unique
- Her background and areas of expertise
- How she feels you could best help her
- How she is handling her own investments
- What information you could provide that would be most helpful
- Whether or not she is familiar with the wealth-management process

Offer to describe your wealth-management process and what makes your process unique. Share briefly your background, and share what kind of prospects you are looking for. Examples:

- People who are retiring or changing jobs
- People facing a change in their life circumstances: divorce, death of a spouse, inheritance
- Prospects who may be unhappy with their current advisor

At the end of the meeting, commit to a follow-up with your new prospect with possible leads and relevant information, and more information on the wealth-management process. Ask if he would feel comfortable referring potential prospects to you if circumstances were to warrant it.

Past Experience and Personal Contacts

"Everyone has a past," goes the old saying, and in our case, your past is a tremendous business opportunity—two of them really. One is the opportunity presented by the people you have come to know over the years, and the other is the opportunity presented by the past experiences and outside interests you have had.

People You Already Know

Everyone brings to this job a Rolodex of personal contacts who could potentially become clients. The number and quality of the people in that Rolodex will determine how much you can use this market action plan. Since everyone has some qualified personal contacts, everyone can use this technique to some degree. The objective is to make sure that your personal contacts are aware of your position as a financial advisor at XYZ Financial, without putting either of you in an awkward position. There are several techniques for accomplishing this.

The first step is to identify the personal contacts you have who are qualified investors. Once you have made a list of those who are likely to be qualified, use one of the five marketing techniques I outline next. Be sure to tailor the technique to fit your relationship and the personality of your personal contact. Feel free to use a combination of these techniques, if appropriate.

No matter which of the five techniques you use, be sure to ask everyone you contact for help in identifying others they know who have money in motion. One successful advisor formalized this technique—she identified one hundred people who really liked her and asked each of those individuals to be on the lookout for anyone he knew who was changing jobs, relocating to the area, retiring, or getting divorced. She checked in with the people on her list regularly to remind them of what she was looking for. This technique provided her with an excellent prospect pipeline.

Letter

Send a letter to your contacts announcing your new job as an advisor at XYZ Financial. I do not encourage mailings except to your most qualified personal contacts. This is a nonthreatening way to open the door to making the transition from a personal to a professional relationship. It's important to stress how proud you are to be associated with a firm like XYZ Financial and the quality of the training you've received. Provide a postage-paid attachment or envelope with a list of follow-up actions that the contact could ask you to take. This is a low-pressure way to make people aware of your position and gives them control over the professional relationship.

Board of Directors

Call your contacts and ask if you could meet with them to get their advice on your new career as an advisor at XYZ Financial. At the appointment, share how excited you are about the training and resources you have received while working at XYZ Financial. Tell them that you are putting together a "board of directors" of influential people you know and respect, to get their insights on building your business. "What advice would you give me in starting this career?" "What's important to you from your financial advisor?"

Perhaps the most important question should be at the end of the conversation: "Can you think of anyone who may be dissatisfied with their current investment situation and who might want a second opinion? Or someone who is going through a change of life circumstances (who is retiring, changing jobs, or going through a divorce or the loss of a spouse)?" Not only are you asking for a referral, but you are opening the door in a nonthreatening way for your contact to talk with you about his own investment situation. Stay in touch with your most receptive personal contacts and truly make them your "board of directors" for business development. Over time, they will provide you with referrals and, optimally, their own business. An excellent source for these personal contacts is successful alumni of the college you attended or fraternity or sorority you belonged to.

Research

Offer to send your contacts your firm's best research reports. Explain that you have been so impressed with XYZ Financial's insights into the markets that, as a friend, you want to share that information with them. Suggest that if they have any questions or need additional information, you will be glad to provide it at no charge. You can also use this technique when you host events for your clients and prospects; inviting a personal contact to a fun or educational event is an excellent way to begin the transition to a professional relationship.

The Rolodex Technique

Write down all the qualified investors that you know from your past work and personal experience. For most people, that is at least two hundred names. Call each one of them, acknowledge the past connection, and tell each person what you are doing now. Offer to visit with them personally and provide a second opinion on their current financial situation, and offer to share with them your unique wealth-management process. Based on the experience of advisors who have used this approach successfully, you will get an appointment for every two people you contact. If your Rolodex is deep enough with qualified prospects, this market action plan alone could be the cornerstone of a new financial advisor's business.

Social Prospecting

There is a fine line that you must not cross in social prospecting, and that is this: Never be obvious about what you are doing. You want to respond to others' requests and never appear to be prospecting them. The technique is the same whether you are at a cocktail party, in a golf game, or on a skiing trip. As you get to know the social prospect, start the process by asking questions that are general and nonthreatening:

- "What business are you in?"
- "How is business going?"
- "Do you have a family?"
- "What do you like to do?"

The prospect will ask you the same questions, and it's important that you have a one-sentence description of your job. For example, when a prospect asks you, "What business are you in?" you might answer, "I am an advisor at XYZ Financial, and I help people reach their financial goals." The door is now open, and the prospect will probably ask for your opinion about the market. When she does, resist the temptation to make a prediction; instead, say something like, "It's impossible to make short-term predictions about the market; I find that everyone's situation is different, and my advice about the market is based on a person's risk tolerance. Have you been getting good advice?" The door is open further. The key is never to get into specifics in the social setting. If the prospect persists, suggest that you can call him at a mutually convenient time. If he seems interested but not pressing, offer to send him your best research reports free of charge.

If the prospect does not give you any door-opening opportunities, it's best not to force it. You don't want to get a reputation that could hurt your standing in the community. The objective is to have the opportunity to prospect socially by asking the right questions and whetting the prospect's appetite.

Example Scripts

Mr./Ms. Personal Contact, as you may know, I'm working with XYZ Financial. As a good friend/business contact/neighbor, I wanted to offer to send you some of our best research. It's the same information I send my best clients. There is no charge or obligation; I just thought it might be of value to you. I have been impressed with the wealth of information available and the quality of XYZ's research, and hopefully you will be too. Would you be interested?

• • • • • • • • • • • •

Mr./Ms. Rolodex, I wanted to reconnect with you now that I am an advisor with XYZ Financial. I enjoyed our past business relationships and would appreciate having the opportunity to share with you what I am doing and how I could perhaps help you. When would be a convenient time for us to get together?

A Letter Example

Dear Mr./Ms. Prospect:

I am pleased to announce my new position as a financial advisor at XYZ Financial. I have been very impressed with the extensive training I've received, and I am convinced that XYZ Financial is the best financial services firm in the industry.

As a friend, I wanted to offer you our best resources and have provided a checklist of free information that might be of interest. I'm sure you will be as impressed as I am with the quality and depth of XYZ Financial's services and research.

Please feel free to call me anytime if I can be of service.

Past Experience

Not only are your acquaintances from your past a place to build your business, but so are your outside interests and past work experiences. The first step is to categorize your background by what you have done and what you are interested in. Every job you have had in the past has given you a level of expertise that you should use to your marketing advantage. As an example, if you worked for a large company or owned your own business, you know how that business operates and how people in that industry think; you should use that background and knowledge for your benefit and develop a market action plan that is focused on it.

In some cases this same principle holds true with your parents' background; for example, if your father was a college professor, you know and understand how college professors think and what marketing approach would most appeal to them. This could also apply to the alumni of your college—most people who attended the same college have a connection.

The same principle applies to your interests. If you enjoy flying, motorcycling, golfing, or some other activity, you can relate to others who have similar interests. It is easy to use your background, interests, and expertise to market to others who are interested in the same activity. You know the clubs these people belong to and the special-interest magazines they read. Use this "inside" information to determine the most affluent individuals and contact them, using your shared interests, background, and hobbies.

Alumni

One of the most effective connections that you can make to your past is to your fellow alumni, because there is a natural connection between you.

The following are proven techniques that can help solidify your alumni connections and relationships.

1. *Contact your classmates about significant events.* Make sure you are on your college's mailing list for alumni publications, then follow your classmates and see what is happening in their lives, both professionally and personally. Mail or call them regarding ways you can help them with transition events. These transition events come about as a result of such things as job changes (IRA rollover opportunities), college planning for children, promotions (more savings opportunities), and being an executive of a public company (stock option education).

2. *Attend alumni events.* This keeps you close to fellow alumni and provides networking opportunities. If you make even small contributions to your alma mater, you will be on the invitation lists for many alumni events.

3. *Offer to be the organizer of alumni reunions.* This works well if you are located in the same town as your college, but it works even better if you are out of state. Fellow alumni enjoy get-togethers, but do not take the time to organize them. Being the organizer puts you in a leadership position and puts you in front of many qualified alumni. Out-of-state alumni might enjoy a virtual tailgating event at a local sports bar—contact alumni from your college and invite them to watch the game at a particular sports bar. Attending a golf event or a major league sporting event is often also popular among alumni. Your alma mater can provide you with the names of out-of-state alumni if you tell the alumni office that you are willing to organize such events.

4. *Be a fund-raiser.* Contact your alumni development office and ask how you can help organize fund-raisers for the college. It will provide you with both names and ideas. This is an excellent way to meet and begin to build relationships with follow alumni.

5. *Offer to do seminars on charitable giving.* These seminars could cover topics such as "Charitable Remainder and Lead Trusts." Your college should be happy to partner with you on such a seminar, provide you with the alumni list, and allow you to use the university logo. The phone calls you make will not violate phone-solicitation and Do Not Call rules because you are calling on behalf of your nonprofit university. (Please verify this with your local compliance officer.)

6. *Contact the business fraternities.* Many colleges have business fraternities or business organizations that welcome alumni of the college, even if you were not a member of that fraternity while you were in college. These groups provide great networking with other alumni members, speakers,

and faculty supporters. These groups also often host alumni mixers with other schools in the area.

This is a relationship-building business, and people naturally gravitate toward and relate to people who share their business experience and outside interests. Using your background for market intelligence and relating to others with this common background from the beginning will go a long way toward effective relationship building and successful marketing.

Scripts

A Shared Employer

> Mr./Ms. Prospect Who Works at ABC Company, my name is Joe Advisor, and I'm a financial advisor at XYZ Financial. The reason for my call is that I used to work for ABC Company before I came to XYZ Financial. I understand the company benefits plan, and I can relate to your situation at ABC. The training I've received from XYZ Financial has given me some important insights that would make a difference in your financial situation, and I would like to share these with you. I'm going to be in your area on Thursday and would like the opportunity to meet with you.

A Shared Occupation

> Mr./Ms. Prospect, my name is Joe Advisor, and I'm a financial advisor at XYZ Financial. The reason for my call is that before I joined XYZ, I owned my own business, like you, and I understand the challenges facing a business owner. At the same time, as the result of my training at XYZ Financial, I've become aware of solutions to some of these challenges. I would like to have the opportunity to share with you some ideas that I know could make a difference. I'm going to be in your area next Thursday and would like to have the opportunity to meet with you.

A Shared Hobby

> Mr./Ms. Prospect, my name is Joe Advisor, and I'm a financial advisor at XYZ Financial. The reason for my call is that I'm an avid motorcyclist like you, and I saw your name as a member of the local Harley-Davidson chapter. As a fellow motorcycle enthusiast, I know we could re-

late, and I was hoping to have an opportunity to meet with you personally and offer my services as a resource at XYZ Financial. Is there a day next week that works well for you?

Parents Had Shared Occupation or Background

Mr./Ms. Prospect, my name is Joe Advisor, and I'm a financial advisor at XYZ Financial. The reason for my call is that my father was a professor at [____ University], and while I was growing up, I was able to gain a good insight into the mindset and financial issues that college professors have. Since coming to XYZ Financial, I am aware of products and services that I believe would be of value to you. I would like to schedule an appointment with you during your office hours to share some of these ideas with you. When would be a convenient time?

CHAPTER 24

Adopt a Town

I n most cases, smaller towns outside a large city are underprospected and provide a good prospecting opportunity for a financial advisor who is willing to commit time there.

Identify and Gather Data

The first step is to identify the town in which you want to make a concentrated prospecting effort. Good criteria to use are that it should be its own entity, not a suburb, and the population should be at least 3,000. You want to focus on a town where there is very little competition for what you have to offer.

Once you select the town, visit it and write down the names of the businesses that look successful and the names of the streets in the nicest neighborhoods. Also, visit the chamber of commerce to gather as much information as possible, including lists of businesses, clubs, and organizations. Subscribing to the local newspaper is also important, as it allows you to see who the movers and shakers are and to view money-in-motion events. Look through the Yellow Pages and identify all the professionals (CPAs, attorneys, physicians) and business owners.

The objective is to immerse yourself in the targeted town and get face-to-face appointments with qualified prospects. Note that you don't necessarily need an appointment with a prospect that you want to see; you can just tell whoever answers the phone that you will be stopping by on a particular day when you are in town. This can work in a small town because of the lack of formality; you only want the person not to be surprised when you show up.

Penetrate the Town

Once you have gathered all the intelligence you can, focus your prospecting efforts on penetrating the town on many different fronts. One of your

objectives is to get face-to-face appointments with centers of influence
and build a trusting relationship with them so that they will refer prospects to you.

There are two excellent channels for reaching centers of influence:
civic and social organizations, and bank directors.

Contact the president of each civic and social organization in the
town, and offer to give a seminar to that group on your firm's current
market insights. Organizations typically are looking for new topics and
presentations for their programs. This gives community leaders the opportunity to see you in a professional "teaching" role.

Bank directors are another excellent source for centers of influence.
They are not employees of the bank or bank officers, but they are usually
the largest depositors of the bank and centers of influence in the community. You can either use the bank's Web site to identify the directors or
call the bank directly and ask who its directors are.

Make a commitment to visit the town at least twice a month for at
least a year. Ideally, you should visit once a week. It takes twenty to thirty
visits to a new town to build a core of clients and prospects who can then
become ambassadors for you in that town.

Ambassadors are what you are after. You want to reach the centers
of influence in each town and have them become cornerstones in building
a client base. Once you have identified the centers of influence and built
a relationship of trust with them, they will become key referral sources.

Every time you visit, see as many existing prospects as possible (no
appointments needed) and drop off information. (For more information
on developing prospect relationships, see Chapter 7.) The community
needs to feel that you are serious in your commitment to the town, and
the more time you spend there, the more credibility you will have. Here
are four prospecting strategies that you can incorporate and that work
particularly well:

1. Build a network of the influencers—CPAs, attorneys, and others (see
    Chapter 28).

2. Host client and prospect events, such as golf, fishing clinics, and educa-
    tional seminars (see chapters 14 and 21).

3. Give seminars for prospects—target affluent neighborhoods and follow
    up with personal calls to your prospects in that town to invite them (see
    Chapter 20).

4. Subscribe to the local newspaper and look for money in motion opportunities. Contact these prospects and set appointments. (See Chapter 32.)

The smallness of the town will work in your favor if you make the time commitment. In touching these prospects in many ways (i.e., appointments, drop-bys, referrals, and speaking engagements), you will increase your credibility. Word will begin to spread that you are serious about your commitment to the community, and that you are a person who can be trusted.

Gradually, you will be able to stop all your prospecting methods except referrals and following up with referrals, and you will not need to visit the town as frequently—you can cut your visits back to once a month or once a quarter after twelve months of concentrated effort.

Use the same techniques for the smaller towns and communities that are on the way to the target town. It is possible to "adopt a region," which is good time management. Also, you can apply the adopt-a-town market action plan to a larger metropolitan area, but you must first divide the metropolitan area into its separate entities; each of these communities has its own newspapers, and in many cases its own chamber of commerce. However, you lose the competitive advantage because all these communities have access to all the firms in the larger metropolitan area.

If you immerse yourself in the town for twelve months, you are likely to get good results, since most of your out-of-town competitors will not make the time commitment they would need to in order to counteract your initiative. These towns do not have many, if any, brokerage firms, and you will have a real competitive advantage. You will also find that some investors are willing to invest outside their local communities for confidentiality reasons, and when they are given the opportunity to do so with a broader platform and with an individual they trust, they will take it.

Scripts

Introduction: Community Leader

Mr./Ms. Prospect, My name is Joe Advisor, and the reason for my call is that I've been assigned to cover [your town name] by XYZ Financial [or my manager]. Since you are a community leader, I wanted to get your thoughts on how XYZ Financial should best approach your town.

I am going to visit on Thursday, and I hoped that you might be available for a short appointment.

Introduction: General

Mr./Ms. Prospect, my name is Jane Advisor, and I work for XYZ Financial. I've been asked to cover your town, [insert name of town here], by my manager, and I am hoping that when I am there on Thursday, I could have a short meeting with you to introduce myself and share with you some ways that I could be of value pertaining to your investments. Would you be available?

or,

Mr./Ms. Prospect, my name is Joe Advisor, and I work for XYZ Financial. I've been asked by my manager to cover your town [insert name of town here]. I will be there on Thursday and wanted to offer to drop by and introduce myself, and give you some information on how the recent tax law changes might affect your investments. Would you be available?

Introduction: Associate

Mr./Ms. Associate, my name is Jane Advisor, and I work for XYZ Financial. I am going to be in [name of town] on Thursday and will drop by to see Mr. Smith. I would appreciate it if you would let him know I will come by to see him on Thursday. By the way, what is your name? Good, I'll look forward to meeting you when I stop by.

Business Owners

Business owners are among the most attractive target markets for three primary reasons: First, you can build your business through them in many different ways; second, they have a decision-making mentality; and third, they include more millionaires than any other group in the United States—a recent survey found that 52 percent of investors with a net worth between $1 million and $10 million are business owners, 67 percent of those with between $10 million and $50 million are business owners, and 85 percent of those with over $50 million are business owners. The higher the net worth, the higher the percentage of business owners.

Not all business owners are successful, so it's important to prescreen owners before you contact them. There are three relatively easy screens to determine qualification:

1. Size of business ($1 million-plus in sales)
2. How long the business has been operating (five years or more)
3. Whether or not the business has been profitable over the last several years

The appointment is critical, as it is essential for building a relationship. Many business owners may object to an initial appointment, but if you can show them that meeting with you will be of value to them, you should secure a ratio of contacts to appointments of about 10 percent. To do this, talk to them about what you can do for their business—their business is their life, and their personal finances are often a lower priority; also explain that by meeting them at their place of business, you can not only gather the necessary information but also see firsthand how the business is run.

You need to get the appointment on the basis of helping the business owner be more profitable, but once you have the appointment, you should discover everything you can about the business owner. One of the reasons this group is so attractive is that there are many ways to do business with them: personal business, retirement plan, the potential sale of their business, and lending opportunities. Base your follow-up on all potential needs, not just on the profitability solutions. This is why, if you make a commitment to marketing to business owners, you need to understand the products and services that are available that will add value to their business.

I recommend two approaches in reaching out to this market: contacting business owners directly, and reaching them through referrals.

Direct Contact

Contacting business owners directly will work better if you follow the six steps I outline here:

1. Develop a list of privately owned businesses that have been in existence for five or more years, have sales in excess of $1 million, and are profitable. Have at least 1,000 names on this list that meet these criteria. Supplement this list with names you gather from local papers that recognize successful business owners.

2. Use a contact script you are comfortable with that identifies you as a specialist who can help business owners bring more to their bottom line.

3. Develop a level of expertise and specialization in the needs of the small business owner. Become an expert in solving the needs of the business owner.

4. Focus your efforts using a specialized approach. Concentrate on one or two industries and get to know everything you can about those industries. Subscribe to and read the industry trade journals, and join the associations that are part of the industries that you've decided to focus on.

5. Make use of trade journals and associations specific to the industries you have chosen. Trade journals will provide you with invaluable information about the "movers and shakers" in a particular industry and will give you a level of expertise that will impress your prospects. Additionally, joining the associations gives you access to the members of your targeted prospect group.

6. When you have the appointment, ask questions, listen, and offer compliments. This will give you important follow-up information and will build rapport. Business owners get too little recognition, so any time you can

find a way to recognize them for their accomplishments in your meeting, do so. Focus on the entire range of opportunities with the prospect, not just the banking opportunities. Ask for a tour of the business—nothing makes a business owner feel better. If the appointment goes well, ask for a referral.

Referrals

When asked how they choose a financial advisor, the majority of business owners respond that it is through a recommendation from a friend or another advisor whom they trust (such as an attorney or CPA). The key to this approach is understanding that the best way to get in front of business owners is through referrals. To do this, create a network of other types of advisors who can help the business owner, and position yourself as the person who can help to solve any problem or challenge that a business owner may have.

Examples of the types of professionals and organizations to make part of your network are:

- Attorneys (corporate, estate, divorce, tax, criminal)
- Public relations firms
- Venture capital firms
- CPAs
- Staffing services
- Human resources experts
- Commercial real estate brokers (lease and purchase)

The idea is that you want to provide your business owner prospects with something that no one else can: the one source that can help them with any problem they might have through the resources you have in your network.

It is relatively easy to set up your network because these professionals and organizations are always interested in expanding their business, and they will usually return your favor and be a source of referrals, which is the point of this marketing strategy. If you refer, you will be referred to.

You need to understand what the business owner's problems and issues are, and you can do this on your first appointment—ask the business owner about his challenges, roadblocks, and pressing issues, and offer to provide solutions for them.

In addition, be sure to read the industry association newsletters and trade journals, the local newspaper's business section, and the local business journal. In the local business journal alone, you can uncover thirty to forty leads per week.

Many business owners have the following concerns:

- Finding, hiring, and retaining personnel
- Financing growth
- Lending
- Balance (time for friends and family)
- Exit strategies

To be successful in this market, you must think like a business owner, not a financial advisor. You should understand business owners' mindset (their business is their highest priority), their challenges, and their industry. If you emerge as a valuable problem solver and facilitator in all areas of their life, not just investments, they will trust you and give you their business.

Scripts

Examples for Contacting the President or CFO of a $5 Million-plus Company

Mr./Ms. Business Owner, my name is Joe Advisor, and I'm with XYZ Financial. The reason for my call is to congratulate you on the success of your business, and also to discuss information that could have a positive impact on your bottom line. We compete very effectively with banks in the areas of lending and cash management. I was hoping to visit with you next Thursday and provide you some of the details of how we can help you. Would you be available?

• • • • • • • • • • • •

Mr./Ms. Business Owner, my name is Jane Advisor, and I'm a business financial services specialist with XYZ Financial. I want to congratulate you on the success of your business. If you are like most successful business owners I work with, you pay close attention to the bottom line. If I could have the opportunity to meet with you and find out more about your situation, I am confident that I could save you money. Would you be available to meet next Thursday?

• • • • • • • • • • •

Mr./Ms. Prospect, this is Joe Advisor, a business finance specialist with XYZ Financial. XYZ Financial asked me to call you to tell you about the services we have available for successful companies such as yours that we believe can help you run your business more efficiently and more profitably. Since it's best to discuss this in person, I'd like to meet with you next Tuesday. Is morning or afternoon better for you?

• • • • • • • • • • •

Mr./Ms. Prospect, my name is Jane Advisor, and I'm a senior financial advisor with XYZ Financial. The reason for my call is, first, to compliment you on your success, and then to tell you that we are offering several new, innovative services for businesses, and I wonder if I could schedule a brief appointment with you to discuss them?

• • • • • • • • • • •

If the prospect asks what type of services:

We have so many that I can best answer that question if I come out and meet with you to find out your specific needs and let you know about the services that are most applicable.

If You Were in the Business Prior to Joining XYZ Financial

Mr./Ms. Business Owner, my name is Joe Advisor, and I work for XYZ Financial. I'm calling you today because I was in your business before I worked for XYZ Financial, and I understand your business needs. Since coming to XYZ, I've been trained on what's available for business owners, and I wish I had known about some of this when I did what you do. I believe that my understanding of your business and of business services could help you. Would you be available for an appointment this week?

Screener Scripts

What Is the Nature of Your Call?

I am calling Mr./Ms. Business Owner to show him/her how to save money on his/her current banking relationship.

• • • • • • • • • • •

I am Joe Advisor with XYZ Financial. The reason for my call is that I specialize in helping successful business owners bring more to their bottom line. I was hoping to schedule a brief appointment with Mr./ Ms. Prospect to find out more about the details of his/her business. Can I do that through you, or should I talk to him/her directly?

Professionals: Medical, Legal, and Sales

n this market action plan, I cover three of the most lucrative professional markets: physicians, attorneys, and sales professionals.

Physicians

This is an excellent target market because physicians are affluent, they are delegators (because they have so little time), they have multiple needs (both personal investments and retirement plans), and they present multiple referral opportunities (because they tend to work in groups). If you pursue this market, it is important that you build skills in asset protection, malpractice, estate planning, and retirement planning. In general, the best way to get access to physicians is through their office managers, whom it is best to approach like business owners by talking about cash management, lending, and retirement plans.

Many of the larger medical practices are overprospected. One strategy is to target the less prospected groups, such as sole practitioners, dentists, orthodontists, ophthalmologists, and podiatrists, because they are often much easier to approach directly.

One of the most pressing concerns of this market is asset protection. The cost of liability coverage has increased significantly and is of great concern to physicians. Many physicians worry about facing a catastrophic malpractice suit, and how to keep creditors from getting their personal assets should that happen. In most states, Employee Retirement Income Security Act assets (ERISA assets) can be protected from creditors, so maximizing their contributions to retirement plans is very appealing to physicians. The best targets are the highly paid specialists, who usually have the highest liability; these specialists are radiologists, pathologists, neurosurgeons, and anesthesiologists.

Your priority, then, is to manage the group's pension plan—the biggest money generally comes from retirement accounts rather than personal accounts. If you can get the group's senior physician's account, there is a good chance that you can get the group's pension account as well.

How to Reach Physicians

- Through the administrator or practice manager
- Through their CPA
- Through seminars
- Through referrals
- By presenting at a convention or meeting
- Through physicians' natural groups

Through the Administrator or Practice Manager

Typically, medical practices have a full-time administrator who, among other things, handles the mechanics of the practice's retirement plan and liability coverage. Typically administrators are not experts, and they need a higher level of expertise than they currently have. Generally, neither the group partners nor the administrator are aware of the fiduciary responsibility that they have. This is an area where you can create concern and provide expertise. Send a mailer outlining these issues and your expertise in providing solutions, then follow up with a phone call. Another good tip is to ask the administrator, or office manager, when business hours start and end each day, and call before or after that, when the administrator will have more time to talk.

Through Their CPA

Many CPAs specialize in physicians, and if you can demonstrate your expertise in retirement plans and knowledge of malpractice liability, you will get the ear of these CPAs. The best way to discover which CPAs specialize in medical professionals is by asking your existing client-physicians or prospect-physicians which CPAs they use.

Through Seminars

Many local medical professional associations offer seminars to their members. Determine the contact person for each such association and volunteer to talk to that group about asset allocation, retirement planning, fiduciary responsibilities, liability, and related topics.

Through Referrals

One of the best ways to build a practice with doctors is through referrals. If you have a client or a good prospect in a medical practice, a medical building, or a hospital, ask for referrals to other doctors she works with or near.

By Presenting at a Convention or Meeting

Most doctors' groups have meetings, and this is the ideal time for you to make a presentation. The best approach is to ask a client or prospect who is a doctor when these meetings are and see if he can get you on the agenda to discuss a topic of interest. Another way is to call his administrator/office manager and ask the same favor.

Through Physicians' Natural Groups

Physicians tend to associate with one another in three natural groups:

1. Doctors in the same practice
2. Doctors in the same hospital
3. Doctors in the same specialty

The best way to develop prospects in the first two groups is to ask for referrals to other doctors in the same practice or location.

Most specialists attend conventions and continuing education seminars. Naturally, many of these conventions and seminars are looking for sponsors to help defray their expenses. A modest sponsorship usually entitles you to a booth, which is a good venue for meeting physicians who are attending the event and for getting them to talk about their financial issues. Sponsorships generally require $2,000 or less. The main objective at these conventions is to get the physicians who are attending to commit to a phone appointment, which is the best way to then set up a face-to-face meeting.

Another possibility is to get a speaking engagement at these events, which is an ideal way to help educate doctors on the economy and investments. Most of the time doctors are very busy and do not have much time to learn about investing, so through such a speaking engagement, teach them the basics.

Scripts

Mr./Ms. Medical Administrator, my name is Joe Advisor, and I'm a financial advisor at XYZ Financial. The reason for my call is that I specialize in advising medical professionals on retirement plans. My objective is to help the partners in your group maximize what they can contribute, and to make sure that they are aware of their fiduciary responsibilities. When was the last time you reviewed your current retirement plan? I know that if I had the opportunity to meet with you personally, I could provide some valuable advice on your plan. Would you be available for a meeting next week?

• • • • • • • • • • •

Mr./Ms. Professional Association Director, my name is Jane Advisor, and I'm a financial advisor at XYZ Financial. The reason for my call is that I have a great deal of experience working with the medical community, and I have developed an expertise on medical retirement plans. I would like to volunteer to speak at one of your meetings to share some insights on retirement planning, and on how to allocate assets effectively. I would follow up with only those members who express an interest. Would you be receptive to my talking to your group?

Attorneys

The following are some effective marketing ideas for the attorney market:

- *Target sole practitioners.* In many cases, these are successful attorneys who have broken off from group practices and need help with retirement accounts, personal investments, and all the services that any small business would need.

- *Attend attorney conferences.* This strategy can be more productive than giving seminars because these conferences are more casual, and it is easier to meet people. For example, many conferences and associations have an annual barrister ball. Buy a table and invite your best attorney clients and prospects.

- *Help sponsor attorney conferences.* Identify opportunities where you can help sponsor attorney conferences. As part of the sponsorship, request an opportunity to talk to the group on a relevant and interesting topic.

- *Focus on judges.* There is a big rollover opportunity with judges. Most judges come from a successful practice and have the opportunity to roll over their retirement plans. Typically this is an underpenetrated market.

- *Focus on money in motion with attorneys (i.e., divorces and estate planning).* Building a business with attorneys has an ancillary benefit—they are in the know concerning money in motion and can refer these opportunities to you.

- *Target young, successful attorneys.* Target the larger firms and their associates. A first-year attorney at a prestigious firm can earn $140,000 and has great potential for accumulating assets. It is relatively easy to open accounts with the junior attorneys who will one day be partners (make $500,000 or more).

- *Specialize in the needs of attorneys.* Let your attorney prospects know that you specialize in working with legal professionals. As professionals, they will appreciate your expertise and interest in their industry. Ask for referrals of other successful attorneys you should be talking to. This is classic niche marketing.

- *Offer continuing legal education credits.* See if you can host a lunch seminar on a topic of interest to attorneys and offer continuing education credit (see Chapter 28 on how to do this).

- *Get referrals.* Ask your top clients who their estate attorney is and set up a meeting about networking opportunities (see Chapter 28 for details).

Attorney Script

Mr./Ms. Attorney. My name is Jane Advisor with XYZ Financial. The reason for my call is that I specialize in working with successful attorneys like yourself with their retirement plans.

I found that in many cases, after a retirement plan review, I can find ways to lower the cost and improve investment performance. Would you be available for a brief introductory appointment next week?

Sales Professionals

Seven of the eleven highest-paying jobs are sales and marketing jobs:

1. Sales managers
2. Manufacturer's representatives
3. Realtors
4. Commercial products sales positions
5. Marketing executives, advertising executives, and public relations managers
6. Insurance agents
7. Financial advisors (securities sales)

Besides having large incomes, sales professionals are not as heavily marketed to as medical or legal professionals, yet in many cases the successful sales professional earns a substantially higher income than either a doctor or a lawyer. This is a good market to start with for new advisors, since affluent investors who are themselves sales professionals are likely to be more empathetic with a fellow sales professional.

Here are three ways you can approach prospects in this market:

- *Recognize their achievements*. Successful sales professionals need more than just having their investments managed well—they need to be recognized professionally. This is a key concept in marketing to this group, and recognition of a prospect's success will go a long way toward building a relationship. Top-performing sales professionals generally feel that society does not adequately recognize them, so always connect their need for recognition with the value of your investment advice. One of the ways to do this is to scan the newspapers and trade magazines and call to congratulate the successful sales professionals; introduce yourself and ask for the opportunity to meet with them.

- *Be a mortgage source for Realtors*. A good way to approach Realtors is to meet their need for a high-quality mortgage source. This is an excellent way to develop relationships with top Realtors in your community. For more detail on this concept, see Chapter 33.

- *Build a network*. Build a network of sales professionals—not only are members of the network good prospects, but they can refer their clients to you just as you can refer yours to them. (See Chapter 22 for ideas on forming a new networking group.) Limit members of the group to the best in their field, and include those that you could easily refer business to.

Script

Mr./Ms. Sales Professional, My name is Joe Advisor, and I'm a financial advisor at XYZ Financial. You have been identified as one of the best sales professionals in your industry, and I'm calling because I believe I could make a positive difference in your long-term investment results. I know that as a successful sales professional, you understand the importance of adding value in order to get business. I would appreciate having the opportunity to show you how I could add real value to your investment results. I will be in your area next Thursday and would like to stop by, introduce myself, and find out more about your situation. Would you be available?

Executives

Senior executives and middle managers of well-performing public companies are a very good market. In many cases, these executives have $1 million or more in restricted stock, options, and cleared stock in the company they work for. They personally earn good incomes, they have saved much of their stock, and in many cases they don't need this stock to maintain their lifestyle.

To be successful in this market, you must invest the time to become an expert in the areas that affect corporate executives. The barrier to entry for most advisors is their lack of expertise in these areas. The following are examples of areas of expertise that you must have:

- Stock options
- Rule 144 trades
- Hedging strategies
- Estate and trust planning
- Concentrated stock strategies
- Alternative minimum tax rules
- Affiliate and insider-trading rules
- Exchange funds
- Lending on restricted securities

There are two excellent ways you can approach this market. The first is to focus on executives' concentrated stock positions, and the second is to focus on the wealth-management needs of senior executives. I outline how to do both of these next.

Concentrated Stock Positions

The key to this approach is understanding that the tax issues, regulations, liquidity, and timing of exercising options are complex. Providing valuable insights into these issues will open the door to this market. Very few executives understand what is the best time to exercise their corporate options and the related tax issues. They also have mixed feelings about the concentrated positions they generally hold. In many cases, their current advisors are not aware of the restricted shares and options that they hold outside of their brokerage accounts. The best way to capture this market is to position yourself as an expert in the rules and regulations affecting these assets, the best options strategies, dealing with restricted stock, and providing liquidity.

During the initial prospecting contact (often by phone), position yourself as an expert in restricted stock and options, and emphasize your ability to provide valuable advice once you have determined the details of the prospect's situation. If the executive perceives you as an expert in this area and believes that you can provide valuable information on his options and restricted stock positions, in many cases, he will take the time to see you.

During the face-to-face appointment, your first objective is to find out as much as possible about the executive's options and restricted-shares situation. Your second objective is to ask for referrals to other executives in the same company. For your follow-up contact, the key is to focus on stock option analysis and liquidity strategies.

Another idea is to invite executives to a conference call on a relevant subject. Invite them by mail and follow up by phone. Examples of such subjects are liquidity strategies, tax exchange funds, and strategies for dealing with concentrated stock positions. This type of virtual seminar appeals to busy executives and positions you as an expert on a subject that affects them. It makes setting the initial appointment much easier after the conference call.

Scripts

Mr./Ms. Prospect, my name is Joe Advisor, with XYZ Financial's Wealth Management Group. We specialize in helping successful executives of public companies handle their restricted stock and stock options. If we could show you a way to manage your equity exposure effectively, would you be interested in a brief meeting?

· · · · · · · · · · ·

Mr./Ms. Executive, my name is Joe Advisor, and I'm a financial advisor at XYZ Financial. I'm calling you because I specialize in working with successful corporate executives who have restricted shares and stock options. The timing, liquidity opportunities, and tax implications of options and restricted shares can have a meaningful impact on your net worth, and I believe I can offer you insights into your situation that can make a difference. I would be glad to work around your schedule and stop by your office. Your time will be well spent. What time would be convenient for you?

Script for Screener

I'm from XYZ Financial, and I wanted to give Mr./Ms. Prospect some information that could affect his/her stock options.

Wealth-Management Needs of Senior Executives

The target here is senior executives; this group is hard to reach but worth the extra effort.

1. Develop a contact list of executives and get as much information as you can about each one.

2. Research each name on this list before you call. Invest heavily in researching the people on this list because the more you know about each executive, the more connections you can make, the more likely she is to return your call, and the more likely she is to meet with you. Some sources of this information are:

    *   *Company Web sites*. These are the best place to gather much of this background information. Senior executives' biographies are generally posted on these Web sites because they are proud of their accomplishments. These biographies talk about the executives' educational backgrounds as well as their past experiences and credentials.

    *   *Hoover's Web site*. This is another excellent source of background information on executives.

    *   *U.S. Search*. This will give you anyone's age, past and current addresses, and spouse's name.

    *   *Local newspapers, magazines, and business journals*. These sources provide information on promotions and relocations, company announcements, and other significant events.

3. Overnight a package to the executive at his workplace. Include:

- A cover letter complimenting the executive on his past successes and a recent significant event that has occurred (if applicable). Also mention that you will follow up the package with a personal call.

- Your biography, including a description of your expertise.

- Your approach to investing.

Try to differentiate yourself as much as possible in the information you send and highlight your experience and expertise.

The goal is to make a minimum of twenty calls per day (approximately two hours of calls), with the objective of either reaching the executive directly or leaving a message on her voicemail. You should expect to contact at least three prospects each day (which is a 15 percent call-to-contact ratio).

Getting to the executive's voicemail is not always easy because of the screener. The best way is to mention the overnight package and that you are following up on it. The screener will probably have seen the package and will know that your call is legitimate, and often will put you through to the executive's voicemail. Leaving a well-thought-out, organized voicemail message is key to getting a return phone call. The following is an example from a team that has had a high success rate in getting messages returned:

> Mr./Ms. Executive, this is Joe Advisor with XYZ Financial. I recently sent you an overnight package, and while I do not know your exact circumstances, I wanted to invite you to have an introductory meeting. Our team has a unique style of money management and has developed a specialty in working with senior executives like you.

This voicemail message does not guarantee a return call, but it does set up the next call.

Try to reach the executive four times. After the fourth call, if he has not returned your calls, you need to make a decision as to whether or not to pursue this lead. In most cases, you should drop the prospect after four calls, but with the following message:

> Mr./Ms. Executive, this is Joe Advisor with XYZ Financial. I am sorry that I have not have the opportunity to reach you. At this point I am

going to leave further communication in your hands. I am confident that we could make a positive difference with your financial situation. Please feel free to call me anytime. (Leave contact information.)

You can recontact anyone you have dropped twelve months later, since the law of receptivity may apply: The prospect's circumstances change and, as a result, so does her receptivity.

The first meeting should be primarily focused on gathering information and should include a short pitch about your team and how you invest money. At the end of the meeting, ask the prospect how and when he would like to take the next steps. Make it a priority to schedule a second meeting right then, and suggest that the second meeting include a specific proposal that will include more detail on your wealth-management process and how much it costs.

You will reach about 15 percent of the executives you call. If you call two thousand executives a year, then you will contact approximately three hundred. Of those three hundred, 10 percent will lead to an appointment (thirty appointments). The team that developed this market plan converts these thirty prospects into fifteen new relationships, with 75 percent of them bringing in over $1 million in assets.

This is a specialized and time-consuming market action plan, but the results will be impressive. If you follow this, you could expect at least $10 million of new assets and ten new affluent relationships.

Influencers

Building a network of influencers is the objective of this market action plan. Influencers are CPAs and attorneys, who are powerful referral sources—these professionals have significant influence with their clients, and when they recommend a financial advisor to their clients, their clients often take heed.

The key to this strategy is quality, not quantity—if you can build a network of three CPAs and three estate planning attorneys who consistently give you referrals, you will have built an excellent network.

The objective is to share your approach with these influencers and to demonstrate that this approach is better than the one that their clients' current financial advisors use. But be aware that referring clients to you will reflect on the influencer, and, therefore, she will be very cautious initially in doing so. Explain to these influencers that you will do everything you can to help them (such as providing cost-basis research on anything they need and provide ongoing education) and to facilitate a professional relationship with them.

The key with this group is to educate them in areas of interest to them and that will make them look smart in the eyes of their clients. Education on the capital markets and current events as they apply to the markets will be of high interest to them. Not only will you be providing value, but the influencers will appreciate your expertise; their confidence in you as someone they can refer their clients to will grow.

The best way to determine the best CPAs and attorneys is to ask your best prospects and personal contacts whom they use; ask permission to call on those they mention.

How to Build Your Influencer Network

Here are three suggestions for starting your network.

Retiree Seminar

When you are presenting seminars to retirees (or to anyone, for that matter), invite one of your CPA or estate planning attorney prospects to join the program. This will add to the depth of the seminar and will create a partnership; it will allow the influencer to see you in action. This is an excellent first step in developing a relationship with an influencer that could be part of your network.

Quarterly Educational Seminars

This is an effective way to both start an influencer network and leverage it after you have built it. Identify all the CPAs in your market area. Personally contact each one of them and invite him to a relevant seminar on tax-related issues that would benefit him. Invite the CPAs a month in advance, and follow up several times before the seminar. I recommend that you present these seminars quarterly to the same group of CPAs.

Make sure that you have expert speakers. Provide lunch, and be sensitive to the timing as it relates to their busy tax season. Take part in the presentation so that the CPAs can see your expertise and professionalism firsthand. Provide continuing education credits. Ideal attendance is twenty to twenty-five CPAs.

The objective of these seminars is to provide a valuable resource for CPAs so that they have a reason to reciprocate—rarely will you be able to provide them with as many referrals as they provide you. Follow up with the CPAs in attendance every month; share with them your expertise, educate them, and familiarize them with your wealth-management process.

The topics of these seminars should not be product related. Here are some ideas for topics:

- Changes in the tax law that will affect their clients
- How options and master limited partnerships are affected by the tax law and how to interpret the reporting received by their clients
- Defined-benefit plans
- Estate planning tax issues
- Medicare and Medicaid tax reporting

- Retirement issues and plan design
- Business valuations as it relates to tax law

How to Get Continuing Education Accreditation

To get continuing education accreditation for your presentations to CPAs, contact your State Board of Accounting and apply for CPA continuing education credits; for presentations to attorneys, submit your presentation agenda to your state supreme court.

Seminar Introduction

Thanks for coming to our seminar. I want to reiterate our commitment to providing high-quality information on timely topics and to providing whatever service we can to the CPA community as a thank-you for the business we get from you. Please take the time to fill out the feedback questionnaire so that we can continue to improve our seminars. We are willing to provide all the resources we have available. We want to be on the list of advisors whom you refer your clients to when the occasion arises.

Face-to-Face Meetings

Identify the CPAs and estate planning attorneys in your market territory. Do this by compiling a list of your clients' CPAs and attorneys, and by calling CPAs and attorneys from the Yellow Pages. The objective is to get a face-to-face appointment with these influencers.

Scripts: Introduction

Mr./Ms. Influencer, this is Jane Advisor from XYZ Financial, and the reason for my call is that I would like the opportunity to learn more about your practice and to share our unique wealth-management process. Would you be available for a brief initial meeting where I can find out more about your practice.

• • • • • • • • • • •

Mr./Ms. Influencer, this is Joe Advisor, and I am an advisor from XYZ Financial. I am building my wealth-management practice in this town/location. If we don't have any mutual clients now, I am sure we will in the future. I know you are a successful professional, and I would like to meet you, find out more about your practice, and tell you about mine. Would you be receptive to a meeting next Thursday?

Script: Introduction (Mutual Client)

Mr./Ms. Influencer, my name is Jane Advisor with XYZ Financial and we have a mutual client, [give name]. I am in the process of building a network of successful professionals like you. I would like to meet you face to face to find out more about your practice and share what we do for our clients. Would you be available to meet?

• • • • • • • • • • • •

In the first meeting, spend the majority of the time understanding the CPA's or attorney's practice and what type of clients she is looking for. Also give a brief description of your practice and wealth-management process. If you feel that there is a good fit and a potential for mutual referrals, schedule a second meeting.

In the second meeting, focus on sharing your wealth-management process and your unique approach to helping your clients. The purpose of this meeting is to separate you from what the CPA or attorney perceives as the typical "stockbroker." Invest as much time as you need in order to understand the CPA's or attorney's practice so that you can add value to her practice by giving her a good understanding of how your wealth-management process is unique. The most common reason for lack of referrals is that the influencer does not know what an advisor really does.

After the first meeting, concentrate on providing valuable information to the influencer so that she looks at you as a true resource. Educate the CPA or attorney with information that can help her and that she is interested in. Some examples of this type of information are your firm's insight into tax laws and changes, market outlooks, wealth-management tools, current issues and how they affect markets, how the capital markets work, and innovative liability products. Provide this information on a regular basis. Once a month, have both a scheduled appointment and an informal drop-by.

This process should generate at least four new referral sources per year. If each referral source provides two new referrals a year and you can convert 50 percent of these referrals to clients, then this process should add at least four new affluent clients per year. This is in addition to the existing CPA/attorney network referrals you already have.

How to Leverage Your Influencer Network Once You Have Started It

Referrals

Once you have started your network of influencers, the most effective way to build it is to refer your clients to your network of CPAs and attorneys. Nothing gets more referrals from influencers than giving referrals. The best time to do this with clients is after a planning session, when you are discussing their current tax and estate planning situation and if they are not satisfied with their current CPA or attorney.

Seminars

Use your CPA network as a source of names for seminars. Suggest to the CPAs that you work with that you would like to hold a relevant seminar for their clients, such as "Planning for Retirement: The Wealth-Management Process." Offer to mail and call the CPA's clients and invite them to the seminar. Provide lunch. Offer to follow up with each of the attendees the next day to discuss his individual situation. CPAs don't always know how to give referrals, and this is an excellent way to stimulate them.

Annual Update

Arrange an individual annual update meeting with each CPA and attorney in your network. Buy the person lunch, exchange ideas, share referrals, and solidify the relationship.

Fun Events

Determine a topic that would be of interest to CPAs and a topic that would be of interest to attorneys, both of which should be eligible for continuing education credit. These events should be separate, since CPAs and attorneys have different interests and requirements. The topics should be presented by outside speakers that money managers or local professionals can provide. A good idea is to present these topics during a lunch, and then follow with golf; the lunch and presentation should take approximately an hour.

CPA Personal Account

Manage the CPA's account, even if it is below your minimum.

> Mr./Ms. CPA, typically I accept only accounts with a minimum qualification of $250,000, but I would like to offer my services to you with no minimum so that you can experience firsthand the quality of our clients' experience.

Monthly Meetings

Invite five or six of your influencers each month to a lunch, breakfast, or dinner intelligence-gathering meeting. Ask attendees to invite their partners and colleagues. Agenda items could include "What do you think of full-service brokerages, discounters, and our firm?" or "How do you decide whom to refer clients to in the financial services industry?" This provides an opportunity for you to gather important information about how your firm is perceived and how these influencers think, and it gives you an opportunity to tell your story—you can make influencers more comfortable giving you referrals if you describe your wealth-management process.

Buy Lunch During Tax Season

Buy brown bag lunches for CPA and staff during the week before tax deadline. Have the lunches delivered with a card that says, "My compliments." This creates enormous good will.

Office Visits

Invite the members of your CPA network to your office, and give them a presentation to explain what a client experiences with you. Share your wealth-management process and the tools you have, and introduce your team and the specialists you use, if any.

Quarterly Parties

Once a quarter, organize a nice dinner and cocktail party for your best clients. Have the dinner at a high-end, well-known restaurant to provide a good draw. Start cocktails at 6:00. After dinner, present a thirty-minute talk on a topic of interest to your clients given by an influencer who has given you referrals. If you have a sponsor for the party, have her share a relevant topic as well.

The purpose of this event is to give one of your best influencers the opportunity to speak to your best clients. The influencer will appreciate the opportunity and will be likely to reciprocate by giving you more referrals. The clients will appreciate being invited to a nice dinner with an interesting and relevant topic. This is also a great opportunity to encourage your best clients to invite an affluent friend who can be added to your prospect pipeline.

Invite twenty-five clients and prospects and expect ten to twelve attendees. You can expect at least one significant referral—from influencer or client—as a result of this event. The advisor who shared this idea has brought in over $20 million in assets as the result of twelve of these events.

Script: Seminar Invitation

> Mr./Ms. CPA, I want to invite you to a luncheon seminar that will provide you with timely tax-related information [give details of the topic]. Additionally, I will apply on your behalf for CPE continuing education credit. The purpose of this session is to give you a high-quality program that is convenient, and to help you serve your clients better. The date and time are _____. Would you be interested in attending?

CHAPTER 29

Diverse Markets: Women, Hispanics, and Asians

In suggesting marketing strategies for women, Hispanics, and Asians, I have made generalizations concerning marketing preferences and cultural traits based on market research; these should not be misinterpreted as stereotyping. My intent is to use market research to provide insights, not to stereotype women, Hispanic Americans, or Asian Americans.

Women

Marketing to women makes a great deal of sense because of their generally favorable demographics. It is estimated that by 2010, the majority of investable money could be controlled by women.

There are several ways you can market to women. In this section, I present some of the best. Note that in many cases, professional women are extremely busy with work and home responsibilities, which means that evening seminars may not be well attended. The best time for appointments with professional women is breakfast or lunch.

Women's Organizations

One way to market to women is to become involved in women's organizations. Examples of these organizations include the National Association of Women Business Owners, the National Association for Female Executives, the Women's Business League, Executive Women's Clubs, and chapters of Executive Professional Women, Inc. You must have a leadership position in order to get the most out of your membership in these organizations—as a leader, you will have the respect of the members, which should lead them to perceive you as being good at your job.

Read the literature from these organizations and volunteer to write articles for their publications. This will encourage this market to see you as an expert.

Many companies have women's organizations within the company. Getting an opportunity to speak to such a group through an existing member is an excellent marketing technique that will get you in front of qualified women investors.

Women Business Owners and Realtors

You can find women business owners through your local chamber of commerce. Position yourself as a specialist in working with female business owners. Realtors are another good group to target. Some of the most affluent women sales professionals are Realtors. Volunteer to speak at the top Realtors' sales meeting on retirement planning.

Speeches

Giving speeches to audiences in this market is very effective. Look for public speaking opportunities at chamber of commerce women's groups, women's business and professional groups, philanthropic organizations, women's investment clubs, and garden clubs. Topics can be general, or they can be as specific as "Investment Needs of Affluent Widows and Divorcees."

A Networking Group

Build a women's networking group yourself that encompasses the many needs of women investors, particularly divorcees and widows. Members of this networking group could include psychiatrists or psychologists, clergy members, estate planning attorneys, and CPAs. The members of this networking group can not only provide referrals to one another, but also sponsor seminars together on topics such as "Women: Are You Prepared to Be on Your Own?" or "Women and Money—Women's Unique Financial Issues." You can encourage attendance at these seminars by advertising in local papers, making local women's organizations aware of them, and calling influencers and suggesting that they invite their clients. Try also to invite personal contacts and existing prospects to these seminars.

Life-Changing Events

There are two life-changing events that the majority of women experience: divorce and the loss of a spouse. Research shows that over 50 percent of women get divorced, and the majority of women who are over sixty years old will lose their spouse. At these times, large sums of money are in motion, and many women need help managing this flow. In many cases, married women have delegated the management of their investments to their husbands, and if they are recently divorced or widowed, their need for professional investment advice is very high.

There are two effective marketing activities that advisors who are interested in marketing to women undergoing a life-changing event can use. One is to give seminars educating women on what their options are when they experience a life-changing event; the other is to build a divorce and estate planning attorney network to generate referrals.

Seminars to Educate Women

Many women who are sixty years old or older have not had much experience in financial planning and realize that they need to learn more. Their overriding concern is to prepare for what would happen to them if they were to lose their spouse (through death or divorce). This should be the topic for talks to women. These women typically are well educated, are married, and do not work. Creating and conducting seminars to educate this target market can be very effective. Also, your CPA and attorney network can be an excellent referral source for attendees at your seminars. Referrals from clients and prospects, especially those who have experienced divorce or the loss of a spouse, are another way to generate attendance. Finding women's investment clubs and offering to speak to them is another way to get in front of this target market.

Attorney Network

Being referred by an attorney during a life-changing event will give you the credibility you need to get the initial appointment. Marketing to attorneys is a good way to get in front of women who are facing divorce or widowhood, and you can make excellent contacts with divorce and estate planning attorneys through the local bar association.

Offer to help divorce attorneys and their female clients decide before mediation which assets to retain to generate income. Getting involved early, before they receive the lump sum, is key. Prepare educational brochures in advance to show your expertise in this area.

For specific techniques on how to approach a targeted attorney or other advisor, or prospect, please refer to Chapters 22 and 32.

A Monthly Luncheon Group

Organize a core group of your women clients for a monthly luncheon. Ideally, you should start the group with ten women who are committed to meeting monthly. Position the luncheon as a combination of fun, charity, and education. The group should identify a women's charity that it wants to support financially (specifically, a charity that benefits women). To support it, each member contributes a small amount of money toward the charity, even if she does not attend the lunch on a particular day. There are many women who do not have the time to spend on a charity but want to be able to contribute to a worthwhile cause financially.

The group invites a guest speaker to speak at the lunch on a topic that is interesting to the group (the topic does not have to be financial). Each member is asked to bring one guest to the monthly luncheon, which is a perfect opportunity for the advisor to meet new potential prospects. The guests can join the group or not, and all new members are encouraged to bring one new guest to the next meeting.

As a follow-up, send each attendee (and members who are not in attendance) a synopsis of the meeting and a reminder of the date of the next meeting, and invite the nonclient attendees to other events that you sponsor in order to develop those relationships further. To ensure good attendance, send a reminder postcard two weeks in advance of the luncheon, and make a call to each group member one week before, reminding her to bring a guest.

This luncheon event is an excellent way to strengthen relationships with existing clients, and it provides a good way for the advisor to meet new prospects through existing clients in a fun, nonthreatening way.

Warm-Contacting Women

Focus on successful women business owners, women executives, women with money in motion (as a result of divorce or the death of a spouse), and women professionals (attorneys, CPAs, and physicians). Job changes, transfers, and promotions are also money-in-motion opportunities for professional women. Develop a list of women in these categories using the appendix. Read the local papers, local business journals, and trade journals to find women who are being recognized and who have money in motion. Before you contact these prospects, find out as much about them as possible in order to make the contact warm. Use search engines to find out as much as you can.

Whenever possible, contact these women at work. Avoid their gate-keeper by calling earlier or later in the day; if your calls are screened by an assistant, try to build rapport by being very open about who you are, explaining that you specialize in working with successful women, and saying that you just want to introduce yourself. If you cannot reach your target prospect directly, leave a voicemail.

Use this script when you reach your target prospect directly:

> Hello, Ms. Prospect. This is Joe Advisor, and I am calling from XYZ Financial. I specialize in working with successful women like you. I know you have done well, as a [business owner/professional/executive], and congratulations. I have a very detailed planning approach that I use with my clients, and I wanted to ask you if you have developed a comprehensive plan with your current advisor. [Wait for answer.] How do you feel about your current investment situation? Are you satisfied with your wealth-management process and the fees, service, and performance of your current advisor?

The goal is to create some doubt about the prospect's current approach, to entice her with comprehensive planning, to identify potential opportunities, and to get her to talk and make a connection with you. Your ultimate objective is a face-to-face appointment with her.

Scripts

> Ms. Friend, this is Joe Advisor. As you probably know, I'm an advisor at XYZ Financial, and I wanted to ask for your help. I have been trying to find a way to meet Ms. Prospect, and I understand you know her as a [neighbor/school mom/work associate]. I wanted to ask if you could introduce me at a lunch or breakfast that I could arrange around your and her schedules.

or,

• • • • • • • • • • •

I wanted to invite both of you to one of my client events scheduled next month. Would you be comfortable helping me with this?

Ms. Prospect, my name is Jane Advisor, and I'm a financial advisor at XYZ Financial. I'm calling you because I've built [am building] my business with women business owners. Through experience, I've developed an expertise in working with successful women business owners like you, and my objective is to show you how to bring more money to your bottom line. Would you be available for an appointment on Thursday to allow me to introduce myself and find out more about your situation?

· · · · · · · · · · ·

Ms. Organization President, my name is Jane Advisor, and I'm a financial advisor at XYZ Financial. I have built [am building] my business with women investors. I enjoy the opportunity to share with women XYZ's best thinking on investment opportunities in the current environment. I wanted to offer to speak to your organization on this or any other investment topic you may be interested in. Would you be interested in my offer?

· · · · · · · · · · ·

Ms. Fellow Networker, my name is Jane Advisor, and I'm an advisor at XYZ Financial. I am organizing a women's networking group of professionals whose expertise and experience complement one another's. The purpose of this group is to exchange ideas on effective marketing to women, as well as to provide one another with business leads. I would also like to organize seminars for women in our community where members of our network can have a forum to share their insights and expertise with the women attending. I wanted to invite you to our next meeting on [date] to see if you would be interested in joining us.

· · · · · · · · · · ·

Ms. Prospect, my name is Joe Advisor, and I'm a financial advisor at XYZ Financial. The reason for my call is that I wanted to invite you to attend our seminar on "Women and Money." The seminar will include experts in many fields who will share their insights on the financial issues that face women. Would you be interested in attending?

Hispanics

If you are going to focus on the Hispanic market, you must specialize in it because you will be more successful if you take the time to develop an understanding of this community. The Hispanic market can be close-knit—you do not need to be Hispanic in order to be effective with this group, but you must be involved in the Hispanic community, and you must invest in relationships and in the community.

To be successful, you must understand the Hispanic culture. Discussing business or asking for business right away can be considered to be in poor taste; instead, invest time in understanding the culture. In general, the culture is conservative and values family, friends, and community very highly. Your marketing will be more effective if you incorporate these cultural traits into your action plan. Some examples of how to do this are the following:

- Fixed income, CDs, and other conservative investments can be very attractive; equities can fit, but before you include them, you must be sure that your clients understand risk.

- Relationships may take longer to develop, but loyalty is very high. Once you have established trust, members of this group will be inclined to consolidate assets with one advisor; this also makes long-term planning very appealing.

- Because of the high degree of loyalty, once you establish trust, you will be able to leverage referrals very successfully.

- Take advantage of the tendency to be close-knit by focusing on building a network of CPAs and estate planning attorneys who have a Hispanic clientele. Estate planning is a high priority for this group because of the value placed on family. As in most demographic groups, owning a business is among the most successful occupations, and getting referrals from CPAs to their Hispanic business owner clients is one of the most effective marketing tactics that you can employ in the Hispanic market.

To get started, read newspapers and magazines focused on the local Hispanic community, join the Hispanic chamber of commerce, and network among centers of influence and respected professionals in the Hispanic community. Your mantra should be network, relationships, and education.

As you do this, focus your attention on two groups: Hispanic business owners and Hispanic professionals. Here are some of the best sources for these individuals:

1. Go to online versions of your local papers and do a word search for "Hispanic" or "Spanish." This will give you names of Hispanic leaders and successful individuals that you can contact.

2. Read the local Hispanic paper, if there is one. Look for recognition and money in motion opportunities.

3. Network by taking a leadership position in as many Hispanic organizations as you have time for, and target key Hispanic community and business leaders for networking opportunities. Most communities have a Hispanic chamber of commerce that provides excellent networking opportunities, as well as other Hispanic organizations that you can use for networking. As a leader, you will cultivate respect and be able to identify who the most influential and affluent members are.

4. Search the phone book for businesses and professionals with Hispanic surnames.

5. Drive through Hispanic business sections and write down the names of the businesses you find there.

6. Contact the Small Business Administration for the names of minority-owned businesses.

7. And use perhaps the best source of names: referrals. The Hispanic community is close-knit, so as you accumulate prospects, be sure to ask for referrals.

The Appointment

Make it clear throughout the conversation that you understand the culture, that you can provide the important personal touch, and that you appreciate the community's strong family values. Demonstrate your knowledge of financial services, listen, and ask questions, but also make sure that you make your commitment to the Hispanic market clear. This will give you an edge over your competition. You and those you are targeting (business owners, professionals, and CPAs) share two important traits: You both have a commitment to the Hispanic community, and you both have a desire to increase business; you can use this commonality to promote a reciprocal alliance where you help each other in your respective businesses.

Scripts

Mr./Ms. Prospect, my name is Joe Advisor, and I'm a financial advisor with XYZ Financial. I work with a number of successful Hispanic individuals like you, and I'd like to have the opportunity to share with you how I can help you and your family achieve your financial goals. I will be in your area Thursday and would appreciate the opportunity to meet with you and find out more about your situation.

• • • • • • • • • • •

Mr./Ms. Prospect, my name is Joe Advisor, and I'm a financial advisor with XYZ Financial. I specialize in working with successful Hispanic business owners like you. I can provide the best business services plat-form to you, and because of my familiarity with Hispanic culture, I be-lieve I can make a positive difference to you, your family, and your business. Are you available for an appointment Thursday?

• • • • • • • • • • •

Mr./Ms. Prospect, my name is Joe Advisor, and I'm a financial advisor with XYZ Financial. You have been identified to me as a leader in the Hispanic community, a market that I work closely with. I would like to meet with you and share some of my best ideas for marketing to the Hispanic community, with the intent of helping each other. Would you be available on Thursday for lunch?

Asian Americans

Research indicates that Asian Americans have among the highest median incomes of all ethnic groups, making them prime customers for a wide range of financial products and services. This market segment is under-prospected, yet has high potential for investment. It is underprospected because Asian Americans generally save and invest more than other Americans and are less likely to spend on signs of wealth. Also, many advisors assume they must be Asian American to be successful with Asian Americans, which is not true; however, you need to understand the mind-set of the Asian American investor.

To be effective in this market you must customize your approach to the specific needs of this market:

• Planning for retirement is very important for Asian Americans of all ages. They were conditioned not to rely on the governments of their former countries. Therefore, pension plans and profit-sharing plans are of special interest to Asian American entrepreneurs, as well as to all self-employed Asian American professionals.

- Most affluent Asian Americans attribute their success to education. They regard high-quality education for their children as essential to their family's continued success in America. Asian American households will seek information and investments that will help them achieve their educational goals.

The first step is to develop a list of names and the best way to approach this market. The following are some suggestions:

- Affluent Asian American prospects in the medical professions are most influenced by their mentors. Mentors can be found in high concentrations among the faculty of medical schools and teaching hospitals. Physicians in specialties such as neurosurgery and orthopedic surgery are particularly affluent. One of the most important lists you can get is that of medical school faculty. Another source of mentors for all professions is accountants and attorneys; scan the Yellow Pages under these occupations for practitioners with Asian American surnames. Once you have built a relationship with these mentors, they can refer you to other Asian Americans, and you will have high credibility because of the respect these mentors have.

- Referrals from leading authorities in the field are considered important endorsements. One idea is to visit a medical school library, examine the current literature, and develop a target list of people who write articles in prestigious journals and live in your market area. If you open accounts with them and are able to gain their endorsements, you can leverage those endorsements to reach affluent Asian American physicians throughout your market.

- Many university faculty members are very well paid, and the highest-paid faculty members are often members of medical school teaching staffs. A growing number of medical school faculty members are Asian Americans. In addition to their base salary, many of these people supplement their incomes by writing books, providing consulting services, and inventing high-tech devices. The important concept here is that medical faculty are important not only for endorsements, but also in their own right as affluent investors.

- An important source of names of affluent Asian American business owners is local Asian American newspapers. Focus on leaders of local business organizations such as the Korean-American Business-

Owner Association. These leaders have a significant influence on the choice of speakers for monthly meetings. Speakers at such meetings are considered to be endorsed by the group's leadership.

• Your image will be further enhanced if you can position yourself as an expert who is quoted in the Asian American press, so place a high priority on developing a good relationship with local Asian American newspapers and other organizations. Identify who the leaders and influencers of the Asian American community are through these media groups, and build relationships with these individuals through networking and by gaining endorsements.

Scripts

Dr./Mr./Ms. Medical Professor/Author/Expert, my name is Joe Advisor, and I'm a financial advisor at XYZ Financial. The reason I'm calling is that you have an excellent reputation as a(n) [professor/expert/author], and I know you are very successful in your field. I have found that many people who enjoy the kind of success you have are so involved with their field that they don't have much time to pay attention to their financial plan. I would appreciate having the opportunity to visit with you during your office hours and share with you how I believe I could make a positive difference in your financial life. My specialties include retirement planning and educational savings for families. Could I come by and visit you sometime this week? When would be convenient for you?

• • • • • • • • • • •

Mr./Ms. Influential Community Member, my name is Joe Advisor, and I'm a financial advisor at XYZ Financial. I am building my practice in the Asian American community, and through my involvement with this market, it has become clear to me that you are a community/business leader. I am convinced that we can help each other find ways to benefit the community and help each other with our businesses. I would appreciate having the opportunity to meet with you, introduce myself, and discuss our mutual interest in the Asian American community. Is there a time in the next week that would work for you? I am glad to meet you at a location that is most convenient for you.

• • • • • • • • • • •

Mr./Ms. Organization President, my name is Jane Advisor, and I'm a financial advisor at XYZ Financial. I am building my practice in the Asian

American community, and one of the things that I have been doing to get better known is to offer to talk to Asian American organizations on any investment topic that they may have an interest in. I understand that your organization meets monthly, and I wanted to offer my services to speak to your group at any time that would be convenient. Would you have an interest in my offer? What date would work best for you?

. . . .

Mr./Ms. Asian American Business Owner, my name is Jane Advisor, and I'm a financial advisor at XYZ Financial. I noticed that you were recently recognized in the local paper [Asian American or otherwise], and I wanted to congratulate you on your success. I have been building my business in the local Asian American community. In fact, you may know some of my clients and prospects [get permission to use names before doing so]. I have specialized in working with Asian American business owners and would appreciate the opportunity to visit with you personally. I will be in your area on Thursday and was hoping to have the chance to visit you then. Are you available?

CHAPTER 30

Retirement Plans

There are two primary targets within this market:

1.   Qualified retirement plans
2.   IRA rollovers

Qualified Retirement Plans

In targeting retirement plans, I recommend the following three steps:

1.   *Specialize.* To be successful with qualified retirement plans, you should focus on retirement plans between $1 million and $50 million in size. This is the most advantageous segment.

2.   *Gain expertise.* Before you begin prospecting, you must be willing to commit to developing a high level of expertise. This is a market in which knowledge is truly essential. Your firm's retirement group can give you much of the training and information you need, as can mutual funds' partner education programs (your wholesaler can guide you to these) or you can read books on retirement plans. Your efforts to continually increase your competencies will give you a definite competitive advantage in winning corporate mandates. The majority of retirement plans have problems with plan design or fiduciary responsibility, so introducing yourself as an expert in these areas is a great way to open the door to getting an appointment.

3.   *Make contact.* Call the person who signed the 5500 form, identify yourself as a specialist in retirement plans, and ask if she will be putting the retirement plan out for bid, either now or in the future (if the firm has just made a change, it is not likely to make another one anytime soon). If she is open to a change, that is an excellent time to make an appointment. You should also find out to whom the firm has given the day-to-day plan-management responsibility and ask if you should speak to that person as well.

Another technique is to look at the performance of the plan in advance of the call (calculate how much the plan is worth year over year), then call the signer of the 5500 and ask if he is concerned about the performance of the investments, reminding him of his fiduciary responsibility. Remember, your goal is simply to gain an audience with the decision maker.

Scripts

Mr./Ms. Prospect, my name is Joe Advisor, and I'm a financial advisor with XYZ Financial. My group specializes in helping corporations create strategies for 401(k) and pension plans, including simplifying their administration and maximizing their performance. If we could help make your administration or performance better, would you be interested in a brief meeting? Would you have time next Thursday?

• • • • • • • • • • •

This is Jane Advisor, and I'm a financial advisor at XYZ Financial. I specialize in working with retirement plans, and I want to ask if you are going to put your retirement plan out for bid now or in the near future. [Or, when was the last time you made a change in your retirement plan?] I would like to have an opportunity to share with you the benefits of considering XYZ to handle your plan. I will be in the area on Thursday and would like the opportunity to introduce myself and show you how we could make a positive difference.

• • • • • • • • • • •

This is Joe Advisor, and I'm a financial advisor at XYZ Financial. I specialize in working with retirement plans, and I wanted to find out if you have been at all concerned with the performance of your plan. If you are open to a second opinion, we offer an open platform with a wide range of investments and managers, and I would like to share with you some alternatives that you might consider. Would you be available on Thursday for a brief meeting?

IRA Rollovers

Three particular situations involving IRA rollover money present unusually good opportunities:

1.   Focusing on people who are nearing retirement

2. Focusing on people who are being laid off

3. Making yourself an outside expert to specific companies

People Nearing Retirement

The first step in this market action plan is to find out who the biggest employers in your market are and determine whether their retirement plans permit IRA rollovers. The best way to do this is to ask people you know who work for these companies; if you don't know anyone there, then simply call the company and ask for someone in HR.

Once you've targeted the company, the next step is to find individuals in the company who are fifty-five or older and who may be close to retiring. To find out who these people are, you must establish a contact within the company. If you already know someone who is at the company, the best method is to simply ask her what people she knows who are fifty-five or older or who may be close to retirement.

If you don't know anyone in the company, then you need to get a company directory. Here are some ways to go about that:

- Ask the receptionist who are some people you can talk to about sales (easy to get), purchasing, service, company information, or something similar. Start calling these people or departments. As you develop prospects and build relationships within the company, ask if they would be comfortable sharing a directory with you.

- It may be possible to get a lead on a directory by checking the company's Web site.

- Many companies post the names of their top employees in the building directory, and you can get names that way.

- Check the local newspaper (especially the online version, which is searchable) for promotions and other announcements.

- You can purchase directories from leads brokers (see appendix).

The Contact

To be successful, you must be able to confidently explain why the prospect should transfer his retirement account to you through an IRA rollover, rather than keeping it at the company.

In most cases, some of the reasons are:

- With you, the prospect has more investment options.
- With you, he gets a professional advisor to help him.
- With you, his investment returns will probably be better than the amount he will receive from his company's defined-benefit plan.

You also should have a thorough understanding of the options, tax implications, and details of the rollover to succeed with this market.

Your calls to employees should include the following:

- Tell them that you have expertise in retirement plan options (and be sure you do).
- Tell them that you would like the opportunity to share with them the different retirement options they have.
- Ask about other people they know in the company who are approaching retirement age and who might want to know more about the options available to them.
- Ask about other people they know who would be interested in a seminar you are offering on the benefits of IRA rollovers. A seminar on IRA rollovers and preretirement options is a nonthreatening, easy way to meet potential prospects and to share your expertise.

You can also send relevant mailers to targeted employees at work (approximately ten per week) with an offer to help them evaluate their retirement options; follow up with a phone call.

The Appointment

Follow these guidelines for your appointments with this group:

- If possible, include the person's spouse in the meeting.
- Keep your presentation simple. Most people in your target market know a good deal about their area of expertise but generally are not sophisticated in investments and their retirement options.
- If a portion or all of their retirement plan is in a defined-benefit plan, you can convince the couple how much more money they can accumulate through the IRA rollover than through the annuity the company provides. Note: They are also assuming a higher risk with the opportunity of a higher return.
- Explain that with a trusted advisor (you), the surviving spouse would

have someone to turn to for advice if anything were to happen to the retired employee.

- Always ask the prospect during the appointment who else he knows who is fifty-five or older and close to retiring. Once you acquire one client in the company, with his permission you can use him as an example of someone you have helped. Often a client will be an advocate within the company and will help you get in front of his friends at work. The more clients you have within the company, the more opportunity you will have.

This market is not easy to penetrate quickly, and you must spend time initially learning the IRA rollover rules and options, but once you develop the expertise and get a few clients within a targeted company, it can be very lucrative and worth the initial start-up time.

People Being "Downsized"

Individuals who have recently been laid off have money in motion, and they need help and guidance immediately. Their highest priority is dealing with their current retirement plan money, and they need to know the intricacies of IRA rollovers and their tax implications.

To be successful in this market, you should develop an expertise in helping laid-off employees with not only the financial issues, but other critical issues as well, such as how they find another job and whether they can afford to retire. If you do this, you can position yourself as the one resource who can help them with their entire situation, either directly or by referring them to other resources (which is also an excellent networking opportunity).

How to Find These People

You can generally find people who are being downsized in several ways:

- Establish a contact at a company that is downsizing. Also see if you can discover whether this company's plan allows lump-sum distributions.

- Get information from your existing clients and prospects. Ask your clients and prospects regularly for the names of associates who were recently laid off.

- Monitor your local papers for news of companies that are downsizing, and ask existing clients who work at those companies if there is anyone they know who might be affected.

- Work with counselors and services that assist employees who have been laid off. You can find these services in the Yellow Pages or get referrals from your HR contacts.

Making Yourself an Outside Expert to Specific Companies

Preparation is required to execute this market action plan effectively. You must develop an expertise in retirement distribution strategies, including NUA and IRA rollovers. You also need to target at least one large company in your area and become an expert in its particular retirement plan—the turnover among HR professionals is fairly high, so if you can establish yourself as the expert on a particular company's retirement plan, you will have great perceived value among the employees of that company and will have a natural "calling card."

Once you have developed the retirement expertise, have targeted the company you want to prospect, and have a good understanding of the company's retirement program, the next step is to build a base of prospects within the company as quickly as possible. The best way to do this is to establish relationships with centers of influence; each center of influence can introduce you to many new prospects inside the company.

Start this process by establishing contact with an insider who can provide you with a company directory, who can identify five or six coworkers who are five years from retirement, or who can help you identify the centers of influence. This means that you must initially be willing to educate employees who are retiring in five years—this may not result in much business initially, but it is an excellent way to build a base within the company and to build a strong foundation for future business. Employees five or more years from retirement are not heavily marketed to and are very appreciative of someone willing to invest time to educate them on their future retirement options.

Once you have identified five or six employees, have lunch with each one and discuss 401(k) allocation and your wealth-management process. In many cases, these employees may not have a lot of assets outside of their retirement plans and will appreciate your free advice on how to allocate their retirement assets. The key is to build relationships with these employees and ask them to refer you to other people who may need your help. Your objective over time is to be considered an insider by the retiring employees of the company.

Another excellent way to reach new prospects within the company is to invite your initial contacts to a preretirement seminar and give each of those prospects five or six seminar invitations to pass out to other preretirees in the company. This will greatly expand your contacts within the company. At each seminar, hand out response cards to set up the follow-up process. You will get people's e-mail addresses and be able to e-mail them with relevant market research, reports, and research on their company, and to set up initial meetings.

Once you have a number of prospects within the company, organizing fun events that are tied to their interests is an excellent way to build relationships and enhance your reputation. Examples are golf, fishing, holiday parties, and tailgate parties at sporting events.

Scripts

Mr./Ms. Prospect, my name is Joe Advisor, and I'm a financial advisor with XYZ Financial. I specialize in working with individuals who are fifty or older who are interested in knowing more about their retirement options. I would like to get together with you and share what we have at XYZ and how we can benefit you and your family. I will be in the area on Thursday and could work around your schedule. What time would be good for you? Is there anyone else you know who is close to retirement that you think I should talk to?

• • • • • • • • • • • •

Mr./Ms. Prospect, my name is Jane Advisor, and I'm a financial advisor with XYZ Financial. I specialize in working with individuals at ABC Company who are fifty or older and interested in knowing more about their retirement options. I am presenting a seminar on IRA rollovers and how they might benefit you next Thursday night at [time and place], and I wanted to invite you and your spouse to attend. Would you be interested? Can you think of anyone else that I should invite who would benefit from knowing more about what their retirement options are?

• • • • • • • • • • • •

Mr./Ms. HR Director, my name is Joe Advisor, and I'm a financial advisor at XYZ Financial. The purpose of my call is to offer your company a preretirement seminar that addresses the concerns and issues that employees who will be retiring in the next five years might have. There is no cost to your company, and we have had very good feedback on our past seminars. I would like to have the opportunity to review the outline with you; would you be interested?

CHAPTER 31

Retirees

In this chapter, I offer two primary marketing ideas for attracting the retiree market; one is to use seminars, and the other is to target retired military officers. I also offer a number of other easy-to-implement ideas.

Seminars

A key to attracting retirees is to recognize that they have the time to work with you and are interested in doing so, but they are reluctant to agree to an appointment without knowing you first. A seminar is an ideal way to position yourself as an expert and give the retiree an easy way to get to know you, making a follow-up appointment much easier. The seminar market action plan provides the techniques necessary to accomplish this.

The place to start is by gathering names. I recommend that you use a list broker to generate a list of prescreened names (see the appendix). For example, you might ask for retirees who have annual incomes over $100,000. Make sure that you screen out names that are on the Do Not Call list in advance of calling them.

Contact retirees personally and invite them to a seminar that is tailored to them, with a free meal included. Raise their interest in attending by telling them how the seminar will benefit them. Follow up the contact with a written invitation, and then a reminder the day before the seminar.

The ideal time for a seminar is from 9:30 a.m. to 10:30 a.m., and you should hold it at a well-known location. Serve coffee and donuts before the seminar and offer brunch after so that you will have a chance to socialize with the attendees.

There are many seminar topics that will be of interest to retirees, such as "The Recent Tax Law Changes and What They Mean to Your Investment Strategy." Break the seminar into two parts: In the first part, present the facts, and in the second part, give the audience three or four ideas or strategies to use. Each part should last between fifteen and twenty minutes.

End the seminar by stating that you would like to meet with each of them to discuss their individual situations, and state that the only price of admission is to accept your follow-up call. If you follow up, a seminar will generate a minimum of one $250,000 client per event.

Retired Military Officers

In the military, it takes twenty years to get a pension, which is why many forty-two-year-olds retire from military service and start another career; when they retire again, they have a double pension. Many of these people spend time at local VFWs or American Legion Clubs. If not members themselves, many have a senior family member who is.

There are two approaches to this pension group: You can advertise as a retirement specialist in one of the veterans association newsletters, or you can host a seminar on "How to Make the Most of Your Retirement Plan." See the appendix for information on finding these people.

Other Proven Strategies

- Contact the recreational directors of retirement communities and assisted-living facilities (not nursing homes), and offer to provide a seminar or a series of classes on investment topics that would be of interest to their residents.

- Referrals are another good way to get in front of retirees. Ask existing clients, prospects, and CPAs for introductions to other retirees.

- Host events for your retired existing clients centered around activities like golf, wine tasting, or cooking classes; ask your retired clients to bring along a retired friend.

- Look for specific clubs and organizations for retirees and offer to speak to them. Many companies have well-organized groups of retirees; an example is the "pioneers" of the Baby Bell companies. Identify these retiree groups and provide investment information through seminars with good follow-up. You can also organize a retirees' group yourself. I've seen this done with excellent results.

- Build a network of influencers, then invite the members of your network to a golf outing and ask them to invite their best retired clients; or present joint seminars to retirees with the CPAs and attorneys in your network. This is a great way to help CPAs and attorneys get comfortable referring their retired clients to you.

Invitation Scripts

Mr./Ms. Prospect, this is Joe Advisor with XYZ Financial. The reason for my call is that I want to invite you to a free seminar and brunch on the tax law changes and how they will affect your retirement plan. Do you currently have any retirement accounts?

If the answer is yes, then:

We have noticed that with many of our retired clients, there is some confusion as to how the tax law has affected mandatory distributions and beneficiary designations, which are topics that we will be going over in our seminar. Would you be interested in attending?

• • • • • • • • • • •

Mr./Ms. Retiree, my name is Joe Advisor, and I'm a financial advisor at XYZ Financial. I am calling you because I am conducting a free seminar on investment issues that affect retirees. The seminar will be held at ——— hotel next Thursday, and breakfast will be included. Would you be interested in attending?

• • • • • • • • • • •

Mr./Ms. Recreational Director, my name is Joe Advisor, and I'm a financial advisor at XYZ Financial. The purpose of my call is to offer your community a special talk that is tailored to the retired investor. Our talks are timely and informative, and we have had excellent feedback on our past programs. I want to ask if you would like the opportunity to review the talk with me to see if there would be an interest on your part.

• • • • • • • • • • •

Mr./Ms. Retiree, my name is Jane Advisor, and I'm with XYZ Financial. I wanted to personally invite you to a seminar that addresses three issues that retirees are concerned about:
1. Inflation
2. Taxes
3. Fees

The seminar is (date, time, location). Would you be interested in attending?

CHAPTER 32

Money in Motion

Money in motion refers to larger sums of money flowing into an affluent individual's life because of a change in her personal or professional circumstances. Examples of this are flows resulting from mergers and acquisitions, a high-level executive leaving a company, receiving an inheritance, a divorce from an affluent spouse, and the death of an affluent spouse. Each of these changes of circumstances generates money in motion, and this market action plan is designed to position you to compete for this money.

If you decide that you want to pursue this market action plan, be prepared to spend the time necessary to develop your expertise. This market is highly competitive. Your knowledge must be specialized, particularly in the areas of mergers and acquisitions, senior executive changes, and Rule 144 transactions. If you don't have the right level of expertise, it will be obvious, and you will be wasting your time.

An Example of the General Approach

Each change of circumstance requires a specific approach, but the overall method is very similar in most cases. To illustrate, let's say there is a business owner whose business is being bought or merged with.

When the news of the merger or acquisition becomes public and you become aware of it, you must move very quickly—if you know about it, chances are your competition does too. Your chances of getting through to the decision maker are much higher if you are among the first to make contact (by phone or overnight package) than if you are the twenty-fifth to do so. The day you become aware of the transaction, ship a package overnight.

The same day, make a call to the prospect. If the prospect does not return your first phone call but sees your name and then gets an overnight package from you, when you make a follow-up phone call two days later, your name will stand out, and he may talk to you.

Keep up your efforts because your competitors can be easily discouraged by the prospect's lack of response, and they will stop their marketing efforts. Eventually the prospect will take your call if you are persistent, if only to tell you that he is not interested. If you have enough of these opportunities outstanding, you will eventually have the opportunity to present to your targeted prospects. Your goal is to get a face-to-face meeting where you can gather information, and where you can impress the prospect with your expertise and your ability to positively affect his situation.

You can use this same process with senior executives who are leaving or retiring from their company, people receiving large inheritances, individuals in divorce situations, and people involved in Rule 144 transactions.

Prepare and Customize

Preparation is essential. You must prepare and organize your different letters and packages in advance of the event. The first and last paragraphs should be customized to the particular situation, but the body of the letter can be the same, depending on the type of money-in-motion event. Also determine the sequence of the packages in advance and customize it as needed.

Here are my specific recommendations for the different types of money-in-motion situations.

Mergers and Acquisitions

Bloomberg is a good source of information on merger and acquisition (M&A) transactions. You can filter by geography, and you can get all the information about the transaction and the individuals involved. The main advantage of Bloomberg is the timeliness of the information; it is available the day the transaction occurs. Also useful are industry-specific trade publications; you can find these in the library or on the Internet. The advantage of both of these sources is that they are not as frequently used and often give you the information before your competition gets it; this is particularly true for smaller transactions.

It's important that you focus on a couple of industries and really specialize in them so that you can stay on top of money-in-motion opportunities. As an example, one advisor who committed to this market action plan was able to uncover as many as twenty-five money-in-motion opportunities every day.

Executive Departures

A senior executive leaving a public company is another excellent money-in-motion opportunity and one that is not as heavily prospected as M&A transactions. Executives who change jobs face IRA rollover and stock option consequences (in some cases, they must exercise their options within ninety days of leaving a company). Executives have less loyalty to their former companies after they leave and are more willing to diversify out of their concentrated positions.

If an executive is retiring, she has more time to evaluate different options and will definitely be receptive to diversification. The role of the advisor also becomes more important, because the advisor becomes the retiree's main connection to the business world and to the information she is interested in. Executives will appreciate you more after they retire than they did before.

The best sources of leads for executives who are leaving or retiring are the local newspaper, Bloomberg, and trade journals. This is where specialization in an industry is especially important because you can more easily be aware of the changes going on in that industry.

Rule 144 Transactions

You can easily identify Rule 144 transactions through a number of different sources, such as www.freeedgar.com. When an executive or past owner sells a block of stock, this triggers a number of different opportunities for you to provide your expertise (tax liability, planning, diversification, and so on). The marketing process described in mergers and acquisitions can and should be followed in Rule 144 transactions.

Inheritances and Divorce

You can find money involved in inheritance transactions by examining state records of probated wills with more than a predetermined amount of money over the past twelve months. You can find divorce filings the same way; it is logical that a divorcee would be interested in having a financial advisor other than the former spouse's. Developing a network of estate and divorce attorneys as described in the previous chapter is an excellent way to get in front of affluent prospects who are receiving inheritances or getting a divorce.

Death

You need to handle the death of an affluent individual very carefully. The best source of information is your network of influencers (CPAs and estate attorneys). Alternatively, follow up with the surviving spouse six months after the death—it typically takes nine months for an estate to settle, and calling after six months takes much of the emotion out of the call and still leaves three months for tax arrangements.

Home Sale

When someone buys or sells a home, large sums of money are in motion. These transactions are a matter of public record and can be easily identified (see the appendix for sources). You can filter this list by dollar amount and date. You have opportunities on both the seller's and the buyer's side (buyers are also often new to the area). These real estate transactions are often listed in local newspapers.

Executive Relocations

All executives who are transferring need a source of services in their new location, and this marketing technique will set you apart from your competition. Scan the local business journal and newspapers in your market for announcements of corporate executives who are relocating to the area. Overnight the most recent copy of the "Best Of" (lists published by local papers giving the best services, restaurants, professionals, and other such providers in your area) to these relocating executives, along with a personalized note introducing yourself. Follow up with a phone call, preferably to where the executive works. Developing a network with successful Realtors® will also help you identify relocating executives. Good Realtors are experts at identifying relocations.

Scripts

Mr./Ms. Business Owner, my name is Joe Advisor, and I'm an advisor with XYZ Financial with experience in working with individuals like you who have had a significant change of circumstances. Hopefully you got the package I sent you that outlines our experience and approach. I would encourage you to give me the opportunity to meet with you and your advisors at your earliest convenience to share our approach and how we could help you.

· · · · · · · · · · · ·

Mr./Ms. Executive, my name is Jane Advisor. I'm an advisor with XYZ Financial, and I have developed an expertise in working with senior executives like you. In changing firms, I'm sure you are considering different alternatives for dealing with the stock and options from your former company. I sent you a package that outlines our approach, expertise, and experience, and I would appreciate having the opportunity to schedule an appointment with you to share what we do and how that can benefit you. When would be the earliest we could get together?

· · · · · · · · · · · ·

Mr./Ms. Retiring Executive, my name is Joe Advisor. I am an advisor with XYZ Financial, and I have built [am building] my business working with retired senior executives. I sent you a package that outlines our approach, expertise, and experience, and given your change of circumstances, I believe we could give you excellent investment guidance. I would appreciate the opportunity to meet with you at your earliest convenience to share our approach and how we could help you.

· · · · · · · · · · · ·

Mr./Ms. Rule 144 Transaction, my name is Jane Advisor, and I'm an advisor at XYZ Financial. I have experience working with executives involved in Rule 144 transactions. Our firm is highly ranked on the execution of large blocks of your company's stock, which reflects our ability to get you an excellent execution price on your stock. Additionally, we offer many products and services that could have a positive impact on your tax liability and investment performance. I would encourage you to give me the opportunity to meet with you at your earliest convenience to share our approach and how we could help you.

· · · · · · · · · · · ·

Mr./Ms. Inheritor, my name is Joe Advisor, and I'm an advisor at XYZ Financial with experience working with individuals who have had a significant change of circumstances. I sent you a package that outlines our approach and expertise, and given your change of circumstances, I believe I could provide you with strong resources and excellent guidance. I would like to meet with you at your earliest convenience so that I can share our approach and provide you with specifics on how we could help you. Would you be available to meet next week?

• • • • • • • • • • •

Mr./Ms. Divorcee, my name is Jane Advisor, and I'm an advisor at XYZ Financial. I have spent a great deal of time working with people in your circumstances and have developed an expertise on the issues involved in your recent [current] divorce. I understand that you might want a second opinion apart from that of your former spouse's advisor, and I want to offer that to you. If I could meet with you in the near future and find out the specifics of your circumstances, I'm sure I could provide you with valuable guidance. Would you be available for an appointment this week?

• • • • • • • • • • •

Mr./Ms. Widower/Widow, my name is Jane Advisor, and I'm an advisor at XYZ Financial. I understand that during the past six months, you have lost your spouse. First, I want to offer my condolences, and second, I want to make my advice and experience available to you. I understand the financial issues you are facing, and I know I could make a positive difference in your situation. Are you available for an appointment next week where I could learn the specifics of your circumstances and provide you guidance?

Mortgages

There are five avenues for marketing mortgage products:

1. Realtor and builder networks
2. CPAs
3. Human resources directors
4. Client referrals
5. Individuals

Realtor and Builder Networks

The idea here is to create a network of builders and Realtors whose clients are best served by unique mortgage offerings. Let's first cover how to do this with Realtors. Both Realtors and builders are excellent referral sources for money in motion opportunities.

Identify High-End Realtors in Your Market

There are four good ways to identify high-end Realtors:

1. Use an Internet search engine (e.g., Google) to search for real estate companies in a certain city or region, or use the Internet phone directories listed in the appendix (such as whitepages.com) and search for the business category "Realtors."
2. Look for real estate guides in your local Sunday paper and in free literature distributions. Agents who can afford advertising are generally more successful.
3. Join or subscribe to the National Association of Realtors, and use its Web site to find contacts.
4. Read Realtor magazine for information on Realtors.

Establish a Connection

Once you have made your list of top Realtors, build a strong network with two to four of them, with their primary loan source being your mortgage product. Do this the following way: Call the Realtors on your list and identify yourself as a specialist in the needs of affluent investors, and specifically in their lending needs; tell the Realtor that you are calling him because you have some unique and very attractive mortgage financing that you know would appeal to his best clients, and that you would like to share the specifics with him. When you meet with your Realtor network, share with them how your innovative mortgage products could help them sell high-end homes by lowering their clients' borrowing costs and, therefore, their monthly payments.

It's important to stay in touch with the Realtors in your network at least monthly to continue to solidify and further develop your relationship with them. Your Realtor network can give you access to:

- Clients who are relocating from other areas of the country and need a financial advisor in their new location
- Clients who are selling or downsizing to a smaller home and could have money to invest
  Clients who are buying larger homes and may be affluent investors

Do the Same with Builders

Your objective with builders is the same as with Realtors: to create a network of two to four builders and to stay in touch with that network monthly. To identify the top builders in your marketplace:

- Search the Web. The best Web site for this is www.homebuilder.com.
- Gather information from the signs on the highest-end custom homes, from home and builder advertisements, and by using your Realtor network.

Approach builders the same way you did Realtors: Explain your experience with the affluent market and your expertise in liability management, and share with them that you can offer their potential clients innovative and very competitive construction financing. Buzzwords about attractive pricing and ease of closing let the builder know that you have a strong product. Lower-rate mortgage options mean that purchasers can borrow more money, which means that the builder can draw up a larger contract. Give the builders information on the construction-loan program, and your business card.

Builders want their clients to finance the construction phase so that they do not have to tie up their own capital or warehouse lines. Thus, they always need some form of lending resource to refer clients to, and typically they will refer them to the most competitive program. If the builder can sell more homes through your lower-cost financing options, he will be eager to partner with you. This relationship can lead to other business as well, such as investment business from the home purchasers you meet and from the builders themselves.

Builders benefit when their clients are comfortable with the mortgage obligation because this will eliminate potential decreases or cutbacks in the project and may provide opportunities for upgrades. The better the structure and the more comfortable the client is with the financing, the more open she will be to enhanced construction terms.

This approach with Realtors and builders has been used by one advisor with three years length of service who generated $52 million in mortgage origination business, resulting in $470,000 in business and add-on business from new mortgage clients.

CPAs

CPAs are typically one of our best mortgage referral sources because they understand the value of innovative mortgage products for their clients. This especially holds true for those clients who are business owners and self-employed individuals. Share with CPAs examples of your innovative mortgage offerings.

Client Referrals

Ask for referrals from clients who have done mortgages through you. You can do this by simply asking, "Who do you know who might be interested in lowering their monthly mortgage payments, or locking in low rates with attractive refinancing costs?"

Individuals

County Clerk and Recorder's Offices

Every mortgage in every county is a matter of public record. You can track down specific information such as addresses of properties, lien information, and property owners' names through the county clerk and recorder's offices. This information is available to anyone. This is an excellent way to identify qualified individual homeowners, and you can then contact them directly and share your offerings with them. I recommend that you obtain individuals' work numbers whenever possible to avoid nonsolicitation regulations.

Title Companies

This is the most reliable source for information on properties and property owners. Title companies can provide lists of properties on which they have pulled title in specific areas. These lists identify the interest rates being paid, which you can turn into a good target list for refinancing opportunities. Many financial advisors have been successful in marketing to a specific geographic area by using leads lists generated by title companies—these lists allow you to market effectively to high-net-worth households or for larger loans. In addition, any title vesting in a trust, corporation, or partnership will provide the potential for cross-selling. Many firms can identify by county, by loan amount, and even by the vesting of title (trusts, LLCs, and so on). You can build a strong information-sharing relationship with title companies because you can refer business to each other.

Scripts

For Contacting Realtors

Mr./Ms. Realtor, my name is Joe Advisor, and I am a financial advisor at XYZ Financial. You have been identified as one of the most successful Realtors in this market, and I would like to help you increase your million-dollar home sales through an innovative mortgage product. I work with affluent individuals and have experience providing innovative liability products to them, and I like having a source to refer my clients to for any real estate needs they may have. I would like to have the opportunity to share the details with you. Would you have time to meet with me on Thursday?

Presenting innovative mortgage products can help Realtors sell larger homes because of the lower payments. You can work this idea into your script this way:

We have a unique program that allows our clients to borrow in the _____ percent range. This allows clients to maximize their monthly cash flow and feel more comfortable with a potentially larger mortgage obligation.

The idea behind this is to show that your products can help the real estate agent sell houses. This is sensitive to the rate environment.

For Contacting Builders

Mr./Ms. Builder, my name is Joe Advisor, and I am a financial advisor at XYZ Financial. I work with affluent individuals and have experience in providing innovative liability products to them. I am calling to tell you about our construction-to-permanent-financing program. Our construction program is one of the most competitive in the market. In addition, our pricing has allowed a number of clients to leverage more of the debt and build a larger property. I can help you increase your higher-end home sales through this product, and I would like to have the opportunity to share the details with you. Would you be available this Thursday?

For Contacting CPAs

Mr./Ms. CPA, my name is Joe Advisor, and I am a financial advisor with XYZ Financial. I work with affluent individuals and have experience in providing them with innovative liability solutions, specifically mortgages. I can help you show your clients how to increase their cash flow by lowering their monthly mortgage payments or locking in attractive long-term rates. I would like to have the opportunity to share the details with you. Would you be available this Thursday for a short meeting?

or,

Hello, my name is Joe Advisor, and I am a financial advisor at XYZ Financial. I wanted to take the opportunity to tell you about some of our creative liability-management strategies that may complement your clients' tax-management strategies. We offer a variety of programs that center on enhancing deductibility, managing personal cash flow, and allowing for flexibility in the repayment of the debt. Would you be available this Thursday for a short meeting?

For Contacting Clients About Referrals

Mr./Ms. Client, I hope you are pleased with the refinancing you did with us this year. I wanted to ask you if you know anyone that you could introduce me to who might be interested in lowering their interest rate and monthly payments.

For Contacting Prospects

Mr./Ms. Prospect, this is Joe Advisor at XYZ Financial, and I specialize in mortgages. I work with affluent individuals who are interested in innovative mortgage products that can potentially make a significant difference in their mortgage payments. Would you be interested in details on this?

If the answer is yes, then:

I would like the opportunity to meet with you to discuss your current mortgage and share in detail how I can help you.

For Contacting a Title Company

Mr./Ms. Title Company Prospect, my name is Joe Advisor, and I'm a financial advisor with XYZ Financial specializing in offering homeowners innovative products that can significantly lower their mortgage payments. I am interested in networking with a title company in a way that would be mutually beneficial. Would you be available next week to meet with me to discuss the details?

CHAPTER 34

Nonprofits

Developing business through philanthropies is a natural approach to the high-net-worth market. Many high-net-worth clients are philanthropic; they may be philanthropic because they feel they can make a difference in society, or they may be philanthropic because the U.S. tax code rewards them with tax credits, or both.

Charitable contributions are tax deductible, and financial advisors can assist clients in a variety of ways in planning the best ways to give. Many high-net-worth clients employ strategies such as charitable remainder trusts, charitable lead trusts, private family foundations, donor-advised funds, and appreciated securities gifting. The beneficiaries of many of these strategies are public and private charities.

Financial advisors have two opportunities:

1. Affluent client relationships with board members and other community leaders
2. Management of a nonprofit's assets

These are not mutually exclusive, as you can do both at the same time and have individual clients who participate in both aspects of your business. However, you need to understand that prospecting within nonprofits effectively can have a longer lead time than other market action plans. Because of this, I recommend that only a portion of your marketing efforts be directed toward nonprofits.

Be Prepared and Be Organized

If you are to be successful in this area, you must understand how nonprofits create investment policy, and how they manage their investments and monitor the performance of those investments. You must understand what nonprofits are looking for, who your competition is, and which products and services are offered in this market. If you target large-market nonprofits, you will also need a high level of expertise—the competition for the business of these organizations is fierce, and most of your competitors will have either their Chartered Institute of Management Accountants certification (CIMA) or their Investment Management Consulting Association (IMCA) certification. You can find out how to get these by visiting the Web sites of these organizations (please see the appendix). Some financial services firms offer special training that leads to these certifications.

No matter how you choose to approach this market, you will be more successful if you are organized and gather the preliminary information that you will need:

1. Find out which nonprofit organizations are located in your area. The local chamber of commerce is an excellent place to start gathering this information. Some chambers of commerce even publish a "volunteer directory" that lists all the philanthropic organizations in the community.

2. Put together a binder of all the nonprofit organizations in your market. This will be your book for data and planning.

3. Gather as much information as you can about each of your targeted organizations. One way to do this is to enter the name of the organization into GuideStar.com, which will give you the organization's board members and largest contributors. Another way is to visit the Web site for each organization. You need to know:

   • The mission of the organization

   • Names, addresses, and phone numbers of board members, executive committee members, and officers

   • Names, addresses, and phone numbers of fund-raising and finance committee members

   • Names of significant donors (contributors who give $5,000 or more, which usually includes board members)

   • Location of current assets

   • Size of the endowment

   • Major fund-raising events and calendar

   • Affiliations with other financial organizations (events sponsored by competitors)

- Brochures and newsletters.
4. Categorize each of the nonprofits in your list by type:
   A. Large-market nonprofits; includes large-market public charities, public colleges or universities, and large private colleges
   B. Small-market public charities, including community colleges and small private colleges
   C. Private charities

Developing Affluent Client Relationships with Board Members

In recent years, philanthropists have been taking a more active role in the organizations to which they give and may often be active members of the boards of directors. In many cases, the opportunity to manage an endowment account does not exist; instead, the business opportunity is strictly networking with board members and other community leaders who are involved with the organization. They are prospects for both your firm's wealth-management services and its expertise in charitable giving strategies.

Although you should have a minimum account level for individual accounts, a small endowment account could lead to affluent relationships.

There are three good ways to acquire affluent relationships with board members of nonprofits:

1. Get on the board of a nonprofit.
2. Become a member of your regional council of foundations.
3. Direct contact.

Get on the Board of a Nonprofit

At the beginning of this market action plan, I recommended that you identify all the nonprofits in your market area, research them and make a list of names, and categorize the organizations by type. Take the list of people you developed and now do the following:

1. Cross-reference your list of people (top donors and board members) across all the organizations on your list to determine which individuals are on multiple boards and multiple donor lists. This overlap list becomes your target list (150 to 200 names is optimal).

2. Make a list of the nonprofit organizations that would give you the best exposure to the largest numbers of people on your target list, and that you could afford to belong to (most nonprofits have minimum commitment levels that you must meet in order to serve on the board of directors).

3. Narrow your list to organizations that you have a true interest in—it would be difficult to spend sufficient time and energy on an organization otherwise.

4. Become a member of one organization in each category and take a leadership position. Leadership is essential to making this strategy work, because if you do not become a leader, your efforts may go unnoticed. (Being on the board is the ideal, but if you cannot meet the minimum level of financial commitment necessary to be on the board, there are other volunteer leadership roles you can take.)

5. Once you are on the board, take a leadership role. Show that you are smart and that you are a leader. The objective is to get on the finance committee, where your expertise will show. For female advisors, it is especially important that you aspire to board positions rather than organizing social events and galas. It is important to hold your own, be willing to work through questions, and emerge as a legitimate, contributing leader of the organization.

6. After establishing a strong reputation as a leader within the board, the next step is to use your firm's expertise to help your organization. Most financial service firms have expertise in philanthropic areas and can provide ideas on raising money through charitable remainder trusts, charitable lead trusts, appreciated stock, and other such strategies. Hold a luncheon for the directors of development on how to raise money. Bring in your firm's experts (or provide this information yourself if you have the expertise) on appreciated stock gifts, charitable remainder trusts, and charitable lead trusts, and how these can save donors money. You can introduce the luncheon by saying,

> I want to help you leverage the resources I have to help us raise money for this organization [the nonprofit]. My clients are wealthy individuals, and philanthropy is a high priority for them—they want to give money away to charities they believe in and reap the benefits of charitable giving. If you know of individuals who need my expertise, let me know, and my firm and I can help them. I would like to introduce our expert who will share with you some insights that can help us raise money for this organization.

7. Identify board members who could be potential clients and focus on building a relationship with them. Invite each of them, and their spouse, to dinner, identify their interests, and find activities you can do with them that are fun. Your objective is to build relationships with wealthy individuals with whom you have a common philanthropic interest. Over time, as you build the relationship, you will be invited into their social circles, and you will meet other affluent individuals. During the course of developing relationships with them, their investment situation will come up or they will ask questions about investments. Let them initiate the conversation; typically it may be, "I have an advisor I have worked with for a long time, and I feel good about our relationship," or, "I feel I am well taken care of." This is your opening to make the following statement: "I am serious about growing my business in the community, and if you are ever considering a change or want to know more about our practice, I would be happy to spend a few minutes with you to share what we do," or, "If you want a second opinion, I would be happy to share how we work with our clients," or, "If you know someone who might be interested in learning about our approach, please let me know."

Become a Member of Your Regional Council of Foundations

Most of these councils give you a chance to get to know both the director of the council and the members who are the decision makers for foundation dollars—these decision makers manage the large pools of nonprofit money. Examples of these decision makers are members of the investment committee of nonprofit organizations ($50 million to $200 million is often the sweet spot), members of the board of directors of police and firemen's pension funds, and board members of municipal defined-benefits plans. Develop your target list, determine who the decision makers are, and begin to develop a personal relationship that could lead to a business relationship using the techniques described in "Getting on the Board of a Nonprofit."

Direct Contact

In most cases, it is probably safe to assume that the individuals who serve on the boards of nonprofits are wealthy individuals who also give large sums of money to charity (often the charities on whose boards they serve). Once you know exactly who these individuals are and how to reach them, you can contact them directly and introduce yourself. Note that some of the individuals on your list will be those who actually started the nonprofit organization. Here is a sample script:

> Mr./Ms. Board Member, this is Joe Advisor, and I am a financial advisor at XYZ Financial. I specialize in giving wealthy individuals access to our advanced tools for increasing the effectiveness of their trust and private planning. Would you be open to meeting with me so that I could show you how we have helped others?

Nonprofit Asset Management

Large-Market Nonprofits

The asset management decisions of these organizations are almost always made by committee and are often turned over to an outside consultant. There are two paths you can take with these organizations (and you can do both, and at the same time):

1. *Organizations seeking proposals.* Part of the fiduciary responsibility that all nonprofits have is to check the marketplace periodically to ensure that they are aware of the available offerings and their pricing. Call your list of nonprofits, endowments, foundations, municipalities, Taft-Hartley plans, and police and firemen's retirement plans, and ask if they are actively searching for a consultant now or will be in the near future. If they are currently searching, you should ask how to submit a proposal. Even if they are not currently searching, you should check back with them every six to nine months because change is constant in this market and you want the opportunity to compete whenever you can. If you submit ten proposals, you have a good chance of making the final cut four times and winning the bid once. As long as you offer a competitive product and have the expertise, you have a chance of winning.

2. *Any other nonprofit organizations you are interested in.* In most of these large organizations, an investment committee makes the decisions, and there is a CFO or business manager who handles the day-to-day operation of the endowment—the CFO or the business manager is the person you want to reach. In my experience, the easiest way to find this person is to call the main number of the nonprofit and ask to speak with whoever handles the endowment. These organizations get these calls daily— not just from solicitors, but also from people wishing to make grants or contributions. Once you have the decision maker on the phone, try this script:

Mr./Ms. Decision Maker, this is Joe Advisor, and I am a financial advisor with XYZ Financial. We have found that we can help nonprofits get better returns and, in many cases, at a lower cost. I would like to have the opportunity to meet with you to find out more about your situation, so that I could potentially improve your returns at a lower cost. Could we schedule some time to meet?

Remember, all you want is a meeting. At the meeting, you can move into a discussion of your firm's competitive advantages.

Small Municipality Funds and Police and Firemen's Defined-Benefit Retirement Funds

These are good leads to pursue. Generally, they fall into the $20 million to $100 million category, and they are often below the radar screen of institutional competitors. If you have the expertise and the product line, you can easily find yourself at the top of the competition with this group. Call the targeted municipality and ask for its annual report; they will send you the report, and that report will list how much the target has in its retirement funds (police and firemen included), and who the board members and investment committee members are. Contact the targeted municipality or retirement fund and use the same marketing process as described in "Large-Market Nonprofits."

Scripts for Finding Out If a Nonprofit Is Seeking Proposals

Mr./Ms. Prospect, my name is Joe Advisor, and I'm a financial advisor at XYZ Financial. I am a CIMA [assuming you are one], and I specialize in working with [nonprofit/retirement] funds like yours. I am calling to ask if you are in an active search for a consultant.

If the answer is no, then:

May I ask who you are currently using to manage your endowment? When do you anticipate that you will be in an active search? I'd like the opportunity to keep XYZ Financial in front of you—when would be a good time for me to check back with you?

If the answer is yes, then:

I would like to have the opportunity to meet with you and find out more about your plan so that I can have the background information to provide a competitive proposal. I will be in your area on Thursday; could we meet sometime that day?

Small-Market Public Charities, Community Colleges, and Small Private Colleges

Traditionally, local banks have dominated this market ($1 million to $25 million in assets), but they are often limited to tools such as money market accounts and CDs. You, on the other hand, can offer much more and can make a big difference in the work these nonprofits do.

Unlike the large nonprofits, these smaller nonprofits rarely have an investment committee. Two people usually run all the finances: the executive director and the board treasurer. Since the executive director is the only one of these two that is a full-time position, I would suggest starting with a call to her:

> Mr./Ms. Prospect, this is Joe Advisor, and I am a financial advisor with XYZ Financial specializing in strategies for smaller nonprofit organizations. We have found that your industry has traditionally not had access to many of the services and instruments used by the largest nonprofit organizations. XYZ Financial specializes in philanthropic services, and we specifically assist organizations like yours. Would you mind if I come out and show you how this works?

Once you have the appointment, you can share with the executive director your firm's services that meet the needs of nonprofits.

Private Charities

Investment Policy Statements

You may find that smaller (and newer) nonprofit organizations are an easier place to start for two reasons: (1) it is generally easier to get a meeting with smaller or newer organizations because they may have a less clearly defined investment policy statement; (2) helping them develop such a policy statement can be a good place to start the relationship.

Start by offering to share your expertise. For example, offer to help the charity develop its investment policy guidelines, and to consult to the finance committee regarding what investments would fulfill the charity's long-term and short-term objectives. In these capacities, you will clearly be acting as a consultant and adding value; this sets you apart as being a leader and facilitator. An appointment should not be hard to get if you offer to lend your expertise at no initial cost.

Board Member Education

You can also begin a relationship with small (and large) nonprofits by offering to educate the board of directors. Since boards are charged with raising money, you can usually get an audience with the board to educate it about charitable trusts. This has the dual purpose of helping board members think about creative ways to approach potential donors and establishing you as an estate planning expert, which could result in business from the individual board members. I know of an example where an advisor spent a great deal of time educating the board of a small nonprofit on their investments (mostly CDs). One of the board members was so impressed, he asked that she handle his personal multimillion-dollar account.

Appendix: Resources

Here are some of the better sources of names for your market action plans. These are grouped into categories so that you can more readily see how each source is applicable to your needs, and the market action plans they can be useful in are also listed. You may want to take some time to look through the entire list of sources and note the ones you want to explore further.

General and Mixed Sources

These sources provide both commercial and consumer information or both general and specialized information.

Bank Directors

Applies to Chapter 24. A list of directors can often be found on specific bank Web sites.

Buy List Online

www.buylistonline.com
Applies to Chapters 20, 24, 25, 26, 27, 28, 29, 30, 31, 32, and 33.
This fee-based site offers business and consumer mailing lists and information, including such things as revenues and revenue history, lines of business, contact data, property value, age range, home value, and gender.

Corporate, Association, and Country Club Directory

www.elusiveleads.com
Applies to Chapters 20, 22, 25, 26, 27, 28, 29, 30, 31, and 32.
This is a phone directory for corporate employees, association members, country club members, university alumni, and other such groups. It often includes direct dial numbers and e-mail addresses.

Free Erisa

www.freeerisa.com
Applies to Chapters 20, 26, and 30.

This Web site provides information from 5500 filings and includes the value of the assets in the plan, annual contributions, the office manager and his phone number, and the names of partners. You can then visit the Web sites of the individual practices for the names of the individual plan members and their phone numbers.

Go Leads

www.goleads.com
Applies to Chapters 20, 24, 25, 26, 27, 28, 29, 30, 31, 32, and 33.
This fee-based site offers low-cost leads for businesses and consumers: names, addresses, phone numbers, number of employees, value of house, and other such information. Filters let you customize a list.

InfoUSA

www.infousa.com
Applies to Chapters 20, 24, 25, 26, 27, 28, 29, 30, 32, and 33.
This fee-based site is an excellent source of names of business owners, names of executives, number of employees, revenues, lines of business, and other such information, and of consumers by name, address, and so on. The site has comprehensive filters. You can search by location, industry code, revenues, employees, key individuals, address, phone number, or other field. Some databases are available in public libraries.

Internet White Pages

www.whitepages.com
www.switchboard.com
www.superpages.com
Applies to Chapters 20, 24, 26, 27, 28, 29, 30, 31, 32, and 33.
You can use these sources to find residential addresses and phone numbers for names. You can also get reverse information: Looking up a phone number will retrieve the person's name and address, and looking up the address will retrieve the person's name and phone number.

Internet Yellow Pages

www.switchboard.com
www.yellowpages.com
www.superpages.com
Applies to Chapters 20, 24, 25, 26, 28, 29, 30, 31, 32, and 33.
Use these sources to find businesses in your area by category, including business names, addresses, and phone numbers. In some cases, the business owner's name is included. The following categories are available:

- Attorneys
- Bankers

- Churches and synagogues
- CPAs
- Home builders
- Medical professionals
- Mortgage brokers
- Nonprofit organizations
- Real estate professionals, Realtors
- Retirement or retiree communities and associations
- YMCAs or YWCAs

Larkspur Data

www.larkspurdata.com
Applies to Chapters 20, 24, 25, 26, 27, 28, 29, 30, 31, 32, and 33.
This site offers databases (for a fee) on high-net-worth individuals and company retirement plans. You can search by all the usual fields you would expect, but also by many unique fields, such as yacht ownership or purchase.

Local Newspapers

www.newspaperlinks.com/voyager.cfm
Applies to Chapters 20, 22, 24, 25, 26, 27, 28, 29, 30, 31, 32, and 33.
Choose your newspaper at this site, which is a listing (searchable by state) of media sources and news sources.

Use this source to find:

- Businessmen and women who have been recognized or promoted or who have relocated
- Networking clubs and speaking opportunities
- News on local companies, individuals, and events
- Real estate transactions and listings, and advertisements from brokers and agents

Marquis Who's Who

www.marquiswhoswho.com
Applies to Chapters 20, 22, 24, 25, 26, 27, 28, 29, 30, and 32.
This source contains a list of influential men and women, including extensive biographies and home and work addresses. Entries are listed both alphabetically and by geography. Separate databases include only women, attorneys, medical professionals, or business professionals. This source is also available in public libraries. Use it to find:

- Executives
- Successful attorneys

- Successful medical professionals
- Successful women

Pension Planet

www.pensionplanet.com
Applies to Chapters 20, 26, and 30.
This source maintains the largest and most timely database of qualified retirement plans and qualified health and welfare plans available anywhere. It is provided by individuals who are experienced in the design, administration, and investment management of qualified retirement plans.

Search Engines

http://news.google.com
www.google.com
www.metacrawler.com
www.yahoo.com
Applies to Chapters 20, 22, 24, 25, 26, 27, 28, 29, 30, 31, 32, and 33.
    Use these sources to search for groups such as:

- Asian American newspapers
- Associations and association news
- Attorneys
- Churches and synagogues
- Company news (promotions, layoffs, and other such information)
- CPAs
- Hispanic newspapers
- Home builders
- Medical professionals and professors
- Names of and news on executives and business owners
- Realtors
- Retirees
- Teaching hospitals and hospital staff
- YMCAs/YWCAs

Search Systems—Public Records Online

www.searchsystems.net
Applies to Chapters 20, 25, 26, 27, 28, 29, 30, 31, 32, and 33.
This fee-based site offers business information, corporate filings, property records, deeds, mortgages, criminal and civil court filings, births, deaths, marriages, unclaimed property, professional licenses, money in motion, and other such information—it has all the public records you could ask for, but you will need to dig and be a little creative.

State Licensure Boards

Use a search engine to search for the terms [your state] state licensure board (example: Nebraska state licensure board). This will return a list of Web sites for various professions that are licensed in your state. Many sites list individual license holders, retired status, continuing education credit status, and other such information.

Applies to Chapters 20, 26, 28, 29, 30, 31, and 32.

Use this source to find:

- Attorneys
- CPAs
- Medical professionals
- Retirees

The Sourcebook of Public Record Information

Applies to Chapters 24, 25, 27, 29, 30, 31, 32, and 33.

This book explains how to find the information you want from municipal, county, state, and federal records. It is available in many libraries.

U.S. Census Bureau

www.census.gov

Applies to Chapters 24, 25, 27, 29, 30, and 31.

Use this source to find census data, including neighborhood ethnic makeup, income, and ages; business types and revenue estimates; and much more.

Business, Companies, Industries, and Executives

American Society of Appraisers

www.appraisers.org

Applies to Chapter 25.

This site provides business valuation reports.

BenefitsLink

http://benefitslink.com/index.html

Applies to Chapters 20, 26, and 30.

Use this site to find:

- Information and articles on retirement and benefit plans
- Information on specific plans

Business Sales Leads

www.biz-sales-leads.com

Applies to Chapters 20, 25, 26, 27, 28, 29, 30, and 32.

This fee-based site provides low-cost leads of businesses and includes contact name, address, number of employees, and other such information. Filters let you customize a list.

Business Schools

Use a search engine, and use the following terms: [your state] association business schools officials (example: Ohio association business schools officials). Business schools host conferences for professional development where it would be appropriate for you to speak. These sites also usually have a list of officers and directors.
Applies to Chapters 20 and 29.

Central Contractor Registration

www.ccr.gov
Applies to Chapters 20, 25, 28, 29, 30, and 32.
Businesses have to register with this site before becoming government vendors. Government vendors have guaranteed income and make a good product.

Click the search tab and use the advanced search function to search for women-owned businesses. You can get all the women-owned businesses in any state or zip code that have government contracts. (You can also do the same for minority-owned, nonprofit, and veteran-owned businesses.) Use this source to find:

• Successful businesses in your area, including contact information
• Women-owned businesses

Chambers of Commerce

www.2chambers.com
Applies to Chapters 20, 24, 25, 27, 28, 29, and 32.
Most of the smaller towns have chamber of commerce Web sites. These sites typically include a business directory that includes business name, address, and phone number. Sites also usually have a link to the local town newspaper. Use this source to find your local chamber of commerce, which can provide:

• Lists of member businesses in your area, which often include owners' names
• Nonprofit organizations

Company Financial and Executive Records of Public Companies

Applies to Chapters 25, 27, 29, 30, and 32.
www.freeedgar.com
This site provides access to insider filings, company annual reports, and other financial filings.
www.investor.reuters.com
This site gives the names of senior executives and directors and copies of the company's annual report (online as well as hard copy).

www.prars.com

This site provides free company annual reports that are public records (hard copy), as long as the report is in the site's inventory.

www.sec.gov

Provides access to insider filings.

Corporate Events That Generate Money in Motion

Applies to Chapters 20, 29, 30, 32, and 33.

Bloomberg at www.bloomberg.com

Bloomberg offers many news services that focus on corporate executives, companies, and industries, for a fee. You can find information on executives, such as news on insider buying and selling, information on filers, filing dates, shares filed, price, and the broker used to sell securities. You must subscribe in order to use Bloomberg's more specialized tools. Bloomberg also has an online tutorial on how to navigate the Web site at www.marshall.usc.edu/emplibrary/basicbloom berg.pdf.

Google News at http://news.google.com

You can search for terms relating to corporate executives changing companies, executive compensation stories, and mergers and acquisitions.

Corporate Yellow Book

Applies to Chapters 20, 25, 26, 27, 28, 29, 30, and 32.

This is a directory of leading U.S. companies, including names of key individuals, executive biographies, and revenues. Listings are by business name, by industry code, and by zip code.

Dun & Bradstreet

www.dnb.com

Applies to Chapters 20, 25, 26, 28, 29, 30, and 32.

This company provides online and hard-copy directories of businesses, for a fee. Available information includes names of business owners and executives, credit reports, business history, financial analysis, and other such information. Both private and public companies are covered. Information is available in many formats, such as in-depth company information and mailing lists filtered by many possible filters. You can search for leads by revenues, number of employees, name, and other categories. Some databases are available in public libraries.

Gale

www.galegroup.com

Applies to Chapters 20, 25, 26, 27, 28, 29, 30, and 32.

This company has a number of fee-based databases covering trade groups and associations (areas covered, contact information, convention information), public and private companies (lines of business, revenues, number of employees, business history, articles about them, competitor information, industry analyses), articles (general interest, academic, specialized and technical, newspaper articles), and health, among others. Many of these databases are available in public libraries.

Hoover's

www.hoovers.com
Applies to Chapters 20, 25, 27, 28, 29, 30, and 32.
For a fee, this site offers comprehensive information on companies and executives, including credit history, lines of business, list of executives, former positions, and other such information. It is also available in many public libraries.

Layoff Reports

Applies to Chapters 30, 32, and 33.

> JWT Employment Communications at www.jwtec.com—click "News and Resources," then select "Weekly Layoff Report."
>
> Google News at http://news.google.com—search using the keyword "layoffs" or "downsizing."

Local Business Journals

http://newslink.org/biznews.html
www.bizjournals.com
Applies to Chapters 20, 25, 26, 27, 28, 29, 30, 32, and 33.
At these sites, you will find a list of business journals published in your area. These journals are a good source of information on local businesses and executives.

Every week the local business journal in most markets will have stories on individuals and companies that often focus on changes of circumstances. Become a diligent reader of your local business journal and read it to find prospects. Use this source to find:

- Businesses being recognized
- Executive relocations and promotions
- Information on specific businesses
- Lists of the top real estate brokers or contractors
- New businesses in the area
- Successful businesses and their owners

National Human Resources Association

www.humanresources.org
Applies to Chapters 20, 25, 30, and 33.
Provides information from the association of Human Resources Professionals.

SIC Codes

www.ehso.com/SICcodes.htm
Applies to Chapters 20, 25, 26, 28, 30, and 32.
This site provides a full list of SIC codes.

Society for Human Resource Management

www.shrm.org
Applies to Chapters 20, 25, 30, and 33.
See also the sites for state chapters, where you can give financial seminars and network.

State Web Sites of Business Registration Information

www.state.co.us
Applies to Chapters 20, 25, 26, 28, 30, and 32.
If you enter your two-letter state abbreviation instead of "co" in this URL, it will take you to the state's official Web site. Most of these Web sites will display public records for every business registered in the state. Each state Web site puts this information in a different place. Look for links such as "Secretary of State," "Corporate Records," or "Bureau of Corporations." You can generally search by business name, SIC code, location, and other such fields. Public records usually list business owners' names, contact information, tax status, and other such information.

Trade Publications

www.tradepub.com
Applies to Chapters 20, 25, 26, 27, 28, 29, 30, 32, and 33.
This site lists many trade publications that you can subscribe to free of charge. Use this source to find information that will help you to become an expert on an industry.

Venture Capitalists

www.vfinance.com
Applies to Chapters 20, 25, 26, 28, and 32.
Venture Capital Resource Library lists over 1,400 venture capital firms.

Attorneys and CPAs

Attorneys

Applies to Chapters 20, 22, 25, 26, 28, 29, and 32.

American Academy of Estate-Planning Attorneys at www.aaepa.com
Divorce Headquarters at www.divorcehq.com
DivorceNet at www.divorcenet.com/money

FindLaw at http://lawyers.findlaw.com

Lawyers.com at www.lawyers.com

National Network of Estate-Planning Attorneys at www.nnepa.com/public;
click "Information for Other Professionals," then "Find an EPA." This
sorts by zip code but returns fewer names and information than AAEPA.

Law offices specializing in land and house sales, estate planning, real estate,
and divorce are great places to find influencers or clients. Attorneys are also a
good source of information. Use these sources to find:

- Attorney conventions and meetings
- Attorneys
- Divorce attorneys
- Estate planning attorneys

CPAs

Applies to Chapters 20, 22, 25, 26, 28, 29, 32, and 33.

CPA associations at www.aicpa.org/yellow/ypascpa.htm; click on the name
of the state you're interested in.

State Boards of Accountancy at www.aicpa.org/yellow/ypsboa.htm; then
choose your state.

CPAs are good sources of information on mergers and acquisitions, divorces, company relocations, and other such events. Use the above sources to
find:

- CPAs
- CPA associations
- CPA conventions and meetings

State Licensure Boards

Applies to Chapters 20, 22, 25, 26, 28, 29, and 33.
Use a search engine to search for terms [your state] state licensure board (example: Nebraska state licensure board). This will return a list of Web sites for various professions that are licensed in your state. Many sites list individual license
holders, retired status, continuing education credit status, and other such information. Use this source to find attorneys and CPAs.

Women

Marquis Who's Who

www.marquiswhoswho.com
Applies to Chapters 20 and 29.
This source contains a list of influential men and women, including extensive

biographies and home and work addresses. Entries are listed both alphabetically and by geography. Separate databases include only women, attorneys, medical professionals, or business professionals. It is also available in public libraries.

National Association for Female Executives (NAFE)

www.nafe.com
Applies to Chapters 20, 22, and 29.
You can register online for information, but there is no online directory as of this writing. There are, however, links and contact information for state chapters. The site also has profiles of local NAFE Award winners and their contact information.

National Association of Women Business Owners (NAWBO)

www.nawbo.org
Applies to Chapters 20, 22, and 29.
You can register online for free, and then you can access chapter directories with names and phone numbers.

National Directory of Woman-Owned Businesses

Applies to Chapters 20 and 29.
This book is available in public libraries.

National Federation of Business and Professional Women

www.bpwusa.org
Applies to Chapters 20, 22, and 29.
You can register online for information, but there is no online directory as of this writing. There are, however, links and contact information for state chapters.

Women's Business Enterprise National Council

www.wbenc.org
Applies to Chapters 20, 22, and 29.
This site offers access to a database of women-owned businesses. There are also excellent networking and speaking opportunities here.

Women's Chamber of Commerce

www.uswomenschamber.com
Applies to Chapters 20, 22, and 29.
This site offers a way to connect to the national women's business community.

Women's Economic Development Council (WEDC)

www.wedc-online.com
Applies to Chapters 20, 22, and 29.

This site provides information on women business professionals' educational, mentoring, entrepreneurial, networking, and community-building advice and contacts.

Women's Vision Foundation

www.womensvision.org
Applies to Chapters 20, 22, and 29.
This is an excellent source for networking and speaking opportunities.

Mortgages, Realtors, and Home Builders

Classified Ads

Applies to Chapters 25, 26, 29, 32, and 33.
Look for top real estate agents by searching classified ads. Look for a Realtor who is looking for a first or even second assistant. If he needs an assistant, then he is more than likely successful and is looking for ways to concentrate his business. Many real estate companies allow brokers to have an assistant only after they hit a certain sales volume. A great online site for looking for these is Monster.com at www.monster.com; you can search for classifieds just for real estate assistants.

County Clerk and Recorder's Office

Applies to Chapters 32 and 33.
Mortgage records are public. You can track specific mortgage information, such as addresses of properties, lien information, and property owners' names, through the county clerk and recorder's office. This information is available to anyone.

Home-Builders.com

www.home-builders.com
Applies to Chapters 26, 29, and 33.
You can find builders in any state through this Web site.

National Association of Home Builders

www.nahb.org
Applies to Chapters 26, 29, and 33.
This site has links to builders' conventions and conferences. Also look for "NAHB Community," which has a link for "Find Your Local Builders' Association."

National Association of Realtors

www.realtor.org
Applies to Chapters 25, 26, 29, 32, and 33.

Click on "Directories," and from there use "Visitor's Link" and then "Associations by State" to get local Realtor boards. Look in their directories for names and contact information for Realtors. For Realtor magazine, look for a link to "Realtor Magazine," which is published by this association. Realtor magazine has a listing of the nation's top Realtors and Realtor teams by sales volume.

Real Estate Brokers

Applies to Chapters 25, 26, 29, 32, and 33.

National Association of Real Estate Brokers at www.nareb.com/members/search.shtml; you can search for broker listings by state for any state and then click on "Find a Realtor."

Council of Real Estate Broker Managers at www.crb.com; click on "Find a CRB" (commercial real estate broker) and choose "accept," then choose a state to get an alphabetical listing of CRB brokers.

Real Estate Guides

Applies to Chapters 25, 26, 32, and 33.

Check real estate guides in your Sunday paper and in free literature distributions.

Search Engine Phrase or Keyword Suggestions

Applies to Chapters 25, 26, 29, 32, and 33.

- "Top commercial real estate brokers" (try using the quotation marks and not using them)
- "Top home builders" (try using the quotation marks and not using them)
- "Top mortgage brokers" (try using the quotation marks and not using them)
- "Top Realtors" (try using the quotation marks and not using them)

Hispanic Markets

Directory of Spanish-Speaking Law Firms

www.1800elabogado.com
Applies to Chapter 29.
Provides information on Spanish-speaking law firms.

Hispanic Business

www.hispanicbusiness.com
Applies to Chapter 29.
This site provides Hispanic business news, research, conferences, and other such information.

Hispanic National Bar Association

www.hnba.com
News, members, publications, board members, affiliate members by state.
Applies to Chapter 29.

National Society for Hispanic Professionals

www.nshp.org

Applies to Chapter 29.

This site provides news, research, conferences, and other such information on Hispanic professionals.

U.S. Hispanic Chamber of Commerce

www.ushcc.com

Applies to Chapter 29.

Local chapters often have annual job fairs and expos where exhibitor booths are for rent.

Nonprofits

American Endowment Foundation

www.aefonline.org

Applies to Chapter 34.

This foundation is an independent sponsor of over $54 million in donor-advised funds. Individuals can start their own fund for only $10,000 and a fee. The AEF does not provide investment advisors, so it is a great resource for advertising. To find endowments that have already been given, enter "endowment" in the "search by charity name or keyword" box on the site.

Chartered Institute of Management Accountants (CIMA)

www.cimaglobal.com

Applies to Chapter 34.

This is a membership organization that offers an internationally recognized professional qualification in management accountancy.

The Foundation Center

www.foundationcenter.org

Applies to Chapters 20, 22, 29, and 34.

This site provides links to resources, regional foundation Web sites, financial reports, and other such resources. It is the largest clearinghouse for all matters pertaining to the nonprofit world.

The Foundation Directory

Applies to Chapters 20, 22, 29, and 34.

This book lists charitable organizations nationwide. It includes biographies, key contacts, addresses, and phone numbers.

GrantSmart

www.grantsmart.org
Applies to Chapters 20, 22, 29, and 34.
This Web site allows you to search based on location and asset size. The site then offers a PDF file of each organization's tax return.

Guidestar

www.guidestar.com
Applies to Chapters 20, 22, 24, 29, and 34.
This Web site allows you to retrieve the records of all public charities in a certain area.

Idealist

www.idealist.org
Applies to Chapters 20, 22, 29, and 34.
Besides information on nonprofit organizations, this site also gives lists of non-profit events that need consulting or volunteer help. You can also list yourself as a consultant in financial services with your profile and contact information.

Investment Management Consultants Association (IMCA)

www.imca.org
Applies to Chapter 34.
This is a professional organization devoted to financial management and cost accounting.

Large and Small Public Charities

Guidestar at www.guidestar.com
Applies to Chapters 20, 22, 29, and 34.
This Web site allows you to retrieve the records of all public charities in a certain area.

Large Colleges, Universities, Private Colleges, Small Community Colleges, and Small Private Colleges

Applies to Chapters 20 and 34.
Simply call the college and ask for the CFO or manager of endowments. If you have access to Bloomberg (see that listing previously), you can find this informa-tion there.

Melissa Data

www.melissadata.com
Applies to Chapters 20, 22, 29, and 34.
This site lists nonprofit organizations by zip code, organization name, or nine-digit tax ID.

National Charity Navigator

www.charitynavigator.org

Applies to Chapters 20, 22, 29, and 34.

This site has listings of charities in each state. Use the search function to browse by region and then state. Click on any charity to see financial information on the organization. You can also see if this organization has a donor privacy policy; if not, the names of all donors will be available on the nonprofit's own Web site. To retrieve contact information for these names, you can use the sources listed under Internet White Pages.

Nonprofit News

Applies to Chapters 20, 22, 29, and 34.

You can find this from the *Chronicle of Philanthropy* at www.philanthropy.com.

Private Charities

GrantSmart at www.grantsmart.org

Applies to Chapters 20, 22, 29, and 34.

This Web site allows you to search based on location and asset size. The site then offers a PDF file of each organization's tax return.

Retirees and Retired Military

Complete Listing of Retirement Communities in All Fifty States

www.retirementhomes.com

Applies to Chapters 20 and 31.

This site gives you the ability to pick any state and includes pictures, phone numbers, descriptions, and links to these communities' Web sites as well as care levels and home pricing. This allows you to prequalify prospects' net worth before calling or visiting.

National Retirement Living Information Center

www.retirementliving.com

Applies to Chapters 20 and 31.

This site has a directory listing under "Retirement Communities and Senior Housing." You can search by state. It arranges these listings by level of care offered, from independent living to nursing homes; you can use it to build your list of properties where residents still handle their own financial decisions (independent living or assisted-living facilities). This site also has a listing of local papers or newsletters from senior housing complexes, which lists decision makers and boards and committees within the complexes. The site also has tax information for seniors by state.

Senioresidences.com

www.senioresidences.com
Applies to Chapters 20 and 31.
This site provides a list of retirement communities.

The Senior Times

www.theseniortimes.com
Applies to Chapters 20 and 31.
This site offers lots of information that is of interest to retirees, with which you may be able to develop leads or sharpen your market action plan.

Veterans

Applies to Chapters 20 and 31.

> American Legion at www.legion.org; you can search for Legion posts in any location, and find addresses and contact information.
>
> Veterans of Foreign Wars at www.vfw.org; under "Membership"; look for links to "VFW Post Websites," where you will often find contact information for the locations you want to focus on.
>
> FindLaw at http://lawyers.findlaw.com; you can find attorneys who work with veterans by searching for legal issues of "veterans" or "military law" and limiting the search to your city.

Veterans of Foreign Wars (VFW)

www.vfs.org
Applies to Chapters 20 and 31.
This site provides only e-mail contact information for each state's VFW chapters, not local chapter information. Under "News and Info," click on a state to call or e-mail the lead contact.

Volunteers of America (VOA)

www.voa.org
Applies to Chapters 20 and 31.
One of the best groups to join is Volunteers of America. This group is very large nationally. Many high-net-worth individuals are on the VOA Guild.

Networking

BNI

www.bni.com
Applies to Chapters 22 and 29.
Although your business networking group will be unique to your needs, you may

want to take a look at the frequently asked questions on the BNI Web site to gain a basic idea of how its meetings operate.

Konnects.com

www.konnects.com
Applies to Chapters 22 and 29.
This is a networking group; its Web site also provides networking tips.

LEADS Groups

Applies to Chapters 22 and 29.
Contact your local chamber of commerce for information.

LeTip

www.letip.com; click your state on the map.
Applies to Chapters 22 and 29.
This is a professional organization with the primary purpose of giving and receiving qualified business tips or leads. Each business category is represented by one member, and conflicts of interest are not allowed. No outside speakers are allowed at LeTip meetings, and you need to be a member of this networking group.

National Professional Associations

Applies to Chapters 22 and 29.
Many special interests have national professional associations that have e-networking or local networking options. Use a search engine to see if your outside interest has a national professional association.

Networking Books Available in Many Libraries

Applies to Chapters 22 and 29.

- Stanley, Thomas J. *Networking with the Affluent and Their Advisors.* Chicago: Irwin Professional Publishing, 1993.
- Allen, Scott, and David Teten. *The Virtual Handshake: Opening Doors and Closing Deals Online.* New York: AMACOM Books, 1995.

Networking for Professionals

www.networkingforprofessionals.com
Applies to Chapters 22 and 29.
This works like a networking "matchmaking" service—you join, you search for professionals you want to speak with, then you contact them and meet.

Online Business Networking Articles and Resources

http://entrepreneurs.about.com/od/onlinenetworking
www.rileyguide.com/enetwork.html

Applies to Chapters 22 and 29.

These sites offer excellent articles about networking, including links and other resources.

Ryze Business Networking

www.ryze.com

Applies to Chapters 22 and 29.

This is a networking tool used in Denver and the entire United States.

State Offices of Economic Development and International Trade

www.state.co.us

Applies to Chapter 22.

Enter your two-letter state abbreviation instead of "co" in this URL, and it will take you to the state's official Web site. Look for links to the state office of economic development. Web sites for offices of economic development offer connections to Internet business resources, guides to small businesses, and offices for minority businesses in the state.

Certifications

Certified Divorce Specialist, Financial Divorce Association

www.fdadivorce.com

Applies to Chapters 28, 29, and 32.

You can take classes (four days) to become certified, or you can study at home. This association also has newsletters and member listings by state.

Chartered Institute of Management Accountants (CIMA)

www.cimaglobal.com

Applies to Chapter 34.

This is a membership organization that offers an internationally recognized professional qualification in management accountancy.

Divorce Financial Planner, a division of Certified Financial Planner

www.cfp.net

www.divorceandfinance.com

Applies to Chapters 28, 29, and 32.

Anyone who is federally registered with the federal Certified Financial Planner Board of Standards, Inc., can be part of the Association of Divorce Financial Planners. This is a great networking opportunity for client referrals, resource listings, and membership events.

Investment Management Consultants Association (IMCA)

www.imca.org

Applies to Chapter 34.

This is a professional organization devoted to financial management and cost accounting.

Physicians

American Medical Association

www.ama-assn.org
Applies to Chapters 26 and 29.
Look for the link "Doctor Finder." You can search by state, city, or zip code for doctors by specialty. The site gives name, biography, education, specialty, and phone number.

University Medical School Web Sites

Applies to Chapters 26 and 29.
Examples:

* School of Medicine of the University of Pennsylvania at www.med.upenn .edu
* Stanford University School of Medicine at www.med.stanford.edu

On some sites, you can search by faculty, alumni, and associations, and you can also access faculty research papers and other such information. In most cases, however, you must go to the library in person if you are not an affiliate of the medical school. Also, you can call the university medical library and ask it where to access research reports. Use this source to find names of affluent medical professionals.

Sales Professionals

Sales Professionals USA

www.salesprofessionalsusa.com
Applies to Chapters 22 and 26.
Here are some search engine phrase or keyword suggestions:

* Supplier awards (then the name or abbreviation of your state)
* "Manufacturers Representatives" (try using the quotation marks and not using them)
* "Business brokers" (try using the quotation marks and not using them)
* "Licensed sales professionals" (try using the quotation marks and not using them)

Asians

Asian American Community Links (Local and National)

www.janet.org/~ebihara/aacyber_community.html
www.asianamerican.net/organizations.html

Applies to Chapter 29.
These sites provide links to Asian American community listings. Use these links
to find:

- Asian American business associations
- Asian American businesses
- Asian American professional associations (attorneys, CPAs, and other professionals)

Asian Chamber of Commerce

www.asianchamber.org
Applies to Chapter 29.
This site offers a way to connect to the national Asian business community.

Affluent Individuals

Businesses for Sale

Merger Network at www.mergernetwork.com
Applies to Chapters 25 and 32.
Business owners who are in the process of selling their businesses have huge
capital potential. You can search by state, city, region, or even internationally.
Lists provide the business owner's contact information and sale price. The basic
membership is free of charge.

Cole Directory

www.coleinformation.com
Applies to Chapters 20, 24, 26, 27, 29, 30, 31, and 33.
This is a cross-reference and reverse directory for residence names and phone
numbers. It includes recent home sales, homeowner's insurance status, and related information. The price varies depending on the type of information you are
requesting. This directory is also available in many public libraries.

CIS Marketing

www.cismarketing.com
Applies to Chapters 20, 25, 26, 27, 28, 29, 30, 31, 32, and 33.
This fee-based site offers leads specifically tailored to the financial industries.

House Values and New Home Buyers

http://newslink.org/biznews.html
www.bizjournals.com
Applies to Chapters 20, 22, 23, 25, 26, 27, 28, 32, 33, and 34.
First, find the Web site for your local business journal using these Web sites.

Then go to the individual site for each journal in your area. Many have links such as "Sales Leads" or "New Homebuyers."

Local Land and House Sales

Applies to Chapters 26, 32, and 33.

Identify individuals with large blocks of land for sale in your community either through the Multiple Listing Service (MLS) directory or through contact with your local Realtors. Often these individuals are facing very low cost basis issues and have a need for professional advice and planning, not to mention someone to invest the proceeds of the land sale.

Your county tax assessor's office can provide a listing of all new deeds to homes or land. Give the parameters of what you are looking for (deeds in the last three months, over $400,000, for example), and it can e-mail or send you a list.

Neighbors of Clients or Prospects

www.whitepages.com
Applies to Chapters 20, 24, 26, 33, and 31.

Do a "people search" and enter data for the known contact: name, street, city, state, zip, or as much as you have. Click "Search." If the person is found, her name and address will be listed along with a "Find Neighbors" hyperlink.

Polk City Directories

www.citydirectory.com
Applies to Chapters 20, 24, 26, 27, 29, 30, 31, and 33.

These are cross-reference and reverse directories, one for each city or for a larger areas. You can search by name of individual, phone number, address, household income, or other such fields. These directories are also available in many public libraries.

Professors and Executive MBA Students

Applies to Chapters 20, 26, 29, and 32.

You can contact professors or admissions people of executive MBA programs, or offer to teach a quick seminar during a class. The average salary for an executive attending an executive MBA program is $93,000, but it can go up to $250,000. The professors are professionals themselves and are usually high-net-worth individuals because schools want successful people to teach their methods.

U.S. Search

www.ussearch.com
Applies to Chapters 20, 24, 25, 26, 27, 28, 29, 30, 31, 32, and 33.

This fee-based site offers basic information (full name, address, and phone number) plus former addresses, basic financial and tax status, age, spouse's name, background check information, value of house, and other such information.

Index

accountability, of team members, 171
account penetration, by teams, 165
administrative tasks
    for client associates, 157–159
    new advisors' time allocation for, 90–91
adopt-a-town market action plan, 241–244
advisors
    "buddy" relationships with, 91
    on multimillion-dollar practice teams, 190
    services broadening by, 148–150
    teams of, *see* teams
    workflow between client associate and,
        158–161
    see also experienced advisors; new advi-
        sors
affluent investors
    number of contacts with, 144
    number of relationships with, 20–21
    referrals to, 110
    rejections from, 12
    resources on, 335–336
    see also million-dollar investors; multi-
        million-dollar investors
agenda technique, 112–113
age range groupings, 138–139
allocation of funds, 78, 81
alternative investments, 127, 133
alumni, marketing to, 204, 237–239
annual planning sessions, 105–106
annuities, 130–131
appointments
    closing, 52–53
    and contact to appointment ratio, 32
    getting, *see* getting appointments
    with Hispanic clients, 277–278
    initial, *see* initial appointments
    for IRA rollovers, 285–286

no-show, 90
    scheduled all on one day, 89–90
    second, 50, 59–60
    "unselling," 38
approach (marketing plan), 28
Asian Americans, marketing to, 278–281
Asians, resources on, 334–335
asset management decisions (nonprofits),
    310–313
asset protection, 251–252
assets at other institutions, 105–108
assets under management, 20
    adding, 125–128
    client ratio for classes of, 21
    increasing, from existing clients, 104–109
    minimums for, 21–22, 124–125
    for multimillion-dollar practices, 187
    new advisor's goal for, 23–24
    preservation of, 181
    see also portfolios
attitude (with prospects), 67–68
attorneys
    market action plan for, 29
    marketing to, 254–255, 263–269
    networking with, 114–117
    referrals to women by, 272–273
away-assets process, 104–108

baby boomers, seminars for, 204–205
bad appointments, 53
balancing clients and prospects, 97–103
    in career stages, 4
    and client contact process, 99–100
    and client monthly contacts, 101–102
    foundation numbers for, 97–98
    by leveraging client relationships, 98–99
    organizing time for, 100–101

banking services, 151
big events, 119, 212–215
"board of directors"
  for event marketing, 217–220
  for natural market, 31–32, 139–140
  in personal contact market action plan, 234–235
boards of directors, nonprofit, 307–310
bonds, 79
"buddy" relationships, with advisors, 91
builders
  network of, 299–301
  resources on, 326–327
  scripts for contacting, 303
businesses
  resources on, 319–324
  seminars through, 203–204, 208–210
business financial services, 130
business owners
  Asian American, 279–280
  marketing to, 245–250
  seminars for, 205–208
  women, 271

career stages, 4
cash, in asset allocation, 78
certifications, resources on, 333–334
Chartered Institute of Management Accountants (CIMA) certification, 306
churches, seminars through, 203
CIMA certification, 306
client advisory board, 217–220
client appreciation dinners, 215–217
client appreciation events, 215
client associates
  client retention activities for, 147–148
  expanding of services by, 148–153
  main responsibilities of, 158–159
  number of relationships for, 144–145
  review meetings with, 91
  rewarding, 161
  time management for, see time management (for client associates)
  workflow between advisor and, 158–161
client retention, 143–154
  factors driving, 145–150
  and right number of client relationships, 143–145
  and scripts to expand services, 150–153
clients
  balancing prospects and, 97–103

contact process with, 99–100
  getting more assets from, 104–109
  investment plan steps for, 77–81
  leveraging relationships with, 98–99, see also leveraging client relationships
  reassigning, 128–129
  setting/managing expectations of, 77–78
  treating prospects like, 66–67
client to prospect ratio, 65
closing appointments, 52–53
clubs
  for networking, 223–224
  seminars for, 202–203
cold calling, 12, 35
commitment (of teams), 171
communication, 146, 171
community colleges, 312
companies
  becoming outside expert to, 287–288
  resources on, 319–324
  seminars for, 208–210
compensation, team, 170
concentrated stock, 132–133, 258–260
confidence, 41–42, 67, 178–179
contacts (personal)
  market action plan based on, 30, 233–237
  networking with, 229–230
contacts (with clients)
  with business owners, 246–247
  for client retention, 146–148
  with CPA and attorney networks, 116–117
  for getting appointments, 38–39
  monthly, see monthly contacts
  new advisors' time allocation for, 88–89
  process for, 99–100
  and recontacting prospects, 44
  warm, 273–275
  see also specific types, e.g.: drop-bys
contact to appointment ratio, 32
continuing education accreditation, 265
county clerk offices, 302
CPAs
  marketing to, 263–269
  mortgage offerings to, 301
  networking with, 114–117
  reaching physicians through, 252
  scripts for contacting, 303–304
credit card services, 152

daily schedules, for new advisors, 85–88
death of affluent individuals, 296

decamillionaire investors, 183–184
delegation of tasks, 158, 190
dinners, client appreciation, 215–217
direct deposit service, 151–152
discovery of assets, 105–106
diversification, 78–80
divorce, 295–296
downsizing, opportunities in, 286–287
drop-bys, 63–64

educational seminars, 264–265
emotions, investing and, 76
equities, 78–81
estate planning, 133, 152–153
event marketing, 31, 212–222
    based on clients' interests, 119, 121–122
    big events for, 212–215
    client advisory board in, 217–220
    client appreciation dinners for, 215–217
    client appreciation events for, 215
    effective techniques for, 157
    to influencers, 267–269
    to interest groups, 139
    to leverage existing relationships, 119,
        121–122
    lunch roundtable for, 220–221
    to multimillion-dollar investors, 189
    in multimillion-dollar practices, 192
    in natural market, 136–137
    small/intimate events for, 213–214
    unique events for, 221–222
executives
    departures of, 295
    marketing to, 258–262
    relocation of, 296
    resources on, 319–324
expanding client relationships, 124–134
    by adding products/services that don't
        compete with portfolio, 125–128
    example scripts for, 129–134
    and minimum level of business per client,
        124–125
    and reassignment of clients, 128–129
experienced advisors
    creating clients out of prospects by, 69, 70
    leveraging of relationships by, 110
    marketing activities time for, 15
    marketing process for, 30–32
    new prospects meetings per week for, 45

face-to-face meetings, 34–35, 265–266
firemen's retirement funds, 311

fit, team, 166, 169
529 plans, 152
fixed income, in asset allocation, 78
follow up
    for initial appointments, 53–54
    to natural market events, 137
    as second priority, 157
    to seminars, 201–202, 210, 211
foundation of career, building, 4, 97–98, *see
        also* million-dollar practice
401(k)s, 131
Fridays, as catch-up day, 89

getting appointments, 34–46
    face-to-face, 34–35
    handling objections in, 42–43
    making contact for, 38–39
    and number of appointments to make,
        44–45
    prequalifying prospects before, 35–38
    recontacting prospects for, 44
    results of confident style in, 41–42
    scripts for, 39–41
goals
    of multimillion-dollar advisors, 195
    for niche marketing, 27
    portfolio performance consistent with,
        145–146
    setting and tracking progress toward, 6–7
golf tournaments, 213
growth, fundamentals of, 9–10
GuideStar.com, 306

Hispanics
    marketing to, 275–278
    resources on, 327–328
home equity lines of credit, 132
home sales, 296
Hoover's Web site, 260

IMCA certification, 306
increasing assets from existing clients,
        104–109
influencers
    marketing to, 31, 263–269
    networks of, 191
information gathering
    at initial meeting, 50, 51
    for mortgage offerings, 302
    on nonprofits, 306–307
    questions for, 54–57

on senior executives, 260
sources for, *see* resources
information request response cards,
    118–120
inheritance transactions, 295
initial appointments, 48–58
    asking questions in, 50–51
    bad, 53
    closing, 52–53
    follow-up to, 53–54
    introduction in, 48–49
    length of, 52
    pitfalls in, 51–52
    sample questions for, 54–57
inside and outside team structure, 167, 172
insurance, 131–132, 153
interest groups, 139, 225–226
internal marketing, 192
Investment Management Consulting Association (IMCA) certification, 306
investment matrix, 82
investment plan, 77–81, 183–184
IRAs, 129–130, 283–288

junior and senior team structure, 167–168,
    172–174

leadership, 195, 226
LEARN fundamentals, 9–10
lending products/services, 133
leveraging client relationships, 98–99,
    110–123
    by inviting clients to events, 119, 121–122
    through CPA and attorney networks,
        114–117
    through referrals, 110–114
    through speaking opportunities, 117–120
liability management, 126
life-changing events (for women), 272
life insurance, 131–132, 153
long-term care insurance, 132
lunch events, 220–221, 268, 273

mailings, 12
managed futures, 127, 132
management fees, 181–182
market action plan(s)
    for adopting a town, 241–244
    for Asian Americans, 278–281
    based on past experience, 237–240
    based on personal contacts, 233–237

for business owners, 245–250
elements of, 28–29
for events, 212–222
for executives, 258–262
for Hispanics, 275–278
for influencers, 263–269
for money in motion, 293–298
for mortgage products, 299–304
for natural market, 136–137
for networking, 223–232
for new advisors, 30
for nonprofits, 305–313
for professionals, 251–257
for seminars, 201–211
marketing
    combination of servicing and, *see* balancing clients and prospects
    contact to appointment ratio in, 32
    determining best activities for, 140
    by experienced advisors, 30–32
    internal, 192
    membership, 192–193
    by million-dollar producers, 8
    motivation for, 11–13
    in multimillion-dollar practices, 191–194
    by new advisors, 29–30
    philanthropic, 193
    as second priority, 157
    time allocation for, 14–17
    traditional, 177
membership marketing, 192–193
mergers and acquisitions, opportunities in,
    293–295
middle managers, marketing to, 258–262
military officers, retired, 291, 330–331
A Millionaire's Mind (Thomas Stanley), 114,
    178
million-dollar investors, 176–185
    adding products/services for, 126, 132–
        134, 152–153
    availability of, 188–189
    offering services to, 149
    proving your worth to, 178–182
    referrals for marketing to, 177–178
    and traditional marketing, 177
million-dollar practice, 19–26
    assets under management in, 20
    broad relationships in, 22
    client ratio in, 21
    elements of, 19–20

formula for, 10, 14
goals for, 22–24
raising minimums in, 21–22
reasons for wanting, 12–14
relationship minimums in, 21
relationships with affluent investors in, 20–21
time frame for building, 7
million-dollar producers, characteristics of, 6–9
minimum level of client business, 124–125
money in motion market action plan, 113, 293–298
money managers, selection of, 79–81
Monte Carlo simulation, 81
monthly contacts
with clients, 101–102
as first priority, 156
with influencers, 268
number of, 143–144
with prospects, 60–63, 71–73
mortgage products, 131, 299–304, 326–327
motivation, 11–18
building and keeping, 11–14
of million-dollar producers, 7–8
of multimillion-dollar advisors, 194–195
superficial, 14
with teams, 164–165
and time allocation, 14–17
multimillion-dollar advisors, personal traits of, 194–195
multimillion-dollar investors, 144, 183–184
multimillion-dollar practices, 186–198
business practices of, 187–194
marketing focus of, 191–194
numbers for building, 195–197
personal financial investments in, 190–191
personal traits of advisors in, 194–195
relationships in, 187, 189–190
service in, 188–189
team business structure of, 190
municipality funds, 311

names list, for marketing plans, 29
natural market, 135–142
"board of directors" for, 31–32, 139–140
creating groupings within, 137–139
determining best marketing activities for, 140

developing plan for, 136–137
identifying, 135
of prospects, 140–141
networking, 223–232
within an occupation, 224–225
building women's group for, 271
building your own group for, 227–229
with contacts you already have, 229–230
with CPAs and attorneys, 114–117
with influencers, 267–269
joining club for, 223–224
with new acquaintances, 230–232
prospect pathing for, 225
with Realtors and builders, 299–301
resources for, 331–333
special-interest or charitable organizations for, 225–227
new advisors
"buddy" relationships among, 91
creating clients out of prospects by, 69, 70
foundation building by, 4
goals for, 22–24
major hurdles for, 75
marketing activities time for, 15
marketing process for, 29–30
new prospects meetings per week for, 45
reassigning clients to, 128–129
time management for, see time management (for new advisors)
new-relationship experience, 150
niche marketing, 9, 27–33
nonprofits, marketing to, 32, 305–313
by developing relationships with board members, 307–310
and nonprofit asset management decisions, 310–313
preparation/organization for, 305–307
resources for, 328–330
with seminars, 202–203
no-show appointments, 90

objections, handling, 42–43
occupation groupings
as natural market, 137–138
networking within, 224–225
online services, 152
operational duties, for client associates, 159

past-experience market action plan, 30, 237–240
pathing, 193–194, 225

personal contacts market action plan, 30, 233–237
philanthropic marketing, 193
physicians
    marketing to, 251–254
    resources on, 334
police retirement funds, 311
portfolios
    adding products/services that don't compete with, 125–128
    asset allocation for, 78, 81
    bonds selection for, 79
    client's expectations of, 78
    diversification of, 78–79
    expectations and performance of, 145–146
    money managers in, 79–81
    monitoring performance of, 81
    preservation of assets in, 181
    returns on, 181
prequalifying prospects, 35–38
presentation libraries, 161
presentations
    continuing education accreditation of, 265
    preparing, 160–161
pricing, 183–184
prioritization
    in client associates' time management, 155–158
    of contacts, 100–101
private charities, 312–313
private colleges, 312
problem resolution, 146
process orientation, 195
products, adding, 125–128
professionalism, 178–179
professionals market action plan, 251–257
    for Asian Americans, 279
    for attorneys, 254–255
    for physicians, 251–254
    for sales professionals, 256–257
prospect pathing, 225
prospects, 59–74
    attitude in dealing with, 67–68
    balancing clients and, 97–103
    customizing process for dealing with, 69–70
    drop-bys with, 63–64
    face-to-face meetings with, 34–35
    initial appointments with, 48–58

introducing wealth-management process to, 82–83
    monthly contact with, 60–63, 71–73
    natural market of, 140–141
    number of, 22, 64–65
    pipeline of, 23
    prequalifying, 35–38
    qualified, 60
    recontacting, 44
    replacing, 68–69
    second appointments with, 59–60
    servicing, 66–67
    who have been referred, 114
    who switch from current advisors, 65–66
proving your worth, 178–182

qualified prospects, 60
qualified relationships, 98
qualified retirement plans, 282–283
qualifying prospects, 35–38

rapport, building, 50
ready-made audiences (for seminars), 202–204
Realtors, 271, 299–303, 326–327
reassigning clients, 128–129
recontacting prospects, 44
recorder's offices, 302
referral plan, 31
referrals
    asking for, 111–114
    to business owners, 247–248
    to influencers, 263, 267
    leveraging relationships by, 110–111
    to million-dollar investors, 177–178
    for mortgages, 301
    in multimillion-dollar practices, 191
    from natural market groups, 136–138
    to physicians, 253
    qualifying, 36
    reluctance to provide, 121
    through event invitations, 119, 121–122
rejections, 11–12
relationship building
    face-to-face meetings for, 34–35
    as first priority, 9, 62
    in multimillion-dollar practices, 20–21, 187, 189–190
    with nonprofit board members, 307–310
relationships
    broadness of, 22

and client to prospect ratio, 65
expanding, *see* expanding client relationships
first experiences in, 150
leveraging of, 98–99
minimum assets for, 21
qualified, 98
right number of, 143–145
replacing prospects, 68–69
resources, 315–336
    on affluent individuals, 335–336
    on Asians, 334–335
    for both general and specialized information, 315–319
    on business, companies, industries, and executives, 319–324
    on certifications, 333–334
    general, 315–319
    on Hispanic markets, 327–328
    on mortgages, Realtors, and home builders, 326–327
    for networking, 331–333
    on nonprofits, 328–330
    on physicians, 334
    on retirees and retired military, 330–331
    on sales professionals, 334
    of teams, 165
    on women, 324–326
retirees
    marketing to, 290–292
    resources on, 330–331
    seminars for, 210–211, 264
retirement plans, 278–279, 282–289, 311–312
rewards, for client associates, 161
risk, 76
risk tolerance, 77, 78, 127
Rolodex marketing, 12, 194, 235
Rule 144 transactions, 295

sales professionals
    marketing to, 256–257
    resources on, 334
schedules
    with all appointments on one day, 89–90
    for client associates, 161–163
    for new advisors, 85–88
screening calls, 160
scripts, elements of, 40–41
second appointments, 50, 59–60

seminars, 31, 201–211
    for age range groupings, 138–139
    for business owners, 205–208
    for companies, 208–210
    for CPAs and attorneys, 116
    follow-up to, 210
    for influencers, 264–265
    key success factors for, 201–202
    at lunch roundtables, 220–221
    markets for, 202
    for natural market, 136–137
    network as source of names for, 267
    for physicians, 252
    for prospects, 141
    for qualified baby boomers, 204–205
    for ready-made audiences, 202–204
    for retirees, 210–211, 290–291
    scripts for, 211
    on topics of client interests, 119
    for women, 272
service(s)
    adding, 125–128
    client associates' tasks in, 159–160
    and client retention, 147–148
    combination of marketing and, *see* balancing clients and prospects
    as differentiator among advisors, 62–63
    drop-bys as indication of, 63–64
    increasing number of, 148–150
    to millionaire clients, 179–180
    in multimillion-dollar practices, 188–189
    and number of relationships, 143
    to prospects, 66–67
    by teams, 164
situational partnering, 192
situational teams, 169
small events, 119, 213–214
social prospecting, 235–236
speaking opportunities, 117–120, 271
specialization teams, 166
spreadsheets, organizing information on, 127
Stanley, Thomas, 114, 178
strengths, assessing, 169
succession-planning teams, 190
superficial motivation, 14
superstar structure (teams), 167, 190
synagogues, seminars through, 203
synergy, team, 166

teams, 164–175
  advantages of, 164–165
  forming, 168–170
  in multimillion-dollar practices, 190
  pitfalls of, 165–166
  resources on, 165
  strengthening, 168, 170–171
  successful examples of, 171–174
  types of, 166–168
telephone coverage, time allocation for, 91
ten-million-dollar investors, 183–184
thank-you letters, 151
time blocking, 158
time management (in general)
  for contacting relationships, 100–101
  by million-dollar producers, 8–9
  motivation and, 14–17
time management (for client associates),
    155–163
  fundamentals of, 155–158
  and rewards for client associates, 161
  sample schedule for, 161–163
  and work flow between advisor and client
    associate, 158–161
time management (for new advisors), 85–93
  for administrative tasks, 90–91
  for client calls, 88–89
  daily and weekly schedules for, 85–88
  for preparation, 91–92
  by scheduling all appointments on one
    day, 89–90

for telephone coverage, 91
title companies, 302, 304
traditional marketing, million-dollar inves-
    tors' view of, 177
trust planning, 133

unique events, 221–222
U.S. Search, 260

values alignment (teams), 171
vertical teams, 167, 171–172
voicemail, 261

warm-contacting women, 273–275
weaknesses, assessing, 169
wealth-management process, 75–84
  articulation of, 180–181
  introducing prospects to, 82–83
  planning and, 182
  set up and maintenance of, 81–82
  steps in, 76–81
web bill payments, 152
web sites, company, 260
weekly schedules, for new advisors, 85–88
welcome calls, 151
women
  marketing to, 270–275
  resources on, 324–326

YMCA/YWCA classes, seminars through,
    203